Eight Septembers

A WOMAN ON WALL STREET
FROM 9/11 TO LEHMAN

Jane Buyers

Eight Septembers: A Woman on Wall Street From 9/11 to Lehman
Copyright © 2025 by Jane Buyers

All rights reserved. No portion of this book may be reproduced, stored in a retrieval system, or transmitted in any form or by any means—electronic, mechanical, photocopy, recording, scanning, or other—except for brief quotations in critical reviews or articles, without the prior written permission of the publisher.

Scripture quotations are taken from the Majority Standard Bible. Public domain.

This work depicts actual events in the life of the author as truthfully as recollection permits and/or can be verified by research. Occasionally, dialogue consistent with the character or nature of the person speaking has been recreated. All persons within are actual individuals; there are no composite characters. The names of some individuals have been changed to respect their privacy.

"Abide with Me" lyrics by Henry Francis Lyte, 1847.
Cover design by Mumtaz Mustafa
Author photo credit: Steven Scrocco

Printed in the United States of America
Hardcover ISBN: 978-1-965253-76-2
Paperback ISBN: 978-1-965253-77-9
Ebook ISBN: 978-1-965253-78-6

Contents

Introduction 9
Part One: Shock 17
   Chapter 1: 9/11 19
   Chapter 2: Evacuation 31
   Chapter 3: Midtown 41
   Chapter 4: Trouble 49
Part Two: Recovery 63
   Chapter 5: Downtown Again 65
   Chapter 6: Family Matters 73
   Chapter 7: Christmas in Hawaii 83
   Chapter 8: Opportunity 93
Part Three: Adaptation 101
   Chapter 9: Surprise 103
   Chapter 10: Step One 111
   Chapter 11: Chosen 119
   Chapter 12: Transitions 127
   Chapter 13: Kabuki Dance 135
Part Four: New Reality 141
   Chapter 14: Outside the Office 143
   Chapter 15: Inside the Office 153
   Chapter 16: Finding Allies 161
   Chapter 17: Turmoil 167
Part Five: Bombardment 177
   Chapter 18: Showdown 179
   Chapter 19: Conservatorship 187
   Chapter 20: Caretaking 193
   Chapter 21: Refco 201

EIGHT SEPTEMBERS

Part Six: Inundation 209
    Chapter 22: Warning Signs 211
    Chapter 23: May Day! May Day! 219
    Chapter 24: Reorg Assault 231
    Chapter 25: Shadow Banking 241
Part Seven: Frenzy 247
    Chapter 26: The Fall 249
    Chapter 27: Valentine's Day 257
    Chapter 28: Bear 267
    Chapter 29: Sabbatical 275
Part Eight: Calamity 281
    Chapter 30: Summer 283
    Chapter 31: Margin Call 291
    Chapter 32: Lehman Weekend 297
    Chapter 33: Immediate Aftermath 303
    Chapter 34: The Year Finally Ends 311
    Chapter 35: Performance Review 317
    Chapter 36: Walking Away 319
Epilogue: Empowerment 325
    September 2010 327
Afterword 331
Acknowledgements 335
About the Author 339
Referenced Sources 341
Reflection and Discussion for Readers and Book Clubs 343

*For my beloved sons, J.J. and William.
This is where I was when I wasn't with you.*

Psalm 23 (Verses 1-3)

My Mother is my shepherd and I lack nothing.
She lays me down in green grass and carries fresh water to me.
I can rest in her watchfulness while my soul is restored.
She leads me along the path to wholeness.
Even when I am lost in my own darkness, I do not give
in to discouragement because I have her with me.

—Barbara J. Monda
Rejoice, Beloved Woman!: The Psalms Revisioned

Introduction

My friend, the late historian and author Christopher P. Moore, insisted I had a story to tell. Chris is the one who called my attention to the importance of the historical arc between my experiences as a banker working in downtown Manhattan on 9/11 and the $5 billion margin call I made to Lehman Brothers on that same date in 2008 — two events that changed the way the United States, and thus the world, operated in profound ways. Responsible for funding brokerage firms' daily activities from my office in lower Manhattan, I was at the epicenter of both of these seminal events.

In the eight Septembers between the deadliest terrorist attack in human history and the global financial crisis, my professional life exploded with a series of escalating crises, and my personal life imploded under the strain of divorce, dementia, and death. It would take many years before I understood how those two aspects of my existence, personal and professional, were connected.

Every time Chris saw me, his eyes would twinkle, and a grin would spread across his face. He'd take my elbow and whisper gently in my ear, "You've got a story, Miss Janey. Tell it."

I dismissed him. "I lived my story, Chris. It traumatized me. I want to forget about it and move on." As if that were a possibility.

In March of 2011, when Chris asked if he could interview me for a play he was writing about 9/11, I reluctantly agreed. I returned home after our three-hour conversation with an overflow of memories and emotion churning for release. I sat down at my computer and, surprisingly, twenty pages poured out. It felt like vomiting as I purged the toxicity roiling inside me.

I worked on this book for the next fifteen years. My writing process was inconsistent as my commitment faltered many times. As much as I love writing, I didn't always have the heart to examine all that had happened to me during those eight Septembers between 2001 and 2008. So I took baby steps. I enrolled in classes, learned about memoir as a genre, and joined writing groups to get feedback. I even walked away from the project for four years. But when I woke from a dream with a complete paragraph in my head, I picked the story up again. With the help of many people, I gradually moved from "if I ever finish" to "when I finish." Sadly, my friend Chris passed away before I could send him a final draft.

I see now that those fifteen years were necessary for me to tell my story with the honesty it deserves. Initially, my plan was to outline my professional experiences without bringing in details of my inner world and personal relationships, but early readers had questions about my personal life, my upbringing, and how I came to find myself as a banker to Wall Street in the first place. Soon I found I was crafting a full-on memoir, weaving together the personal and professional, which required me to evaluate and understand my experiences from a different, and perhaps more generous, perspective.

One thing I learned in the process is that a memoirist strives to tell the truth. While not a verbatim recount of events, a memoir tells the emotional truth of the writer. It is important to remember, though, that her truth is not the whole truth. It's not even *her* whole truth. It's simply a window into situations and experiences that are relevant to the overall story. Thus, there are many voices and perspectives that are not included here because the story is told from my point of view only. I have tried to be fair and accurate in my representation of events, people, and myself. Some names have been changed and some events conflated in the interest of good storytelling.

As 2026 marks the 25th anniversary of the 9/11 terrorist attacks, and 2028 brings the 20th anniversary of the Lehman Brothers collapse that led to the Great Recession, I hope you find my story a welcome and enlightening addition to the existing narratives around these significant world events. Probably both events touched your life, too, and perhaps you faced hardships that were similar to my personal struggles. No matter how our experiences may have differed in the details, I hope

INTRODUCTION

you have also come to appreciate the tremendous human capacity for resilience, healing, growth, and transformation.

***

Like most of us, I brought my history and emotional baggage into the office. We are largely blind to how much our personal lives impact our workplace dynamics and we charge ahead, forging alliances and facing obstacles, replicating strategies we learned to protect ourselves when we were young. With our professional masks in place, we rarely acknowledge the wounds of our inner child and freely project our biases onto those who cross our paths. From the remove of more than four decades, I can see clearly now what I carried into my professional life.

Primary among the baggage I carried was a deep-seated sense of abandonment. In 1975, when I was fifteen, my family unit exploded like a rocket, scattering debris across the country. My parents parachuted into a new life in Honolulu, liberated from parenting and barely casting a glance at what they'd left behind in Philadelphia's Main Line. Hawaii was exotic and exciting. Dad wielded power as the CEO of one of the biggest companies on the island, and Mom supported him as a gracious hostess and enthusiastic cheerleader. They made friends, immersed themselves in the culture, and reveled in being the new toasts of the town.

My oldest sister, twenty-one, took shelter in Carlisle, Pennsylvania, for her senior year of college, determined not to lose her roots or her bearings. She doubled down on the importance of family and stability, maintaining meaningful relationships with our Pennsylvania-based grandparents and older cousins. She finished college and went on to grad school, securing her career as an educator. Within two years of our parents' move, she married and started a family of her own.

Our middle sister, eighteen, drifted into hostile territory at the newly co-ed Princeton University as a freshman, unwillingly following Dad's path while also mourning the loss of his proximity. She suffered under the weight of expectations and competition, unmotivated by the Ivy

EIGHT SEPTEMBERS

League credentials and values that had propelled Dad's success in the business world. She dropped out, reenrolled, and dropped out again. After a number of false starts, she found herself in Maine, a place she loved, and chose a college that better suited her creative and humanitarian sensibilities.

And I, the baby, crash-landed in Long Island at the Christian boarding school my dad, uncles, cousins and sister had attended, confused and disoriented. A moody and resentful teenager, I felt entitled to reject my parents and relieved to be five thousand miles away from my overbearing father, but I wondered why the decision to send me to boarding school had not been reconsidered when they chose to move to Hawaii? I suspected they had simply decided not to tell me about the move until after I'd been admitted to boarding school, afraid that I'd choose to go with them and they'd continue to be saddled by their "difficult" daughter, whose emotionality and choice in boyfriends embarrassed them. I felt betrayed and rejected by my parents, certain they were glad to be free of me.

Our family dynamics fractured. Communication nearly ceased. This was before the age of cell phones and the internet, so we were confined to snail mail and phone booths. But even when we'd been in one another's company, honest dialogue and emotional transparency were in short supply.

I simultaneously conformed and rebelled. Externally, I went to my classes, got good grades, followed the honor code, and participated in athletic and social activities. I had been well-trained to do as I was told and leave my complaints unvoiced. Internally, however, I chafed against the rules and withdrew emotionally, building walls to protect my heart. I vowed to make my own decisions before my parents could make them for me; decisions like applying early decision to a single university that wasn't a good fit just so I could avoid my sister's Princeton fate. I tried to isolate myself from their influence even though their voices were loud in my head.

My heart ate resentment, malice, and anger, which eventually turned into self-loathing.

INTRODUCTION

That's what happens when you bury your feelings. Because of the distance, it was easy to hide what was happening inside me. I could feign the obedient, well-behaved daughter in my letters home while keeping my hurt and anger masked.

Since I only saw my parents for Christmas and summers, it was easy to adhere to our normal family dynamic and avoid difficult conversations and confrontations. This allowed my parents to see only what they wanted to see, the girl who — on the surface — was "fine." My sisters were in different stages of their lives, so we didn't have much in common, and it was easy to fool them, too. I visited them more frequently than my parents, but not that often, since one was in Pennsylvania raising a family, the other in Maine trying to live off the grid, and I went to college in Boston after boarding school.

For thirty years, that was our family. Physically separated, emotionally stunted, and essentially unknown to one another. What is the consequence of this kind of avoidance? What price did I pay for not going through an age-appropriate maturation and separation process?

Five years after my parents moved to Hawaii, when I was twenty years old and still in college, I fell head-over-heels in love and followed my oldest sister's lead and married. The allure of having a partner to face the world with — a little family of my own — and making a fresh start I could control called to me. My parents made a flaccid attempt to stop me, but when I ignored their perfunctory effort, they threw a big wedding instead. It was obvious to me that they were delighted to have someone else take responsibility for me.

I followed my heart, but it was wounded and thus more reactionary than trustworthy. In hindsight, I can see that my lack of self-awareness and limited life experience stunted my capacity for growth. I stayed nearly thirty years in a codependent marriage with my college sweetheart, a musician and gambler, replicating the passive-aggressive dynamic I'd forged as a teenager—conforming on the outside and rebelling on the inside. In order to lie to and hide from others, it meant I had to hide from and lie to myself, which made it hard for me to know who I was and what I truly wanted. It also made it hard for others to know me, including my sisters, with whom I was not always close and in whom I did not easily confide.

College prepared me to be a social worker, and I worked in foster care for a year or so. Then, in an effort to become more financially stable, and following my father's advice, I transitioned into banking. I didn't expect to stay in that industry long as I was counting on my husband's success in the music business. But that didn't happen. And as it turns out, I was quite good at being a banker. Whether in the bank's formal training program or learning on the job, I picked things up easily and my career progressed accordingly.

I was almost fifty when the strategies I'd used to cope my whole life — hard work and denial — stopped working. My life erupted in a series of calamities, and with the support of professionals, I finally found the time and courage to go deep within to understand and know myself.

The multiple crises detailed in this book allowed me to reconnect with my sisters in a way that I had not been able to when I was keeping secrets. We joined forces to handle our family problems, which not only strengthened our sisterly bonds but also gave me the opportunity to improve my relationship with my parents.

Gradually, I became willing to live my life authentically instead of hiding behind the "good girl" persona. I could dare to be honest instead of telling people what I thought they wanted to hear. I learned to let go of people and practices that were hurting more than helping me, to replace negative self-talk with more supportive language, to widen my capacity for uncertainty, and to strengthen my healthy will. This became my new way of being in the world. Spaciousness, freedom, and joy blossomed in my heart and self-acceptance replaced self-loathing. I gained the capacity to tell my story.

It still saddens me that I waited until after my parents were both gone to do that inner work. Why couldn't I accomplish this level of growth while they were still alive? What kind of relationship might I have had with them if I did? Who can say. But as it is, I am grateful that I was able to at least reconcile with them and show up to support them in ways I wished they had done for me.

INTRODUCTION

I imagine a scenario where my younger self is emotionally fearless: able to stand in her own power, speak what's on her mind and heart, make hard choices, and do it all with compassion and respect. Choosing to be that person now sets an example for my sons and is my gift to that young woman who wasn't yet ready.

That's the spirit with which I wrote this book.

PART ONE
Shock

"September 11, 2001, revealed heroism in ordinary people who might have gone through their lives never called upon to demonstrate the extent of their courage."
—*Geraldine Brooks*

CHAPTER 1
9/11

Since it was before nine o'clock, I didn't feel guilty about being on a personal call at the office.

My older sister Becky and I were making plans for our mother's seventieth surprise birthday party when a low, rumbling thud jolted me. The sixty-story high-rise shook with a loud, abrupt, yet oddly muffled *thump* — as if a derailed train had smashed through a concrete wall in the lobby twenty-one floors below. The subtle swaying that followed disoriented me, like a wave of nausea.

I immediately understood that wherever the noise had come from, it was not the subway, which ran beneath Chase Manhattan Plaza in lower Manhattan where I worked for the newly merged J.P. Morgan Chase.

"Something's not right," I said, interrupting Becky mid-sentence. "I'll call you back."

Standing to look out the window behind my desk, I put my hands on my hips, pushing them forward to stretch out my lower back. It was a cloudless, sunny day and I could easily see a handful of workmen in white overalls on the roof of the Federal Reserve Bank next door. They craned their necks and turned in confused circles, looking for the source of the sound. Suddenly, one of them pointed west, and they all scattered off the roof. The speed at which they went and the fear on their faces made me think they had seen Satan himself.

What the heck did they see? Is something going on that I should worry about?

I rushed to the windows on the other end of the floor to look in the direction the workmen had pointed. White smoke billowed into the brilliant blue sky. It appeared to be coming from the top of the building across the street, which occupied the entire block from Nassau Street to Broadway. I saw bits of paper floating in the air and wondered if a bomb had gone off. There had been a bombing at the World Trade Center

EIGHT SEPTEMBERS

in 1993, so that wasn't such a farfetched idea, but still, it wasn't exactly a common event in Manhattan. The building blocked my view of the Trade Center, and I couldn't see much else, so I went back down the corridor to my boss's office, next to my cubicle, to find out what he knew.

I leaned against the open doorway of his glass-walled office with my arms crossed. "Was that a bomb?"

Bob's tall body sprawled across his ergonomic chair as he leaned back and ran his left hand through his thick brown hair, pushing his bangs to the right. He shook his head with a grimace and leaned forward, elbows on his desk, shoulders hunched. "No bomb. Initial reports are saying a commuter plane has flown into one of the Twin Towers." He pulled at the knot of his tie, loosening it at the neck.

I furrowed my brow and tilted my head. *WTF? That doesn't sound right.*

As we were considering this scenario, Therese and Vincent burst in through the glass doors opposite Bob's office. I wondered why Therese had confetti stuck to her black hair.

Bob and I hurried out of his office to talk with them. Bob leaned against the edge of the cubicle wall and swayed, rubbing his back like a grizzly bear scratching against a tree.

Breathless, Therese said, "We just came from the World Trade Center. That was no commuter airplane. It was a jet liner! We saw it hit." Her words were clear and definitive, but her almond-shaped, dark-brown eyes were wide, her eyebrows raised above lightly freckled round cheeks, as if she herself didn't believe what she was saying.

Seriously? We looked at each other and tried to comprehend the meaning of her words.

Vincent, always nattily dressed and inclined to tell you he was "super fantastic" whenever you asked, nodded in silent agreement.

Pandora, our loan documentation expert, rushed in behind them, wound up and on the verge of tears. Doug, the head of our department, hustled down the hallway to join us, and we clustered together, listening.

Pandora's voice rose and her words tumbled out in a rush as she tugged at the scarf around her neck. "I was on the last PATH train they let into the Trade Center and nearly got crushed by all the people rushing up the escalator. Cops were everywhere, yelling, 'Run! Run!' and the stores were all closing their gates. When I got outside, I could see people hanging out the windows, calling for help. Oh my God! I think I even saw someone jump." Tears filled her eyes, and she paused to take in a gulp of air.

Doug put his arm around Pandora and walked her away from our group, steering her back to his corner office to calm her down. The intimate gesture surprised me given the usual animosity and tension between them.

A few moments later, Doug came running out on the floor and shouted, "A plane hit the other tower! That's no accident. Get the *fuck* out of the building. *Now!*"

I watched Doug sprint by — suit jacket over his shoulder, tie flapping behind him as he hightailed it down the hall — and stood there, stunned, not quite absorbing his message. It didn't occur to me that our sixty-story office was the next-tallest building in the Financial District and could be a target. Officially, we had not been told to evacuate. In fact, the loudspeaker announcement kept saying, "This is not an evacuation!" So much was happening so quickly that I couldn't process what was going on.

Not everyone followed Doug downstairs. Certainly not me, since I avoided crowded elevators due to the claustrophobia that has plagued me for most of my life. My greatest fear has always been being trapped alive.

While debating what to do, my phone rang, so I returned to my desk to answer it. It was Jimmy, my husband, calling from his recording studio at home. I heard the TV blaring in the background.

"Janey, CNN says it's a terrorist attack! You need to get out of there!"

I stalled. Despite the announcement not to vacate, people were leaving the building in droves, and the elevators would be packed—at least in my imagination. "We haven't been ordered to evacuate, and I really don't want to ride down in a crowded elevator."

After twenty years of marriage, Jimmy was well aware of my claustrophobia and usually tolerated it, even if he did think it was silly.

EIGHT SEPTEMBERS

"Okay," I promised Jimmy when he continued pressuring me. "I'll go down in a little bit."

Maybe I will, and maybe I won't.

Used to pandering to my phobia, that morning I did the same. I waited for the elevator traffic to thin out, then rode down to the Plaza to see things for myself. I exited the building through the revolving doors in the thirty-foot-high, glass-walled lobby, disoriented and unsure where to focus my attention.

Executives in suits and clerks in casual clothes milled about the Plaza, a wide-open, granite-tiled space bordered by Nassau Street, Pine Street, and William Street and known for its artwork: the *Group of Four Trees* sculpture by Jean Dubuffet and Isamu Noguchi's *Sunken Garden*. I looked to my right and saw angry flames bursting out of the South Tower, where several of our clients were located. Roiling plumes of dark smoke wreathed the building, and the pungent scent of fire assaulted my nostrils. Sirens blared nonstop.

Papers burnt at the edges swirled around my feet, so close I could read them. I thought it odd that financial records from Cantor Fitzgerald, one of our customers located at the top of the North Tower, were over here by our building, four blocks east of the Trade Center.

Our heavyset, officious head of operations stood nearby. He had a transistor radio and one earphone plugged into his ear.

"A plane just hit the Pentagon," he reported. "They're evacuating the White House."

Are you shitting me? What the hell is going on?

No one's cell phone worked, and we were not sure what to do. Everyone stood around, aimless and confused. Time seemed suspended.

Diane, another client manager, walked across the Plaza on her way back from a client meeting. Already a vice president when I joined the Wall Street group at Manufacturers Hanover Trust in 1987, Diane had been my colleague for a long time. We had already survived three mergers together. Her short dark hair, pushed back with a headband, framed her delicate porcelain features. She gave me a lopsided grin and raised her eyebrows as she cocked her head toward the building. "I need to pee. Can we go in?"

"Yeah, actually, we can," I said as it dawned on me slowly. "It's not an official evacuation." I glanced at my watch. It was not even ten a.m. Having something to do felt better than standing around.

Diane and I went into the lobby and took the elevator up to the twenty-first floor. No need to worry about crowded elevators now, since no one else was going back up. Already, our office was scattered. Some of our staff members were on the twenty-first floor, some were down on the Plaza, and some had gone to our backup offices at 4 New York Plaza. Some might have even gone home. No one knew who was where. So much for our well-thought-out disaster-recovery plan, outlined in painstaking detail in the department policy manual. As with a lot of what happened on Wall Street, our plan had failed to factor in the human element, which, in this case, was panic.

***

Our department, once the Wall Street Group, was now called the Broker Dealer Division. Broker dealers buy, sell, and trade securities for their own account and for their clients. All of our clients were broker dealers, most of them located downtown. As bankers, we supported the infrastructure of Wall Street. We lent money, moved cash and securities, issued letters of credit — the bank's guarantee that the broker dealer "promises to pay"— and settled with the clearinghouses, which is the process used to pay for all those stocks and bonds. The pace was fast, the dollars at stake enormous, and the consequences of a mistake could put a firm out of business. It was our job to manage and control risk, to understand the bank's credit exposure — potential losses — to the Street at any given moment. And that was about to get incredibly difficult.

My husband called again. Jimmy had been fielding phone calls at home from family and friends who wanted to know if I was okay. I was surprised and flattered, unaware of the extensive media coverage of that morning's events. Our office phones were ringing off the hook, forcing me to focus on my job.

EIGHT SEPTEMBERS

"What do you think about J.J. and Will? Can you go get them?" I asked Jimmy. Our sons, ages ten and six, were at PS9, an elementary school nine blocks north of our apartment on the Upper West Side. "Don't you think they should be at home?"

"No," he argued. "They're safer at school. Best to keep their normal routine."

Did he mean that? Or was he preoccupied with his own projects? I often made the mistake of assuming we had the same priorities.

"Really? This could scare them," I said, not convinced by his logic. I would have gone and picked them up myself if I'd been able to, but I had to depend on Jimmy, who worked from home, and stay at the office to deal with the intensifying chaos of the financial markets. "Maybe school will keep them busy? I guess they don't need to know about the details just yet."

After all, I told myself, our boys were only in the fourth and first grades. Since their school was ten miles north of my office, a seemingly safe distance away, I reluctantly agreed with Jimmy that the best course of action was to leave them in school. Little did we know that all the other parents were rushing to get their kids, so things were definitely not "normal" for them at school.

Just after I'd hung up with Jimmy, we heard an explosion like a clap of thunder, loud and rolling like the roar of fighter jets. Thick brown fog immediately enveloped our building. I thought maybe the Federal Reserve Bank next door was being bombed, so I ran to look. Someone shouted, "Get away from the windows!" and I jumped back quickly. About ten of us gathered in the file room in the center of the building, trying to figure out what had happened. I had the sense of being disembodied, as if I were physically in the room, but mentally somewhere else entirely. I stood without really comprehending anything—blank and numb.

"One of the Twin Towers collapsed!" someone said in disbelief. I looked around at my colleagues, dumbfounded.

What?! My mind couldn't process what that meant. Trained as a social worker and Sunday school teacher, then as a banker, I saw the world through relationships, psychology, and religion. I understood balance sheets and income statements. I did *not* understand engineering or physics. The possibility of one of the one-hundred-and-ten floor towers collapsing had simply never occurred to me.

"They're reporting a plane crashed in Pennsylvania too."

This information floated slowly into my already addled brain.

Oh my God! Is it related? Was that an accident? Where was it headed? What is going to happen next? Events were unfolding too quickly for me to process.

After a bit, we returned to our desks to try to collect ourselves and deal with the incessantly ringing phones. The air outside was so thick with smoke I could not see out the windows. It felt as if we were inside a cyclone, and if anyone had second thoughts about staying in the building, there was nothing to be done about it. We were trapped for the duration. But I felt safe in this familiar place with critical work demanding my attention.

Then it happened again. *Boom!* More smoke, more noise and confusion, more earth shaking beneath us. My mind flitted over the thought that there were still people outside on the Plaza. A colleague explained that the other tower had now fallen, and I tried to make sense of his words.

How is this even possible? Will more buildings fall? Is lower Manhattan going to sink?

Someone reported that one of our operations colleagues had fainted. It took me a while to understand she was having a panic attack. I didn't seem to be having any reaction at all, certainly not panic. Shock and confusion, yes, but I seemed to be functioning just fine.

Our department, which occupied half of the twenty-first floor, was divided into two sides. My side, where Doug, our department head, was located, had offices and cubicles for the client managers and credit analysts. The operations side was behind locked doors, where clerks sat at desks on an open floor handling loan advances, collateral, and daily settlement activity. Therese went over to the other side to see how she could help our panic-stricken colleague. Diane and I continued to answer the phones on our side, maintaining some semblance of business as usual while we triaged work and personal issues. The typical adrenaline that drove our business kicked into high gear. Working kept me focused, while all around me, confusion reigned. The phones never stopped. Calls came from family members, friends, colleagues in Midtown — everyone trying to contact loved ones working in or near the World Trade Center. Somehow, they thought we might know where they were or how to find them.

But we didn't, and we had to move on to other calls, many of which were about funding our clients.

"Bob!" I yelled, swiveling my chair toward his office as I put the phone on hold, receiver still in my hand.

"Yo!" he answered, poking his head out of his office, looking shell-shocked like the rest of us.

"Salomon Smith Barney wants to know if they can borrow $5 billion tonight. *Un*secured. They can't get their money out of Bank of New York," I said, rolling my eyes and grimacing. We always referred to Bank of New York (BONY), our chief competitor, as Brand X. We fought for clients constantly, extolling our own capabilities and casting doubts on Brand X's ability to deliver. Now, from their location next to the World Trade Center, Bank of New York was completely — and unexpectedly — off the grid. Their clients were left in the dark, unable to move cash or securities. The financial services industry is its own ecosystem, and a competitor also plays the role of service provider, ally, and market participant, so BONY's absence threatened to seriously destabilize the marketplace.

"No word yet if the Fed is relaxing the regulations," Bob said. "So they can't borrow from Citi."

In order to prevent banks from exposing themselves to unnecessary risk, which could threaten the stability of the entire banking system, a regulated broker dealer like Salomon Smith Barney was prohibited from borrowing unsecured money from their affiliated commercial bank, in this case Citibank. Instead, Salomon Smith Barney typically borrowed from Bank of New York, its settlement bank. A settlement bank provides funding backed by collateral, so at the end of the day the broker dealer can pay for the securities it bought for itself or its customers. With Bank of New York out of commission, Salomon was scrambling to find the money it needed to operate.

"Any word on BONY?" Bob asked.

"I was told Brand X was gonna be back up and running any minute," I said, "but *that* hasn't happened. What are we going to do?"

We had authority to lend up to $2 billion for a collateralized loan that would be paid back on the same day. We definitely needed special approval to make a large, unsecured overnight loan of $5 billion.

"I'll call George and get it approved, just in case," Bob volunteered. George was the senior credit officer for the Investment Bank, and a good partner to our group. Bob picked up a phone in one of the empty cubicles and leaned against the divider while he made the call, his own phone line out of commission since both Twin Towers had fallen.

I turned back to my phone. "Okay, we'll try to get approval. I'll call you back as soon as I can," I informed the client, pushing the disconnect button abruptly to grab another call.

"Jane!" Diane called. I stood and looked over the cubicle divider and saw her sitting at her desk, the phone glued to her ear. "Is our wire transfer system operating?" The wire system is what the clients use to send and receive money.

"Yeah, I think so, DiDi. Why?"

"Lehman's complaining their funds are being held up."

Diane had been Lehman's banker for years, and they counted on her to get things done. Forced out of their offices in the World Financial Center, they were now relying on the bank to let them know what was happening in their accounts.

"Well, you know *nothing* is coming in from Bank of New York. Maybe Lehman's hitting their intraday overdraft line?"

Timing issues — otherwise known as intraday or same day liquidity — were a big problem, even on a normal day. We had intraday credit lines in place to "grease the skids" for a few hours — allowing clients to send money out when they hadn't yet received money in — but there were limits to those credit lines. Once those limits were hit, outgoing wires were stopped. It was possible Lehman had already hit their limit, and that's why they were still waiting for their money.

"Shit!" she said. "Guess they'll just have to wait." She frowned and shook her head, frustrated we couldn't help. Cash was the lifeblood for broker dealers. Being able to move it where it was needed, when it was needed, was a critical aspect of the broker dealer role, and more than one broker dealer had gone out of business by miscalculating their cash needs.

Therese came back from the other side of the floor and reported that our fainted operations colleague was resting. "Apparently DTCC is up and running and expecting us to settle for clients," she informed us, her whole body tense and her eyes still wide from the shock of the morning.

DTCC, the Depository Trust Clearing Company, was located a few blocks away on Water Street, overlooking the East River. Owned by the banks and broker dealers who used their services, DTCC kept the books and records to make sure stocks and bonds were paid for and ownership was transferred to the proper owner after every purchase and sale of securities. In the mid-1960s, the process of exchanging paper checks for physical stock certificates became so onerous that Wall Street had to close every Wednesday afternoon simply to catch up with the paperwork. DTCC was created to clear and settle all those transactions electronically.

Like Bank of New York, we were a settlement bank for many broker dealers, obligating us to either receive a payment from, or make a payment to, DTCC at the end of each day. If sales exceeded purchases, the broker dealer would receive cash from DTCC at their bank account with us. Easy enough. If purchases exceeded sales, the broker dealer owed money to DTCC. If they didn't have the cash to make that payment, they borrowed it from us in an act known as a broker's loan. In return for the loan, they gave us a lien against their securities at DTCC as collateral, so if they didn't pay us back, we could sell the securities to repay the loan.

With clients out of commission and money transfer problems escalating, it began to look like we would be extending a lot of broker's loans. And if Bank of New York didn't come back online soon, we would have to finance all of the government bonds our clients sold but couldn't send to BONY's clients, too, since that bank's systems were down.

We spent the next hour or so responding to client calls and personal requests. We were so busy and reactive that we had no time to assess what might be happening outside our little universe.

9/11

Shortly after noon, a security guard walked by my desk. A layer of thick, brown dust covered him head to toe. I didn't understand why, not quite computing he must have been outside when the Twin Towers fell. I had no idea how bad things were out there. He looked young and wore a grim expression, yet he strode purposefully down the hall, silently counting heads.

His presence interrupted our hectic activity, and he made it clear that this was now an official evacuation.

"Time to go!" he barked, his voice hoarse. We barely had time to grab our personal items before he led us briskly to the service elevator to take us down to the ground floor, one level below the Plaza. As we stepped into the elevator, I took a deep breath, closed my eyes, and pushed my fear down into my belly. I couldn't rely on my usual strategy of waiting for the next empty elevator; we had to go *now*. My twenty or so colleagues were gracious in accommodating my claustrophobia and gave me plenty of personal space on the ride down.

My heart pounded the entire time.

CHAPTER 2

Evacuation

In the ground floor lobby, people were lined up to get cash at the wall of ATMs near the entrance to the subway. Others were congregating in small groups, talking, and crying. Noise bounced off the white tile floor and echoed through the low-ceilinged, block-wide lobby as a steady stream of people exited the building onto the street.

The subways were not running, and our team hesitated in the lobby, unsure where to go or what to do. Bob, Diane, Therese, and I talked options. We had an obligation to both the bank and its clients, but we also had a million questions.

"Is it still a workday?"

"Are markets open?"

"Is the bank functioning?"

"*Where is Doug?*"

Our department played a critical role in the daily functioning of Wall Street, and we took our responsibilities seriously. While most people went about their day unaware of the machinations of Wall Street, what happened there allowed our economy to function — not just for corporations, but for individuals too. What we did helped money flow, supporting the availability of goods and services, allowing credit to be extended for the purchase of houses, cars, and college educations, and facilitating the financing of the US government.

"Since we haven't heard otherwise, let's assume it's still a workday," Bob said. "We need to be able to operate." We all agreed, and with that assumption made, we began to organize a plan.

The head of our customer service team said, "Mike, Ann Marie, and I will get to our homes on Staten Island and set up our remote access." Their team provided an important link to our clients, and new technology made working from home with remote access possible. We assumed the Staten Island Ferry was running.

The head of loan operations spoke up. "I'll take a few of my team and go to 4 New York Plaza and see if I can activate our disaster-recovery space." Accessing our loan operations and collateral management system would be critical to maintaining our responsibilities, and our disaster-recovery plan included office space in a building a few blocks away that used a different power grid — something we once thought would be sufficient in the event of an emergency.

Next we had to figure out where our staff could work if we couldn't get back into our building.

"Let's head uptown to 270 Park and see if we can find out what senior management wants us to do," I suggested.

Some of our group went south, some went north, and some simply disappeared.

I headed north, along with Bob, Diane, and Jeff, our department business manager. We stepped outside into another world. Everything was covered in thick ash particles that were falling like snow from above. Warm, slightly humid air pressed in on us, a contrast to the crisp air conditioning in the lobby, and dust caught in my throat. The sun was muted in the dark sky and the air was cloudy and yellow. The city was hushed, and the energy was akin to the morning after a wild party — deflated, messy, hungover. Yet it was also surprisingly organized. First responders were already handing out water bottles and dust masks, ordering dazed people where to go: *Walk away. East. North.* In Chinatown, an old man stood holding a cardboard sign bearing a handwritten message that said "UPTOWN" with an arrow showing where to turn. His smile revealed a missing tooth as he waved us on with his gnarled hand and nodded to encourage us.

There were lines at the pay phones on every corner. Groups of people were standing outside store windows and bars, wherever TVs were visible, staring at live videos of the carnage. The streets and sidewalks were crowded with refugees from downtown offices. We kept walking. *Away.* We could see and smell the smoke and fire behind us, hear the steady stream of sirens piercing the afternoon silence. We noticed the trail left behind by people who'd fled hours before us — a random shoe, broken eyeglasses, a pocketbook.

I was wearing high heels, part of my everyday uniform. I had recently purchased a beautiful new silk suit for fall: a skirt of gold, brown, and green geometric shapes with a beige silk blouse and a tailored green jacket that matched my eyes. The heat of the day paired with the effort of the walk forced me to remove my jacket, but I kept my heels on.

The farther away we got, the clearer the blue sky became. When we got near Madison and East 24th Street, I remembered my client, Credit Suisse First Boston, had offices there. Earlier in the day, I had been on the phone with their operations guys at 5 World Trade Center, a nine-story building that was part of the WTC complex. They'd already been worried about how they were going to finance themselves that night, and that was *before* they realized they needed to worry about getting out of their building alive.

It suddenly occurred to me to stop at Credit Suisse. I needed to find a working phone and figure out what was going on. Plus, I was hot and tired from walking for well over an hour.

Jeff came with me. An older gentleman who had worked for Doug for many years, Jeff was courtly and deferential, humbly keeping his balding head down and his watery, pink-rimmed eyes averted as I pushed my way into 11 Madison Avenue.

"We're not letting anyone without an employee ID into the building," the guard informed me, halting us at the security desk and blocking our entrance.

"You have to let us in," I argued. "We just walked up here from downtown, and I'm their banker. Please!" I was adamant, not to mention on the verge of tears.

The guards located someone who knew me, and finally we were let in. We ran into the operations guys I'd been on the phone with earlier. They'd walked uptown, too, after running out of their building, which had been on the verge of collapse. They looked fried, totally stressed, but they were here, doing their job, just like I was trying to do. Wasn't everybody? We were all racing to contain the chaos, rushing to salvage a world that might soon be irretrievable, unsure of what was happening.

We commandeered an office. I gratefully kicked off my heels, sat at a desk, and began making phone calls and madly scribbling in my notebook. Jeff stood behind me — silent, curious, watching over my shoulder, lending moral support. I don't think he'd ever seen me in action before. He clasped his hands behind his back, shifting back and forth on his feet.

It was about 2:30 when I picked up the phone and consulted my list of my colleagues' emergency phone numbers. "Jerry! Good, you made it home. Are you safe? Are your systems operational?" I'd known Jerry, the head of our customer service team, since I'd joined the group in 1987. It felt like a victory that he'd gotten home safely.

"Yes, I've got access to the system. Not to worry," Jerry assured me.

I now knew that we'd be able to track our clients' bank accounts, see cash come in and go out. That visibility into money flows was a key part of our ability to manage risk.

"Hang in there, Jerry. Talk soon!"

I hung up and made my next call.

"Al, what's happening down there?" I'd known Al as long as Diane and Jerry. We had all worked together at Manufacturers Hanover Trust, where I first became a banker.

Al ran the bank's US Government Securities Clearance department, one of our biggest operating services for broker dealers. Bank of New York was still completely out of commission with all their systems down but Al, who was at his office on the twenty-first floor of 4 New York Plaza, reported, "We're all good here, Jane. Systems are running. We're finding space for Patel and his team. Doug was here a little while ago, but when the lights flickered, he shot out of here and headed up to 270."

270 was the bank's world headquarters on Park Avenue.

Al laughed. "Feet, don't fail me now!" He sounded normal, as if it were just another crazy day on Wall Street.

After the 1993 World Trade Center bombing, Al had gone to the top floor of the North Tower to obtain Cantor Fitzgerald's trading records,

EVACUATION

the only civilian to do so. He embodied our commitment to our clients, and he wasn't about to abandon his post.

"Brand X keeps saying they're about to come back online," he told me, "but we're not seeing anything coming in or going out from them. Bonds are piling up down here."

Al meant that bonds were being delivered to the bank's account at the Fed. We'd been paying for them as they came in, and since we had nowhere to send the bonds, we might get stuck holding — and financing — them overnight. I needed to talk with Doug and senior management.

Now that I had touched base with the team and had some idea of what was going on, I began to settle myself. I called Jimmy to let him know my game plan and to check on the kids. He told me most of the other children had already been picked up from school by the time he got them.

"How are they doing? What did you tell them? Are they okay? Were they scared?" I asked.

"I told them a bad thing happened near your work but that you are okay and will be home soon," Jimmy reassured me.

"Great, thanks. What are they doing now?" I asked, drawing lines of connected triangles in my notebook.

"Downstairs on the computer playing a game." Okay, this was their normal routine when they weren't in an after-school program. Those hadn't started yet, as the school year had just begun. My triangles turned into hearts.

"Fucking terrorists!" Jimmy shouted. "How dare they?! We ought to hunt them down and kill all of them!" I could hear the news in the background. I remembered how he'd stayed glued to the TV every minute during the O.J. Simpson car chase and murder trial, obsessed with the minutiae, emotionally involved with the drama. I'd lost interest quickly, uneasy with the hype and fearmongering, bored with the relentless commentary.

My doodles turned to Xs. "Please don't let the boys hear you talk like that!" I said sharply. "They're too young to understand." Self-conscious that Jeff was in the room and could hear me, I quickly redirected my conversation. "Tell them I love them and that I'll be home soon. Love you too. Gotta go."

EIGHT SEPTEMBERS

Jeff and I left Credit Suisse First Boston and walked the twenty-four blocks uptown to join Doug at East 48th and Park Avenue. Jeff peeled off and continued on his quest, like so many others stranded in the city, to find a way over the George Washington Bridge to his home in New Jersey. We awkwardly wished each other good luck, an odd and unexpected intimacy between us.

A small crew had convened at the bank headquarters at 270 Park Avenue. The message was clear from both the Federal Reserve Bank and senior management: *The bank is open for business. Provide liquidity. Keep cash and securities moving.* It was a matter of national security to maintain functioning financial markets. The alternative was financial panic.

The message we received was loud and clear: "Doug, you and your team just keep doing what you do. Your country needs you!"

Before I became a banker, I'd been unaware of how the banking system supported the infrastructure of our economy. Now, of course, I knew there would be chaos in the streets if the banks stopped functioning. If people couldn't access their cash and their credit cards wouldn't work and the supermarkets and gas stations shut down because they couldn't borrow money to fund their inventories, civil unrest would be right around the corner. If the US government stopped paying its employees and sending out social security, unemployment, and welfare checks because they didn't have enough cash, panic would sweep the country.

Making sure the United States government could finance its operations was a huge part of what we did. The federal government issues debt, borrowing money to have the cash to meet its obligations. Known as US Government Securities, this debt is the world's safest, soundest investment and is traded extensively and owned worldwide.

The Federal Reserve Bank of New York, the government's central bank that implements our nation's monetary policy, is responsible for the issuance, settlement, and clearance of all government debt issued by the US Treasury Department. The Treasury sells the securities through an auction process that allows authorized bond dealers — known as "primary" dealers —to bid on the securities. In 2001, there were only twenty-five of those authorized bond dealers, all physically located in New York City, all impacted by the attacks.

The transactions between the Treasury and the primary dealers clear and settle electronically, mainly through two regulated clearance banks who play the role of middleman — J.P. Morgan Chase and Bank of New York — providing the government with cash and the dealers with the securities.

Every day, *trillions* of dollars of government securities transactions are conducted through this banking system, which is connected by technology. The terrorist attacks that morning disrupted almost every participant in the system, both in terms of personnel and physical assets, creating unprecedented turmoil in the market — ostensibly what the terrorists wanted. But the loss of Bank of New York created a very tricky risk situation for J.P. Morgan Chase.

Most government bond trades settle on the *same day* — meaning that they are exchanged and paid for on the same day they are traded, which means those trades needed to settle *on* 9/11, despite the attacks. Over $500 billion of government bond trades had already happened before the first attack at 8:46 a.m. If our clients were unable to pay, then we, their clearing bank, had to do it on their behalf.

Late that afternoon, our little group at 270 Park Avenue decided that part of "maintaining functioning financial markets" meant reducing chaos in the government bond marketplace. Specifically, J.P. Morgan would accept all the bonds that were delivered to our clients on 9/11, even though a consequence of the technological disruption from the attacks meant that *we didn't have the normal instructions from clients authorizing us to do so.*

Al and his back-office personnel would have to settle the trades that happened that morning. If we couldn't redeliver the bonds that came in, we would be financing them with the Fed on behalf of our customers. That's why we kept waiting for Bank of New York to get back online. We couldn't deliver anything to them while they were out of commission, which meant we couldn't offload and get paid for the securities we received. We were aggravated because they kept saying they'd be back up within the hour, only to push it back again while the rest of Wall Street waited in limbo.

On a normal day, my job required me to stay until settlement occurred. On 9/11, settlement with the Fed had been extended beyond the normal three p.m. deadline, and still hadn't closed by seven p.m. There was nothing left for me to do but sit around and wait. Since I wasn't actually needed to complete settlement and could be reached on the phone if a loan was required, I decided to head home while it was still light outside. I figured it would be nearly impossible to get a cab, and I did not want to walk to my apartment on the Upper West Side in a dark, deserted Manhattan. It turned out that I got a cab immediately. No one was allowed in or out of the city, the cabby informed me. Too busy to keep up with the news, I had no idea they'd closed Manhattan. It was the fastest, cheapest cab ride ever. The streets were deserted.

The cab dropped me in front of our brownstone. I walked inside to the sight of my family eating dinner in the small kitchen at the back of the apartment, much like any other night. I kicked off my heels, now covered in ash, and threw my jacket and purse on the dark-red leather couch that sat outside the kitchen against the exposed brick wall. I hugged my husband and kids and told them I loved them. I had no energy to discuss the day and rushed upstairs to change my clothes. The last thing I wanted to do was look at the news. My body reverberated and my mind was blank as I lay across the bed on my back, listening to the stillness, numb. I took a few deep breaths and felt tears slide down the sides of my face to my neck. I wiped them away and rolled over, pushing myself up on my elbows and squeezing my eyes tight to summon the willpower to push through.

Get it together, Jane. The boys need you.

After a while, I went downstairs to put J.J. and William to bed. Always my favorite part of the day, I considered it the most important thing I did. J.J., age ten, lived inside his imagination, creating stories and games, happy to read and watch funny TV shows. William, age six, was sensitive and moody, less talkative than his brother, anxious to do well, quicker to cry. I had always marveled at how my labor for each son mirrored their personalities. J.J.'s lasted forty-two hours. He gave up his comfy spot in my womb reluctantly, deciding to join the world at his own leisurely pace. My one-speed wonder, I always joked, and to this day, he is not one to be rushed. William came ten days late, but when he did, the labor was fast and hard. Slow to make decisions and uncomfortable with transitions, William is impatient to act once he's ready.

After they changed into their pj's and brushed their teeth, we snuggled on one of the twin beds in their tiny bedroom, the cheerful Looney Tunes wallpaper a stark contrast to my mood. I could feel them carefully watching me as I read from a book my mother had given us, tears gathering under my eyelids, then dripping down my cheeks as my throat closed up.

"I'll love you forever, I'll like you for always, As long as I'm living, my baby you'll be."

CHAPTER 3

Midtown

My cell phone woke me from a deep sleep the next morning. I hadn't bothered to set my alarm the night before, having had enough for one day.

"Where are you?" I asked, trying not to sound groggy.

"At 270 Park," Bob informed me, his voice husky. It was already after nine a.m.

Shit. Bob made it all the way to Midtown from Jersey already, and I'm still in bed.

"I guess we're working today?" I lifted myself up onto one elbow and tried to focus, my hopes of retreating from the world vanishing.

"Yeah, we need the client managers in today. There's a *lot* going on. We're setting up outside of George's office for the time being. See you there," Bob said, then clicked off the line.

Okay then.

I got up, showered, and dressed. It would only take about twenty minutes in a cab to get to 270 Park Avenue, but I still needed to get moving. The kids would remain safe at home with Jimmy, which was one worry off my plate.

I went downstairs where they were playing.

"Hey, guys!" I called. "Mom's gotta go to work, but you've got the day off! Come give me a hug and a kiss goodbye." I held their warm, young bodies in my arms a little bit longer than usual as I breathed them in and kissed their faces and necks, prompting them to giggle and pull away.

"See you tonight. Be good for Daddy!" I turned away quickly so they wouldn't see my tears.

Jimmy was already in his studio flipping through the cable news channels. I stood outside his doorway in our small entry foyer as I gathered

41

my pocketbook and keys. "Please don't let the kids see any of that!" I implored.

"I won't," Jimmy said absentmindedly, then glanced at me. "They'll be fine. Just go. Be safe!" He got up and came to give me a hug, reassuring me he would take care of things on the home front. "Go get 'em, tiger." He grinned, kissing the top of my head, which rested gently against his heart.

Outside, the city was eerily quiet, with very few people on the sidewalks. The smell of the still-burning Trade Center permeated the air all the way up on the west side, a strange contrast to the gorgeous fall morning. I found a cab quickly on Columbus Avenue, and we drove straight across Central Park and cruised easily down Fifth Avenue. The proliferation of American flags hanging above all the storefronts confused me.

Were the flags always there? When did that happen?

I felt out of sync with the rest of the world.

***

I thought back to the night of my first Wall Street crisis: Black Monday on October 19, 1987, when the stock market crashed.

I had just started working as a loan officer in the Wall Street Group at Manufacturers Hanover Trust, one of the predecessor firms for J.P. Morgan Chase. We lent money to stockbrokers and bond dealers, and they pledged us their stocks and bonds as collateral. I learned there were all sorts of rules — some regulatory, others simply the bank's good sense — that governed what kinds of securities we could take, how much we could lend against them, and what we could do in the event of a default.

Our broker-dealer customers could borrow between 50 to 80 cents on every dollar of securities they gave us. Normally, we would reprice collateral every morning with the prior day's closing prices. We had to make sure the ratio between the security value and loan amount didn't go below what we originally lent. If the stocks and bonds had fallen in value, we'd call the customer, and they'd either pay down the loan or send us more collateral. This was known as a "margin call." If they didn't do one of those two things, we had the right to sell their securities and pay ourselves back with the proceeds.

When the stock market crashed that Monday in 1987, dropping 22 percent — still the *largest ever* one-day percentage drop to date — the value of our collateral fell so dramatically we couldn't wait until the next morning. We had to stay late the night of October 19 to manually reprice all our securities collateral so we could make margin calls to ensure we had enough collateral to cover our loans. The margin calls would flow from the banks to their broker-dealer clients to *their* clients, the individual stock owners. The regulators were worried the cascading margin calls would cause mass bankruptcies within the industry and beyond. I realized then how critical my job was and how we needed to respond in an urgent, real-time manner to market events. I liked that aspect of working on Wall Street, the sense that what we did mattered. In 1987, I didn't yet understand exactly how the stock market fit together with the overall economy, but I did know that a stock market crash in 1929 led to the Great Depression, so doing my small part to stabilize the banking system seemed like a worthwhile endeavor.

Back then, we crowded into the cramped Brokers Loan department, an area behind locked doors usually filled with clerks tasked with booking loans, disbursing proceeds, monitoring collateral, and making margin calls. Their large metal desks, inches apart, were covered with reams of computer printout paper, ashtrays, and ledger books. On a normal morning, two of the junior officers would go over, coffee or tea in hand, to sign off on the collateral and loan advances while cracking jokes with the clerks and smoking — a casual but critical part of our day.

On the night of the crash, however, all hands were required on deck, from the head of the department to the vice presidents, assistant vice presidents, analysts, and associates. Instead of the usual convenience of a computer upload with the information we needed, we had to search on the Quotron terminal — a device that replaced printed stock ticker tape with an electronic screen — for the closing price for every stock or bond we held as collateral, then manually calculate the value by multiplying the closing price by the number of shares pledged to us. We had over $500 million in loans across an estimate of seventy-five borrowers, each of which had a *minimum* of five stocks supporting it, but many had twenty or thirty apiece. We had a lot of work to do.

We finally finished around nine p.m., and our boss offered to take us all out for drinks. "Work hard, play hard" was the Wall Street motto in the '80s, when "play" still included Jell-O wrestling and wet T-shirt contests on the pier. I didn't participate in what I considered to be misogynistic events — not that I was invited — but drinking was fast becoming my specialty. We piled into the elevator, maybe ten of us in all, laughing and talking, ready to decompress.

When we got to the first floor, the doors wouldn't open. It may have been only sixty seconds before they did, but in that time, my face had gone white, my palms became sweaty, and my heart pounded so loudly I could hear nothing else. I flew out of that elevator, taking deep breaths to settle myself, and couldn't get to Captain's Ketch fast enough for that drink.

***

When I arrived on the seventeenth floor at 270 Park Avenue on Wednesday, September 12, the place was already bustling. We had commandeered a corner outside the office of the chief credit officer. We were about fifteen people trying to work in six cubicles, sharing the few phone lines with limited computer access. Most of our operations staff were working remotely, so it was just the client managers and credit officers, scrambling to meet customer needs and figure out our exposure: how much money we had at risk and how much we could possibly lose. Standing up, leaning over, and reaching behind, we navigated around each other in the limited space, triaging like we were in a war zone. And in a way, we were.

Doug, together with two of his team, ran around trying to procure more "permanent" space for us, including computers, phones, and whatever connectivity we needed to be functional. It would take days before we were settled on another floor in some semblance of normality, but thank goodness our remote access disaster-recovery plan was working, since all our clients were in crisis mode and wanted immediate answers. We struggled to respond, balancing work demands with personal concerns.

My mother, who lived in Pennsylvania, had been visiting friends in Canada, and no one had heard from her. My father, who lived in Hawaii with his new bride, finally tracked me down, no doubt getting the phone number from Jimmy. Our relationship had been strained the past few years, ever since he had divorced my mother and remarried a woman my older sister Becky's age. He longed for forgiveness, which I resolutely withheld because his remorse seemed related only to the consequences of his actions. Besides, he'd never admitted what he'd done that needed forgiveness.

"Janey! Oh, thank goodness you are safe! We were all so worried about you." I could hear his relief and enthusiasm ooze across the phone lines.

"Thanks, Dad. I'm actually okay. Super busy though. Things are crazy here." I could barely hear him; the phones were ringing, and people were talking and shouting all around me.

He started asking me questions, trying to keep me on the line. We spoke for a few minutes before I cut him off.

"Dad, I'm so sorry, but I can't tie up this line. We only have a few phones for the entire department, and we're under a time crunch. I've got to go." Six hours behind New York, it was morning for him in Honolulu but afternoon for me, and almost settlement time. As a CEO who refused to retire, worked seven days a week, and sat on multiple profit and nonprofit boards, he certainly understood prioritizing work above all else.

"Okay. I love you. We're all so proud of you . . ." He drifted off, reluctant to say goodbye. He'd taken to repeating himself lately, leaving long-winded messages on our answering machine, striving for connection, for acceptance — or so I thought.

"Bye, Dad!" I said, then punched the disconnect button.

The phones continued to ring with unusual requests we couldn't begin to meet.

EIGHT SEPTEMBERS

"Can you move money from my corporate account to my personal account so I can write payroll checks for my employees? We can't access our systems." Simple transactions like payroll had become impossible because with offices destroyed, there were no checkbooks and no computers. If folks didn't have remote backup capabilities, they were stuck.

"Can you get me access to the vault in your branch at the Financial Center? Our backup tapes are there."

Um... no. Even if the vault wasn't practically underneath the World Trade Center now, it was occupied by US Marines and military — no civilians allowed.

"Can you get us copies of our 250 tri-party repurchase agreements? All our files were lost when the building collapsed."

Managing tri-party repurchase agreements, more commonly known as *tri-party repo*, was part of Al's government clearance business and a big operation for us. We assisted our clients with their financing needs by acting as the third party in their transactions. We kept both the lender's cash and the dealer's collateral and moved them to the other party when certain conditions were met. The agreements they were asking for were what governed those conditions. In response to this request — the answer to which was *Sorry, no* — we glossed over the reason the files were missing, since the enormity of it was incomprehensible.

"We lost nearly seven hundred employees. Will you still continue to settle and clear for us?" Cantor Fitzgerald, whose New York headquarters was located at the top of the World Trade Center, had lost every single person in the New York office on 9/11, an unfathomable tragedy. We were their main bank, and they were desperate to keep their business afloat, as we'd helped them do after the World Trade Center bombing in 1993. Without our support, they would likely be out of business by the end of the week.

Bob and Doug left to meet with Cantor's CEO, Howard, in his home to figure out what we could do without taking on too much risk. Howard had lost his brother in the attacks and only escaped being there himself because he had taken his son to his first day of kindergarten. Yet he, too, had to put his grief on hold for a larger purpose.

It went on and on like that all week, one situation more critical than the next. Our clients were searching for physical locations where displaced employees could work, relying on vendors and banks to process their work for them, and trying to reconcile positions by reverse engineering what trades might possibly have happened when and between which parties. Those same employees were also grieving their colleagues, friends, and relatives as the 9/11 victims were disproportionately concentrated in the financial services sector. Compounding their losses, many came from families and communities with heavy concentrations of first responders, some of whom were missing, dead, or still working at the site. The pervasive grief pressed against my chest, making it hard to breathe. Taking a moment in the conference room to participate in one of the many televised funeral services helped release some of that pressure.

The actions we would take, and the decisions we needed to make, would be life-altering for people who had no idea what we were doing or that we were even doing it. The weight of responsibility hung over us all, adding tension and adrenaline to every interaction. Doing our jobs felt crucial: toiling behind the scenes, keeping the country's financial infrastructure functioning to prevent the economic chaos that would ensue if we failed.

There was no lack of commitment from anyone on our team. We all showed up, willing to do what needed to be done.

CHAPTER 4

Trouble

When I joined the Wall Street Group at Manufacturers Hanover Trust Company in 1987, my boss suggested I meet with Al to learn about his side of the business with our mutual clients. Walking from my department through a labyrinth of hallways and locked doors to Al's cramped office on the other side of the fourth floor at 40 Wall Street, I literally moved from the "front office" to the "back office" — Wall Street terms for our different roles. I was part of the department that lent money and sold bank services like check cashing and money transfers to Wall Street companies — brokerage firms, investment banks, and, apparently, inter-dealer brokers, whatever those were. Al ran the government securities clearance business, a mysterious and complicated operation I was eager to understand. He'd been in the business nearly twenty years, and I'd been in it about twenty minutes.

My front office group worked at big mahogany desks in a spacious, hushed carpeted room with large windows overlooking the New York Stock Exchange. The Exchange is a massive structure with six Corinthian columns and a 110-foot-wide sculpture above the columns titled *Integrity Protecting the Works of Man*. Surprisingly for Wall Street, Integrity is a woman, classically robed and wearing a winged cap. She stands at the top of the triangle with arms outstretched, fists closed, watching over toiling men, women, and children.

Al's group worked noisily under fluorescent lights on metal desks stacked with computer printouts, surrounded by overflowing cardboard boxes lining the linoleum floor, looking out over the far-less-inspiring Pine Street through dirty reinforced windows.

In my bright-red suit and white bow-tie blouse, I was certain I looked out of place — the lone young female in a blur of preoccupied men, shouting and joking with one another. The haze of cigarette smoke and ringing phones reminded me of my college internship in an East Boston police station, when I was studying to be a social worker.

Being the only female was okay, but I never liked being the center of attention. I'd developed a woman's body at the age of twelve and suffered enough construction worker catcalls and unwanted male advances ever since that I was hypersensitive to the objectification of women. Even now, at the ripe old age of twenty-six, being stared at made me uncomfortable. While I enjoyed looking my best, I wanted to be taken seriously and seen as a woman of substance, not a sex object. I did recognize that I often received special treatment because of my looks — a slender, evenly proportioned, green-eyed brunette — but it was a double-edged sword. Just as often, I'd been discounted for the same reason.

When I received enthusiastic compliments on understanding some routine aspect of the business, it seemed like the men were unnecessarily surprised: "Oh! The pretty girl can think!"

Or maybe I had a chip on my shoulder, as Dad often said. *His* highest praise, of course, was that I "thought like a man." Another double-edged sword.

Weaving through the busy workers, I kept my head down and plastered a pleasant expression on my face, self-conscious about my presence there. We met in a small, dingy conference room off the main "cage" area, where workers were locked in to protect the valuable securities they handled. I was ready for my tutorial.

"What the hell is an inter-dealer broker?" I asked as we shook hands hello.

Al laughed as he took a seat in the cramped room. "That's a good question, Jane. It is Jane, right?" He caught my eye to be sure I nodded. Over time, I'd learn his trick for remembering everyone's name: Use it right away, the first time you meet someone, and as frequently as possible.

"An inter-dealer broker is basically a middleman. The big boys like Salomon and Lehman don't want each other to know their trading positions, so they use an anonymous middleman to buy and sell government bonds." He sat straight up in his chair, arms folded across his broad chest, feet planted firmly on the floor. He looked to be about forty, and his close-cropped hair and disciplined posture gave away his military background.

I sat across from him in a hard plastic chair, anxious to learn. "Huh. How does that work exactly? And why don't they want their positions known?"

I was a blank slate. I knew nothing. I'd only been a banker for three years and a lender for less than a year. I'd joined the bank in an entry-level position, and after two years in that job, I was accepted into the twelve-month credit training program — which I had completed just six months earlier. My first assignment out of training had been in the Utilities group, something I found so uninteresting that I jumped at the chance to transfer to the Wall Street group, even though I knew nothing about Wall Street. I barely knew how to make a loan, let alone how trading worked. My entry-level job and training had not covered the operating intricacies of how securities were bought, sold, and exchanged.

I pulled out my pen and pad so I could take notes, my legs crossed at the ankles, the pad balanced in my lap. I loved the freedom of being without a pocketbook, so I'd left it behind and walked over with my ID in one suit pocket and my cigarettes in the other, the pad and pen in my hands. I tried to forget about a phone call I'd gotten right before I left for the meeting with Al: American Express telling me a cash advance check had bounced, and I owed them $2,000. It made me upset and angry, not to mention mortified, to get such a call at work.

I forced myself to focus on Al.

"The dealer, let's say Lehman, buys and sells bonds on behalf of their customers. They also trade using their own money to speculate on which bonds will go up or down in value. They don't want their competitors, like Goldman or Salomon, to know what they or their customers are doing. If everyone's on the same side of the trade, Jane, they won't make any money." Al raised his eyebrows, shrugged his shoulders, and lifted his palms as if this was the most logical thing in the world.

"I guess that makes sense, Al. Is it kind of like a card game, where you never show your hand to the other players?" I grew up playing cards, and it was the closest I'd ever come to trading, so I grasped for an analogy.

Basically, my clients were in business to make money by buying and selling securities, and they wanted to keep those transactions secret.

"That's right! You got it, kid." He leaned forward and slapped his knee. "And the inter-dealer broker makes it okay for you to switch cards without anyone else at the table knowing what you're doing."

Oh, okay. Buying and selling through the inter-dealer broker is how they keep their secrets.

I thought about that while I lit a cigarette, breathing in deeply and slipping my lighter back into my pocket. "How do they actually do it?" I asked, thankful that the topic was complex and interesting enough that I had to focus and couldn't think about that bounced Amex check.

"Well, Jane, I'm glad you asked!" He settled in, tilting his chair back against the desk behind him as if telling me a story. "Dealer A calls up the IDB and says, for example, I want to sell $100 million dollars of the five-year note."

"What's a five-year note?" I interrupted him, never afraid to ask a stupid question.

He nodded, stroking his chin. "Good question, Jane. A *note* is a name for a short-term bond. The government is basically borrowing money for five years, during which time they'll pay the holder of the note interest, and at the end of the five years they'll pay back the entire thing. Usually by borrowing more money!" He chuckled and continued. "The IDB calls around to the other dealers to find out who's interested in buying the five-year note, quotes a price, and makes a match. The one who wants to purchase it on those terms is the buyer. We'll call him Dealer B."

Al paused to see if I was with him and I nodded for him to go on.

"Both Dealer A and Dealer B set up their instructions with the inter-dealer broker. In our example, Dealer A *sells and delivers* the bonds to the IDB, while Dealer B *buys and receives* the bonds from the IDB. The IDB stands in the middle and takes a commission, and the dealers never know who's on the other side."

Al took a yellow legal pad off the table and drew me a diagram. "Remember, Jane, bonds settle *delivery versus payment,* so when the bonds are delivered to us, the cash automatically goes out."

Geez, Louise. It was like an algebra equation where both sides cancelled each other out.

"But if all the trades are perfectly matched, and everything clears and settles on the same day, why would we ever need to lend money to the IDB?" I asked. Part of my job included signing off on collateral when we made overnight loans secured by government bonds, but I couldn't see the need for a loan to the IDB in this scenario, which essentially seemed to be a pass-through transaction.

"Well, Jane, welcome to clearance!" Al laughed again, his good nature outweighing his cynicism. "It doesn't always work the way it should. In a perfect world, the IDB gets the bonds from Dealer A, immediately redelivers them to Dealer B, and doesn't need anything more than a same-day loan from the clearance bank — that's us — to grease the skids for a few hours. But we don't live in a perfect world. Sometimes the dealers or the IDB don't get the instructions to us in time."

In the late 1980s, the transition to fully automated back offices hadn't happened yet, so every dealer and IDB had to give written instructions to their clearance bank for every security they were going to receive in or deliver out. The instructions gave the bank the description of the exact security and the agreed-upon price to be exchanged. I knew written instructions were usually sent electronically, but they could also be printed out or handwritten and sent over on paper. Sometimes those instructions got waylaid when the messenger stopped in at the local bar instead of coming to the bank. I'd heard the legendary story about the messenger who left a bag of bearer bonds behind when he stopped at McAnn's pub for a beer.

"Even if they do get us the instructions on time, the bonds don't always show up before the cutoff," Al continued.

Securities had to be delivered to us before the Federal Reserve Bank's securities wire closed at three p.m. If the bonds were coming to us from another bank, they might miss the deadline.

"Sometimes it's an error, and sometimes it's deliberate!" He leaned forward, his neck and face flushing red. "Gotta watch for these guys playing games, especially on quarter end," Al said, his voice rising as he explained how things could be manipulated. "It's kinda like playing hot potato. Everybody wants to manage what positions they report to the regulators, so they might refuse to take in a security at the last minute. When there's a mismatch, we call it a fail. If we get one side in but the other side doesn't go out, we're stuck with the bond, and *you* have to finance it!" he exclaimed, pointing at me with more emotion than I expected. Al obviously took it as a personal affront that his clients would intentionally create fails. "Fool me once; shame on you. Fool me twice; shame on me," he said with stern deprecation.

His comment made me think about that American Express call about the bounced check. It had startled me because I hadn't taken a cash advance. I didn't even know how to. It angered me because it must have been Jimmy, who hadn't told me about it, and I suspected the reason he hadn't was because he'd been gambling again. The knot in my stomach made me want to throw up. I had been fooled by him way more than twice.

I forced my mind back to the meeting. "Well, here's the thing, Al," I said. "Dealers like Salomon or Lehman have $50 million, or even $100 million dollars of capital." I'd been learning how to analyze the dealer's financial statements, and capital represented the amount of their own money at risk. "But these inter-dealer brokers only have $5 million dollars in capital, maybe less. How can I justify lending them ten or even twenty times that amount?" By this point, I'd kicked off my black pumps. My big toe poked through the "reinforced toe" of my nylons, so I tucked my feet under my chair to hide them.

The lending part of the business technically resided outside Al's domain, but he continued to answer my questions. The truth of the matter was: *Every time a government security was delivered to the bank, our account at the Fed was automatically debited to pay for it.* That meant if we didn't send it out to someone else, or if our client didn't pay us back for the intraday loan, we had to finance it overnight. In other words, we'd have to pay for it ourselves.

Since fails — legitimate and otherwise — were a regular part of the business that led to overnight loans, any client who wanted to have our bank clear and settle their government bond trading activity had to be credit approved first. That's where I came in — a junior credit officer who had been trained by the bank to analyze balance sheets and income statements to determine how much money a company could borrow. In essence, the question I was answering about each company was: Do they have the capacity to pay the loan back?

Lending to Wall Street was a whole different kettle of fish than lending to a retail clothing company like Calvin Klein, whom I'd had as a client during a previous assignment, so I had to learn everything about Wall Street lending on the job. Some of the same concepts applied, such as making loans against inventory, but in this case, the inventory was stocks and bonds, not dresses and shoes.

The bank essentially lends a company cash so it can purchase goods to sell to their customers later. This is similar to a cash advance but collateralized by the goods purchased, in the same way your house is collateral for your mortgage. That was something I already understood. Other concepts, however, like how much money a company could borrow, were totally different when it came to lending to Wall Street. Whereas a retail shop might have $2 in debt for every $1 of their own capital, a broker dealer had more like $50 in borrowed money for every $1 of their own money! Theoretically, debt secured by marketable securities, especially government bonds, is safer because the collateral is considered "liquid," meaning it can be repriced every day and easily liquidated — sold — in the open market to repay the debt. Thus, higher debt levels had become acceptable and commonplace for Wall Street firms.

"Two things to remember, Jane," Al said as he held up his pointer finger. "One, you've got the collateral. US government bonds are the safest investment in the world. And I've got it all locked up for you in an account with an indisputable claim on the bonds. Not to mention" — he laughed jokingly — "possession is nine-tenths of the law!" He put up another finger. "And two, the IDBs only do matched trades. Meaning, they never buy without having an offsetting sell. And they submit those paired transactions to us simultaneously. They don't speculate or keep bonds in inventory. The fail is usually just a technical foul-up, so the next morning we make the delivery and get the cash to pay you back."

EIGHT SEPTEMBERS

He leaned back and folded his arms across his chest, satisfied he'd made his point.

Ah, okay, I thought as I headed back to my desk, absorbed in what I'd just learned. It wasn't so much a credit decision as an operational accommodation. Honestly, when you looked at it like that, it was pretty straightforward. Even in a worst-case scenario, we had the government bonds in hand and the right to sell them to pay off our loan. Simple.

Until 9/11.

***

On Friday, September 14, I called our department's in-house counsel. "Peter, we need to talk."

Peter and I met alone in a conference room, assuring attorney client privilege, and I explained the situation as he took notes.

"Remember that inter-dealer broker we haven't been able to reach? The one located in the South Tower?" I kept my voice low and my expression serious.

Peter looked at me across the table. He'd put his suit jacket on the back of his chair to reveal a striped button-down shirt and wide brown tie. "I know Cantor is working with us from their offices in London. And Garban is working with us from Jersey." Garban's main office had been in the North Tower, and their backup site was in the South Tower, so they were in a temporary location. Like Cantor, they'd lost people and offices.

"Yeah, no, the other one. Eurobrokers." I took a deep breath. "The one that's been *completely* MIA. The one with the $20 billion overdraft."

Amidst all the death and destruction from the terrorist attacks, there had been two kinds of reactions on Wall Street. One was to work like crazy around the clock trying to salvage the situation. The other was to decide life was too short and simply walk away.

"They finally resurfaced and called today. They asked what we were planning to do with all those government bonds we purchased on their behalf," I said, watching his reaction. "Since their systems went down with the building, they claim they hadn't given us any instructions."

Normally, clients gave us instructions both to *receive in* and *deliver out* securities, and it was our obligation to compare those instructions with any bonds that came in. If they didn't match, they were kicked back to the sender.

I swallowed the lump in my throat and continued. "By their logic, if we received securities in without instructions and paid for them — which created the overdraft in their account — then the securities must be ours. They're saying they have no obligation to figure out where those securities were supposed to be delivered or pay us interest for financing the securities." Repeating their stance to Peter sounded as crazy as it had when Eurobrokers said it to me. My reaction then and now was the same: *Fuck!*

They were trying to argue that the terrorist attack had suddenly turned the bank from being their middleman into owning the transactions ourselves. And not millions of dollars of securities. *Billions.* I thought I might throw up.

As I sat with Peter, I tried to gauge how much trouble we were in. He hunched over his legal pad, taking copious notes. I hated the feeling of dread that accompanied thinking I'd done something wrong, even though I knew I hadn't.

"Peter," I continued, "you're aware the bank agreed that we should accept all incoming securities deliveries on 9/11, right?" I'd been part of the conversation that had come to that conclusion.

Peter nodded. He glanced up from his notes and pushed his glasses onto the bridge of his nose with his index finger. "We knew we were taking a risk when that decision was made, Jane, so now we'll have to deal with the consequences."

Peter's matter-of-fact response helped me to relax slightly.

The decision to accept all incoming securities was intended to reduce turmoil in the markets and came as a result of the message passed from the president of the United States, the president of the Federal Reserve Bank, the president of the Bond Market Association, and the president of our bank to maintain orderly markets. The rallying cry was, "Capital markets must keep functioning! We cannot let the terrorists win!"

As a result, we'd used our bank's cash and balance sheet to purchase the securities delivered to our clients — even without the "receive" instructions. Since we were also missing the "deliver" instructions, we had no place to send those securities — and even if we did, the Bank of New York was not functioning and could not receive them. Between BONY and ourselves, we cleared nearly 100 percent of the primary dealers and inter-dealer brokers, and virtually every one of us had technological issues to some degree on 9/11. It was as if someone had dumped a jigsaw puzzle on the floor and we had to gather and arrange the pieces while wearing a blindfold and trying to beat the clock.

As more securities were delivered each day, we had no choice but to borrow from the "lender of last resort" — the Federal Reserve Bank — not just on the day of the attacks, but on the days that followed. The stock market had been closed for the rest of the week after 9/11, but the bond market had not, and trading continued despite the growing inability to clear and settle the trades. The Fed had clearly announced that it was open for business and would provide funding for whomever needed it, in whatever amounts were needed, and as a result, while loans from the Fed to its member banks usually averaged $200 million on any given night, on 9/11 they were $37 *billion*, and on 9/12 they were $46 billion.

Al's team had spent most of the week working with clients and the Government Securities Clearing Corporation (GSCC) trying to figure out which bonds belonged to which dealer without the benefit of instructions. GSCC had been created by the industry to centralize and "net" government bond trading activity — essentially, add up all the buys and sells between two parties and net it down to one cash payment between the two. In the aftermath of 9/11, that work was being done manually, by folks who hadn't yet gone home to rest and emotionally recover. They had been sleeping in their offices all week, working around the clock to reconstruct instructions from the bits of information they had.

All hands had been on deck all week, except this particular IDB, Eurobrokers, who had only just resurfaced.

"Peter, we bought in more than *$20 billion* in government bonds for Eurobrokers! And we've been borrowing from the Fed to cover that $20 billion overdraft in their account for three nights and counting. I really thought we were doing the right thing." I looked at him, eyes wide, and he nodded slowly, understanding the gravity of the situation.

I shouldn't have been surprised by what Eurobrokers was trying to do. Apparently, not everybody felt obligated to do what was in the best interest of the markets, and this client was trying to take advantage of the turmoil 9/11 had caused and leave us holding the bag. I didn't know that they'd lost more than two hundred employees in the attacks, some of whom were senior management. But even so, their approach, once they'd reestablished contact, differed significantly from the other IDBs. Cantor Fitzgerald and Garban looked to us as their allies, not adversaries, and so did the rest of our clients.

"Okay, Jane," Peter reassured me, peering over his glasses, which had slid down his narrow nose again. "Let me look at the contracts over the weekend. We'll talk on Monday to figure out how to proceed. You'd better brief Doug."

But 9/11 had shaken Doug. He'd been at the epicenter of the financial fallout since the first moments of the terrorist attacks, and the pressure on him was enormous. Decisions that would determine the fate of companies and individuals, billions of dollars in overdrafts, unreconciled securities positions, defaults in the unsecured short-term corporate debt market — the list of burdens on Doug went on and on. Given all he'd had to deal with that week, the news of the problem with Eurobrokers only caused him to sigh deeply and shake his head. He said he trusted me to work with Al to resolve it. He had enough on his plate.

As for me, I'd deal with it on Monday. We'd made it through the week without the bond market crashing, so we'd done what we needed to do. I had nothing left to give.

EIGHT SEPTEMBERS

***

Saturday, September 15, was my first day to rest, my first day to see what they were showing on TV. I couldn't bear to watch the news during the week when I arrived home so late, frazzled from working, and I tuned out my husband's increasingly animated calls for retaliation against Bin Laden. I sought peace and normalcy in my evenings, so I played with the boys, helped them with their homework, and read them bedtime stories. I was still in shock, still crying every day.

The images on the television were too overwhelming, too sad and grievous, and the commentary — the blaming, fighting, and warmongering — was even worse. I couldn't stand it. So I focused on my need for a haircut. But my hair salon was downtown, buried in rubble. Which made me cry again. Loss appeared everywhere in unexpected places.

"Jimmy, I have to get out of the house. I'm going to see if I can find a place to get my hair cut."

He didn't mind my leaving yet again.

I walked over to Columbus Avenue and into Dramatics, the hair salon closest to home. My brain was mush, and I sat dazed in the chair as the hairdresser tried to understand what I wanted.

Gradually, I became aware of the woman getting her hair done next to me talking. Her words pierced my foggy mind like a screeching owl.

"Oh my *gawd*! Everyone is making such a fuss. I mean really, there is nothing else on the TV! It's so upsetting. We can't travel, the kids' activities are all cancelled, and all we hear about are the attacks."

Really? I shook my head to clear the cobwebs.

I started to cry. Maybe I misunderstood her, but I simply couldn't believe how oblivious and callous she was behaving about the chaos and tragedy downtown.

"Get me away from her," I choked to my hairdresser, tears streaming down my face. She graciously took me to another chair in the back.

TROUBLE

***

The following day was "Welcome Back Sunday" at our church, the first gathering after the summer hiatus. West End is part of the Collegiate Churches, a Dutch Reformed Protestant denomination, and the oldest corporation in Manhattan, dating back to the days of Peter Stuyvesant. The West End motto is "a neighborhood church for all people."

I loved my friendly, close-knit church community, and I loved being a Sunday school teacher. It was great to walk just two blocks north to get there, hand in hand with the kids. Both of my sons had gone to the church's preschool before they started kindergarten, and we all felt safe there.

We went into the sanctuary and sat in our regular pew on the burgundy velvet cushions, Jimmy on the aisle and the boys nestled on either side of me. When it was time for Sunday school, the boys and I got up and headed towards the classrooms.

I was one of a handful of Sunday school teachers that day, including my friend Kim, who also had two young sons. The younger boys were in her class, and the older boys in mine. We decided that instead of engaging them directly about the attacks, we would give them crayons and paper and let them draw during our lessons. I couldn't get Will to talk about his feelings and hoped this activity would give me some insight into how he was coping.

The historic Dutch Colonial church, built in 1892 and modeled after the Vleeshal in Haarlem, the Netherlands, was more crowded than usual that Sunday. The dark-wood sanctuary and colorful stained-glass windows depicting Jesus knocking at the door and "morning cometh and the shadows flee away" reminded me not of the clean, bright, modern, suburban Presbyterian churches of my parents, but rather of the old-fashioned, small-town Pennsylvania churches of my grandparents that we visited on special occasions. The coziness and familiarity of the dark coolness in the historic building made me feel welcome and safe. The prayers, the hymns, and the sense of community embraced me as I sat, sorrowful and spent, pondering the role of hatred and violence in the world.

EIGHT SEPTEMBERS

When the sun shone through the round Tiffany stained-glass window directly onto the minister standing at the large, carved oak octagonal pulpit at the very moment he preached about love and forgiveness, it seemed as if God had illuminated his message.

The world needed love.

Not fear, not hate, not anger.

Love.

PART TWO
Recovery

*"Every worthy act is difficult. Ascent is always difficult.
Descent is easy and often slippery."*
—Mahatma Gandhi

CHAPTER 5

Downtown Again

I heard the dog whimpering before my alarm went off.

"Tar, shush!" I commanded, my voice low and hoarse.

My response only served to increase his cries. I groaned, sat up, and shut off the alarm, casting a glance at my oblivious sleeping husband, who never got up at the crack of dawn to take care of the dog. I pushed back the wave of resentment and rose in the darkness.

"Just a minute!" I called to the dog, who tap-danced noisily in his metal cage at the foot of the spiral staircase. I went into our tiny bathroom to pee and brush my teeth, unconcerned if my actions or the dog's happened to wake Jimmy. I peered at my tired face in the mirror, grimaced, and looked away, snapping off the light switch.

I walked cautiously down the floating wooden stairs — I'd slipped and fallen years ago when pregnant with William — and reached around the bottom step to release the black cocker spaniel. "Hello, pretty boy. Why are you up so early?" I stroked his ears and kissed his cold nose, his body wriggling with joy. I opened the sliding glass door and stepped out barefoot to lift the heavy iron security grate, which rose with a short but deafening screech. The dog raced into the concrete backyard, sniffed, and then relieved himself on the corner of the cinder-block planters. The early fall chill drove me inside to fill his food bowl and put on the kettle.

After I let Tar back in, I settled myself with a cup of tea on the couch, across from the stairs and the baby grand piano I'd bought myself with my first serious bonus from the bank. Picking up my Bible and devotional, I turned to the day's entry. Isaiah 41:10: "Do not fear, for I am with you; do not be afraid, for I am your God. I will strengthen you; I will surely help you; I will uphold you with My righteous right hand."

My throat closed and my eyes watered. I'd been working long, chaotic hours every day in the three weeks since 9/11. This added structure

EIGHT SEPTEMBERS

and purpose to my days, but I had endless daily reasons for the tears to flow. The tenderness of holding my children. The frequent sound of bagpipes marking yet another funeral. The frustration of trying to solve problems with insufficient information. The magnitude of the impact on our clients and industry.

I grabbed my spiral notebook and started writing: *If I just have faith, I can get through this day. I am not alone. God loves me. I choose the living God.*

Shutting my notebook, I closed my eyes and lay very still on the couch. I wanted to carry this moment of peace with me through my hectic day, hoping it would help me to be patient with my children, tolerant of my husband, brave at work, and strong in the face of adversity.

It was almost six a.m. I needed to shower, dress, and be out the door in an hour. Chase Manhattan Plaza had just been deemed safe for occupancy. The telecommunications that had been destroyed when 7 World Trade Center collapsed onto the nearby Verizon building were now sufficiently restored.

It was time to go back downtown.

***

Walking the three blocks to the subway, I inhaled the acrid, metallic air, a constant nauseating presence that had barely dissipated in the past three weeks. The fire still smoldered at Ground Zero, but the spiraling brownish-gray smoke was less visible now. I knew what I kept in my office desk drawers — hairspray, nail polish, Wite-Out, paper clips, staples, photographs, shoes, pantyhose, papers, pens. Imagine thousands of desks on fire. Not to mention human bodies.

Combustible, flammable, incinerated.

All...reduced to ash.

The city still felt subdued. Shaken, grieving. People flowed quietly into the small, picturesque subway station at 72nd and Broadway, and I joined the early morning commuters with some trepidation. I hadn't been back on the subway since the morning of September 11, instead taking cabs back and forth to 270 Park every day. I knew people who'd been trapped in the subway that day, and I wasn't in a rush to ride it again. Plus, taking the subway to the southern tip of Manhattan meant switching from the express to the local at Chambers Street, then taking the train all the way to South Ferry — through the closed stations underneath the World Trade Center.

I sat in silence on the smooth, cool silver bench in the first car of the express train, watching the stations rush by, grateful the train wasn't crowded. The local train idled at Chambers Street as the express pulled in on the opposite track. I crossed the dirty platform that smelled like stale urine and wet concrete to board the local, one of only a few people in the heavily air-conditioned first car, the molded, plastic orange seats waiting for passengers that did not come.

The doors closed and the conductor shouted, "Passengers getting off at South Ferry must move to the first five cars of the train!" The train started inching forward much more slowly than usual, as if it, too, was reluctant to proceed.

As we neared the World Trade Center, I felt the tension rising, the weight of the tragedy above me, the heaviness of the sorrow pressing in on me. I didn't understand how it was even possible for the train to run beneath the collapsed towers.

I closed my eyes and recited Psalm 23 over and over again as the train crawled under the Trade Center, my breathing shallow, my stomach clenched. The train moved so slowly through the closed Rector Street station that I thought my heart would lurch out of my chest. I put my hand over my heart as if to hold it in place, thinking about all the displaced commuters and lost lives. How busy this stop used to be; how vacant and abandoned it now was. The first of the day's tears arrived.

Wheels screeching, the train made the sharp turn into the final station where only the first five cars could fit. Impatient for the doors to open, I bounced out as soon as they did, rapidly climbing the stairs and pushing my way out into sunlight and blue skies.

When my department evacuated downtown on 9/11, the streets had been covered in debris, a thick, chalky layer of dust coating the sidewalks and buildings and the people who had been outside when the Twin Towers fell. But now, the streets and buildings had been washed clean; so clean that they looked fake, like a Hollywood movie set. Armed guards, automatic rifles, and camouflage fatigues were everywhere, and markedly fewer people were on the streets. There were no tourists snapping pictures of themselves with George Washington on the steps of Federal Hall, no lines waiting for the ferry to the Statue of Liberty.

Concrete barriers stood in front of the New York Stock Exchange where cars were no longer allowed. Long lines formed outside of the Exchange and office buildings as people tried to get to work, navigating new security procedures. Small shops — shoeshines, barbers, and delis — were closed and boarded up.

Thousands of handmade signs seeking missing loved ones lined the streets — stapled one on top of the other, already fading and frayed, rippling in the wind. I stumbled past, my chest tight and my eyes moist.

And the stench. So much more intense than on the Upper West Side, where the faint metallic burning mixed with the scents of falling leaves and cooling air. Here there was no dilution. The Pit was still smoking. Excavation was still happening.

Fragments of lives were being retrieved, bit by burnt bit.

Get back to work, I told myself. That's what we do.

***

Al and I had an appointment to meet with Dominick, head of the Government Securities Clearing Corporation, to discuss our 9/11-related inter-dealer broker financing problem. Our conversations with Eurobrokers had led nowhere, as they were still refusing to take any responsibility for the bonds we accepted, so now we were trying a different angle.

Collectively owned and funded by all the major Wall Street banks, GSCC had been created to streamline the back-office settlement of government bonds. They were in the middle of the IDB financing debacle,

DOWNTOWN AGAIN

as well as coordinating the Herculean reconciliation effort underway to find the proper owners for all the bonds traded on September 11.

GSCC provided a guarantee on some of the IDB transactions we processed that day. The billions of dollars of securities we financed on behalf of the inter-dealer brokers following the terrorist attacks arose, in part, from those GSCC guaranteed trades.

We planned to get GSCC, as the guarantor, to pay our financing costs. Not just for Eurobrokers, but for our other customers, Garban and Cantor Fitzgerald, as well.

On the walk over from 4 New York Plaza, Al confided in me. "I've known Dominick for a long time. We're good golfing buddies and friends," he said. "But when it comes to business, he can be difficult. He's a tough negotiator and smarter than anyone else I know. Deep down he has a heart of gold, but I don't think you'll see it in this meeting." He chuckled.

I didn't really know the guys at GSCC, but I was determined to get them to cover our interest costs. I knew how to read contracts, and I knew certain verbal assurances were made on 9/11, so I intended to collect. If Eurobrokers wasn't going to pay, then *somebody* would. There was no way we were going to let the Street stiff us for being the good guys and financing billions of dollars of government securities when the market was in chaos. We'd been helping to stabilize the market in the name of national security, after all.

"It's bullshit, Al!" I complained. "What's the fucking point of a guarantee if they're not going to honor it?"

Al, a self-described Irish-Catholic altar boy from Queens, didn't swear, but he tolerated a lot of it from the rest of us. "You're right, Jane." He nodded agreeably. "Let's see what we can work out."

As pissed as I was, I knew we were lucky that the only thing we had to recover was interest costs. In a crisis, there's usually a "flight to quality," which means investors move their money into the safety of US government bonds. This means the bonds rise in value, which means they're worth more than what we paid for them on 9/11, which means we didn't lose any money from buying them in. But we *did* have the expense of financing them until we figured out who actually intended to buy them — and interest on $20 billion for three weeks and counting equaled a lot of money.

I walked into the conference room on the thirty-first floor of 55 Water Street with an attitude. The room had a curved glass wall covered by a drawn curtain. The large oval conference table dominated the space with chairs both at the table and along the wall. It was way too big for four people.

Dominick was at the far corner of the conference table, his brown eyes narrowed and his expression inscrutable, and he stood to greet us. His shoulders, broad in his houndstooth jacket, made him appear commanding and taller than he was. He made me think of Napoleon with his Romanesque nose and imperious bearing. Jeff, the general counsel and Dominick's longtime collaborator, sat beside him at the head of the table, his broad, open face and laid-back posture a bit more welcoming and conciliatory. Jeff had written the rules for GSCC, which Al told me Dominick claimed to have invented, and as Al and I took our seats on the opposite side of the table from Dominick, I felt like we had walked into the lion's den.

After Al made the introductions, I launched into my spiel, determined and direct. "Look, we did the right thing buying in those securities. You know it, the Street knows it, the regulators know it. Eurobrokers is refusing any responsibility. But their trades were done under GSCC's guaranteed product. It's time to honor that guarantee and pay our interest costs. While you're at it, you can pay Cantor's and Garban's, too."

Dominick drummed his fingers on the table, giving the impression that we were boring him. He raised his eyebrows and glanced at Jeff, who looked bemused.

Al chimed in to break the tension. "Dominick, Jeff, give us a hand here. We're the good guys."

I watched Dominick purse his lips before he chose his words carefully. "It's not our problem."

Jeff tried to soften the blow. "We know you are the good guys, Al, but we don't see any legal rationale for covering your interest costs. That's a business decision J.P. Morgan made." He flashed me a smile.

My heart started to quicken with anger as I realized they planned to stonewall us. The conversation went around in circles, with increasing stridency on my part. How many different ways could I say the same thing? How many different ways could they condescend and obfuscate?

We left without a resolution.

Frustrated and furious with Dominick, who was clearly calling the shots, I was more determined than ever to get GSCC to pay.

CHAPTER 6
Family Matters

Amidst all the death and despair in New York and the nation, life pressed forward.

William, in second grade, would be turning seven on October 28, 2001. When he was in kindergarten, he wrote in his journal that he wanted to visit the Twin Towers. Now it would never happen.

He refused to talk to me about the terrorist attacks on 9/11 and the destruction of the Twin Towers. Instead, he buried his face in his pillow at night, his long legs tucked up beneath his torso, making him look like a beetle. He shook his head vigorously when I asked if he wanted to share his feelings while I softly stroked his back. How much did he know? How much had he seen on the television that constantly played in his father's music studio at the front of our apartment? What did the kids talk about at school? I worried about his little heart.

His Sunday school drawing from the first Sunday after the attacks, drawn with thick magic markers on cream-colored construction paper, clearly depicted the Twin Towers on fire with violent orange flames, a plane crashing into them, and angry black swirls of smoke. My sweet, silly, sensitive son was struggling to make sense of this huge event. How glad I was that we were teaching our children to love and not to hate. Life is hard enough without the weight of bitterness in your heart.

At a recent Friday Night Club, the children's play group at church, he'd flung himself into my arms, his slender body hot and sweaty, sobbing uncontrollably. On my knees, his head burrowed into my shoulder, he heaved his sorrow and frustration onto me. I held him close and kissed the top of his head and let him cry himself out. It was just a game of musical chairs, but the fun ended when no chair remained for him, shoved out of the way by a bigger, more aggressive child.

EIGHT SEPTEMBERS

Competitive games filled William with anxiety, and competing for his older brother's attention made him jealous and angry. J.J., almost four years older, played the imaginative Pied Piper of the group, admired by the younger children and in high demand. What should have been a fun night became a frustrating emotional cauldron for William, so I wasn't surprised that his overwhelming and unspoken feelings about the terrorist attacks rose to the surface at Friday Night Club.

Other times, William was a happy child, all giggles and wiggles, singing and dancing, comfortable in his own skin. Was it wrong for a mother to want more of that for her son and less of the emotional turmoil?

I understood him. As the youngest of three girls in a hierarchical family where I was clearly the least important member once I'd outgrown the adorable baby phase, I shared his sense of impotence. "Be quiet. Sit still. Stop that," were constant admonitions throughout my childhood. Always in trouble for being my talkative, fidgety self, at his age I threw temper tantrums, prostrate on the floor, arms and legs flailing in frustration. My parents either ignored me, which gained me neither the attention nor the control I was after, or spanked me, which added to my misery. I wanted better for my son. Allowing him to use his words, validating his feelings, and holding him during a crying spell were generational wins, progress in the annals of family parenting styles.

My mother always made a big deal out of birthdays when we were growing up, baking cakes and offering to make whatever we wanted for dinner. It's a sweet feeling to be celebrated just for arriving in this world — no other accomplishment required — and I enjoyed passing that on to my sons, so as his birthday approached, I happily focused on the occasion, making William's favorite cake — chocolate with chocolate chips, chocolate icing, and chocolate sprinkles — and choosing a fun place to have his party: Act Up, an acting studio where kids could dress up in different kinds of costumes and play improv games.

I didn't even mind that we had to take an elevator up to the tenth floor to get there. It was a balm to watch the children trying on colorful wigs and choosing silly props to express themselves and entertain one another. The boys and girls shrieked and giggled as they ran around the big open room, not a care in the world, and their innocence made me hopeful about the future. Had it really been only two months since the terrorist attacks?

It made me happy that Mom was in town to join us for the party, too. She hadn't always been so readily available to participate in my sons' lives. She used to live in Hawaii with my father, until they suddenly announced they were getting a divorce and she moved back east. Although it had been three years, the divorce still rankled. It had been completely unexpected, revealed on a conference call in early 1998, not long after my thirty-eighth birthday.

Mom and Dad had arranged the conference call with my sisters and me two weeks in advance. While not typical, it wasn't completely out of the ordinary. My sisters and I lived in three different states — Ellie in Pennsylvania, Becky in Maine, and I in New York. Given the six-hour time difference, the call was scheduled for early Sunday evening on the East Coast, when Mom and Dad would be in Dad's office after attending the morning church service in downtown Honolulu. My sisters and I were excited and curious, wondering if they might be planning a family vacation or wanted to discuss estate plans.

Dad cleared his throat before his voice came over the speakerphone with a slight timing delay. "Your mother and I have something we want to share with you," he said, using his brusque, authoritarian voice, the one he learned in the Marines and employed to preempt back talk. I knew it well.

Hearing his voice, I feared a lecture — most likely on how not to spend the money he planned to give us at some future date when we were "old enough to be trusted with it," as he would often admonish.

"It will just be easier if we read you this letter," Mom said, sounding nervous. "We wrote it a few months ago but didn't get around to sending it."

This was puzzling. A few months ago, we'd all celebrated Christmas with Mom and Dad at their farm in Pennsylvania. They hadn't said anything then about the need for this conversation.

"There is no easy or appropriate way to tell you sad news." Mom's voice wavered and she sounded a little teary, but she plunged ahead.

"After much deliberation, discussion, and prayer, we have decided to live separate lives and get an amicable divorce."

Stunned, I could not speak. Becky's involuntary gasp was barely audible. I could hear Ellie softly weeping. These were the same parents who taught us not only that *divorce* was wrong, but who'd also implied that divorced *people* were wrong and morally weak. Our Pennsylvania Presbyterian family heritage had always been a point of pride to Dad. What they were saying didn't make any sense. One of the reasons I never considered divorce as an option for myself was because my parents wouldn't approve. Mom and Dad's parents had each been married sixty-four years before one of them died, and "Til death do us part" was taken very seriously in our tribe.

"Mom is ready to 'retire' from her role as corporate wife," Dad said, "and live at our farm in her beloved Pennsylvania, where all her family is..."

Wait, wasn't his family there too? We knew Mom expected they would move back to Pennsylvania together after living nearly twenty-five years in Hawaii.

"Dad is launching a new career and is busier than ever," Mom continued. "His business, assets, and friends are all in Hawaii."

Yeah, and his fame and fortune too. Gotta feed that ego, I thought, feeling the familiar resentment toward Dad arising.

Like a responsive reading in church, back and forth they went, reading the letter. Then, half plea, half order, they delivered the final blow. "Please do not be upset with us, and do not place blame. Our painful decision has been made, and we are at peace with it. So please do not put us through any more agony as the divorce proceedings are well underway."

Are you kidding me? Were they really still telling us what to think and feel, ordering us to behave like good little girls?

I stared at the fireplace across from my bed, where I lay stretched out in the fading light of early evening, and blinked my eyes. The sound of my heart knocking against my rib cage began to slowly fill my ears. Generally slow to "name and claim" my feelings, even in normal circumstances — and this was definitely *not* a normal moment — I wondered if I was going to say anything. Almost forty years old and I still kept my mouth shut to avoid getting in trouble with my parents for saying what I thought.

Just the year before, during one of my trips to Honolulu, I told Mom we were considering moving to Hawaii, something I thought she'd welcome. J.J. and Will were six and two at the time, young enough to make a transition — although six-year-old J.J. informed me that I'd have to drive him everywhere if we moved, and he didn't think he'd like that very much. Jimmy could teach or write music anywhere, and I had never been truly fulfilled in my banking job and thought I could work for Dad, instead. I was already on his board of directors and learning the business — macadamia nuts, guava farms, and real estate development.

"Oh, that's probably not a good idea," Mom said as she stood stiffly in their windowed penthouse kitchen on South Beretania Street, avoiding eye contact. "We're getting older and could die, then you'd be out here all by yourselves." I'd been surprised by that and taken aback by the abrupt rejection. Now I understood. It had been easier for her to talk about death than to let me know they were contemplating divorce.

Dad, the businessman who took care of all the family finances, said, "We saw an attorney in Pennsylvania in December and started the process."

We'd soon learn that the divorce had actually already been finalized. They'd shared an attorney, who'd allocated 90 percent of their assets to Dad, 10 percent to Mom. My fury about Dad's self-serving manipulation had nowhere to land. When I later brought up this injustice to Mom, she chastised me for being an ungrateful daughter and scolded me for being critical of my generous father, in whose brownstone we lived.

My sisters asked a few more questions on the call, but I still couldn't wrap my head around this conversation. I may not have been in touch with my feelings, but my bullshit detector was in overdrive. The divorce being presented as a joint decision didn't add up.

The phone rang a little later that same evening. I stood in the kitchen, lights off, the boys in bed for the night. Becky's voice floated over the airwaves, her words dreamy and calm. "How ya doin'?" she asked. Maybe she was stoned.

"I'm okay, I think, just processing. Well..." I laughed. "I *am* on my third glass of wine and having a cigarette, so maybe I'm not doing so well! Can you believe it? What a fucking hypocrite. I don't believe for a minute it was a mutual decision. Dad wanted out and maneuvered Mom as usual. Everything is always about him." Becky and I had a long history of Dad-bashing.

"I can't believe they didn't tell us when we were together over the holidays!" Becky said. She didn't like confrontation any more than the rest of us but felt affronted at being blindsided. "I mean, the picture-perfect Christmas at the farm with the matching stockings, the horse-drawn carriage ride, all that pressure to attend and put on a happy face."

Every year Becky, the middle sister, struggled with the expectation from Mom and Dad to come to the farm for Christmas, and her husband's desire to stay at home in Maine. She'd confessed that coming home under false pretenses felt like a slap in the face.

I snorted. "I know. It's so typical. Mom smoothing the way for Dad, the Almighty. Keeping up appearances at all costs. Even in divorce they're united against us." It was frustrating how Mom always took Dad's side. She might admit he shouldn't have lost his temper, or note a certain topic made him "crazy," but if she ever called him out on anything, it was most certainly behind closed doors.

"Two peas in a pod," Becky said wistfully. She'd been calling them that for years and had even given them one of those cute little sets of peas sitting together on a log. "I still don't understand it. Do you think there's someone else?" There'd been rumors from time to time about Dad, the occasional gossip in the local Honolulu papers about the big CEO spotted with beautiful young women, but it was hard to reconcile that with the Sunday school, Boy Scout persona he presented to us.

"I'd bet my life on it," I said. "No way they just decided to go their separate ways. Mom probably got tired of stroking his ego, and he found someone else to do it. There has got to be a backstory."

I always hated the way Dad stacked the deck in his own favor, even in small things, while purporting to be a proponent of playing by the rules — like his tendency to assign the strongest and fastest male cousins to his football team at Thanksgiving so his team would win. It really burned me that he was such a stickler for *us* to follow the rules, but he would change the rules for himself. We girls had been forbidden to go to the movies or parties on Sunday, the Sabbath, yet he routinely ran to the store after church to pick up Breyer's ice cream and get the car washed, and sometimes even went into the office to work. This high-gloss, no-fault divorce explanation smelled of the same self-serving behavior.

"Jimmy's already trying to ferret it out," I said.

Jimmy's emotions always came out fast and furious, often overpowering my own. We'd been married nearly twenty years, and he adored my mother and looked up to my father, so he took this news as personally as I did and vowed to get to the bottom of this mystery. He presumed Dad was ditching Mom for another woman, so he went on the hunt.

Fueling Jimmy's indignation and distrust of my father was an episode a few years earlier, when Dad had called him, excited to say he had a film composing job for him. He presented an opportunity for Jimmy to work on a project that Dad had financed for a Hawaiian producer. "Jimbo, we're going to put you on the map!" Dad declared gleefully.

Jimmy had been trying for years to break into the film scoring business, so he jumped at the chance to be involved. And then...radio silence. No explanation, no rationale, just evasion and avoidance. The documentary came out in 1996. It was a nativist view of the development of Hawaii at the expense of the indigenous peoples, an indictment of the missionaries and White men who "came to do good and did very well indeed." Dad proudly boasted about the film, an odd incongruence since, as the head of one of Hawaii's "Big Five" corporations and a son of missionaries himself, he was clearly on the side of the film's villains. He conveniently forgot the conversation with Jimmy had ever happened and ignored the pain in Jimmy's eyes.

Jimmy knew the producer of the documentary was a woman, which made him suspicious about why Dad had kept him away from the project, so that's where he started his snooping.

"I'll keep you posted if we find out anything," I told Becky, then hung up and dialed Ellie, our oldest sister. I lit another cigarette and refilled my wine glass.

EIGHT SEPTEMBERS

As we all did, Ellie spent a lot of time and effort trying to live up to Mom and Dad's expectations. She emulated them in some ways through her more traditional stay-at-home lifestyle. She strived to remain true to the Presbyterian values of service, fellowship, and worship we were taught, while trying to give her family the emotional stability ours lacked, yet she herself was emotionally sensitive and wounded easily. The sudden divorce cut her deep.

When she answered, Ellie sounded hoarse and her nose stuffy. She seemed deflated, crushed, her voice barely audible.

"It feels like such a betrayal of everything I thought our family stood for," she lamented.

"I know! I don't know which is worse, the divorce or the deception."

Ellie sighed deeply. "This feels like being abandoned all over again."

When our parents had moved from Philadelphia to Hawaii to follow a once-in-a-lifetime job opportunity for Dad in 1975, I was fifteen years old. I headed to a Christian boarding school on Long Island, a complicated decision that never got revisited after Dad accepted the job in Honolulu. Becky faced her tenuous first year at Princeton, a confused teenager pressured into following in Dad's footsteps while also wrestling with depression. Ellie began her senior year in college, with many life decisions looming over her. Each of us struggled to adjust to our new situations while Mom and Dad were fully engaged with their new life five thousand miles away and six hours behind us. Our parents may have considered us successfully launched into the world, but we felt the loss of our home base. Children are supposed to leave their parents, not the other way around.

"Abandonment indeed," I echoed, vigorously stubbing out my cigarette in the overflowing ashtray.

A copy of the letter Mom and Dad had read from arrived in the mail a few days later, part of a mass mailing to family and friends.

They'd been married for forty-five years.

But now, three years after that conference call, Mom not only lived at the farm in Pennsylvania, she also had an apartment upstairs in the brownstone, which she now owned, courtesy of the divorce. This meant she could visit us whenever she wanted without disrupting our day-to-day lives. We'd had fun renovating and furnishing her apartment, and the boys loved it when she would pick them up from school and walk them home, bringing them up to her place to play games and hang out and do homework, which somehow never got completed until after I got home from work.

Born in 1931, the youngest of four siblings, the rest of whom had already passed, Mom would be celebrating her seventieth birthday that fall. Ellie, Becky, and I had long planned a surprise party to be held in Manhattan on December first. The first week of September I had booked a block of hotel rooms for out-of-town guests, secured a location for the dinner, and sent out "save the date" emails to all her nieces and nephews and selected family friends on September 10th. Mom's party was what I'd been talking to Becky about in my office on the morning of 9/11 when the first plane hit.

Three months later — despite the trauma of the attacks and the constant terrorism alerts keeping everyone on edge — nearly every guest accepted the invitation to travel to New York City for Mom's party. We even managed to finesse the arrangements and got everyone to the Crane Club early.

"Mom, Ellie's running late and can't find a place to park," I lied. We were gathered in our apartment, waiting to go to dinner. Becky had arrived from Maine the day before with her husband and teenage daughter and they were staying upstairs with Mom. "She says to meet her at the restaurant."

In reality, Ellie was at the restaurant already, greeting guests and making sure food and decorations were in place. Our group of eight walked the few blocks up Amsterdam Avenue in the dark, unseasonably warm night, and it was all I could do to keep my young sons from spilling the beans, squeezing their hands to silence them when necessary. They looked so handsome in their blue blazers, ties, and khaki pants — an upgrade from their usual T-shirts and jeans.

As we opened the heavy, carved wooden door and walked down the polished steps of the restaurant, the noisy street disappeared into

EIGHT SEPTEMBERS

the hushed silence and I felt excited for the first time since 9/11. My mother looked lovely with her closely cropped wavy white hair, black-and-white checked suit, and regal bearing. She was thrilled to have us all together: three daughters, three sons-in-law, and six grandchildren. On the landing at the bottom of the stairs, where a dark-purple, heavy velvet curtain blocked off access to the party room, we met up with Ellie, her husband, and three kids. Hugs and smiles all around, quick furtive glances, and then we were ready.

"Mom, this way to the table," I announced, parting the curtain and letting her go in first. We crowded quickly behind her so we could see her reaction. The art deco room sparkled with chandeliers and balloons. Her ten nieces and nephews and their spouses, as well as her lifelong best friend, gathered at the foot of the raised-entry landing to greet her, the long wooden bar and dining tables glistening in the background.

"Surprise!" everyone roared, clapping and smiling.

My mother gasped and laughed out loud, clasping her hands together. "You fooled me!" she cried, delighting as her eyes fell upon one guest after another.

My sisters and I laughed and hugged each other, congratulating ourselves on pulling it off, happy to be together.

We'd done our part to choose love over fear.

CHAPTER 7
Christmas in Hawaii

First, there was the idea of a nameless, faceless female at the center of our parent's divorce.

Unacknowledged, unspoken, unknown.

Gradually, the truth seeped out. It wasn't a no-fault, amicable divorce. There *was* another woman. There *had* been an affair. There *was* a desire for the son and namesake our father never had.

Details emerged. The woman was an actress and former Miss Hawaii, thirty years his junior. He'd bought her a house, financed her documentary, and paid for her PhD — all before the divorce.

We only just met. It's a whirlwind romance, a love story, Dad wrote in a letter to family and friends, trying to circulate his version of the facts, as if seeing the words in black and white would make them true.

It appeared Dad couldn't bear the guilt, the negative feedback he received, and the suspicion about his cover story. He kept soliciting Mom, his historical number-one cheerleader, seeking her approval, sending flowers on their anniversary, trying to keep her close even as he sent her away.

He begged our forgiveness without acknowledging the lie. We withheld it, hoping for honesty.

Then the idea of the other woman became flesh: Leilani.

It was bad enough that Leilani was forty-three, my sister Becky's age, and just three years older than I. An actress and a beauty queen, she triggered all my judgments and stereotypes about second wives.

They married in 1999, on his seventy-first birthday, just eighteen months after Mom and Dad's divorce. My sisters and I, along with our families, were invited, but we all declined. His lying and manipulative tactics still had us feeling raw. No one wanted to be up close and personal with Leilani to witness this strange new chapter in Dad's life. No thank you.

EIGHT SEPTEMBERS

I'd had the unpleasant job of telling Mom about the impending marriage. With the date fast approaching, Dad still had not told her, and my sisters and I decided it was the right thing to do. All her friends in Hawaii would know about it, and Mom would look like a fool if she didn't. I was *not* going to let that happen. We made sure Mom's best friend came to spend the weekend with her at the farm in Pennsylvania so that when she got off the phone with me, she could process the news with a friend, not with the daughters she was still trying to keep from criticizing Dad.

Dad, of course, considered me a traitor for telling her. He sent me a seven-page handwritten letter accusing me of jumping the gun and spoiling his plans. But since Mom was not entirely surprised by the news, I felt justified. She finally admitted that Dad had wanted this all along, and she had managed to delay it from happening for *five years*. It was cold satisfaction learning the truth after so many years of deception, and a small consolation that at least we daughters wouldn't have to deal with a sibling since Leilani had aged out of her childbearing years.

A year after Dad and Leilani's wedding, the summer of 2000, I had yet to meet my father's new wife. Jimmy and I were visiting the Big Island to celebrate our twentieth wedding anniversary. We coordinated the trip in conjunction with a board meeting and gala in celebration of Dad's twenty-fifth year as CEO of C. Brewer & Co. Ltd.

We booked a romantic mountainside bed and breakfast, using our anniversary as an excuse to avoid staying with Dad and Leilani. I would have been happy ignoring her indefinitely, but Jimmy had been prodding me: "You can't pretend she doesn't exist, Jane."

We turned down the secluded road that slanted off from the main highway and parked across the street from the entrance to the traditional white clapboard plantation manager's house Dad's company owned. It sat on a small rise across from the now-empty fields of the former sugar mill and the abandoned concrete sugar warehouses. I'd never been there before, but I'd heard Leilani had been staying there well before they got married. The wood frame house had asymmetrical lines, a wide corrugated metal roof, and a large, covered wraparound lanai. Beyond the white picket fence and lava stone pillars, a circular driveway led to the front steps through a yard full of deep-green grass, exotic tropical plants, and tall trees — palms, Norfolk pines, and sprawling monkey pods. You could see the Pacific Ocean in the distance, a vast expanse of shining, moving, shifting shades of blue and grey.

Jimmy drove slowly through the open gate and up toward the porte cochere. "You ready?" he asked, his lanky body halfway out of the car, grinning at my nervousness.

"I guess," I said, grimacing, not as enthusiastic about confrontation as Jimmy. I got out of the car and slammed the door shut, steeling my nerves. We walked up the steps to the front door and knocked, my heart beating wildly. Wearing a headset and talking on a cell phone, Leilani answered the door, her long, straight black hair a stark contrast against her white T-shirt and jeans. Her big brown eyes widened and teared up, and she quickly got off her call, surprise and fear flitting across her face.

"Oh, Janey," she whispered, almost cooing. I balked at this stranger using my family nickname. "I can't believe you're here."

We hadn't arranged to come, just popped in unexpectedly. I can't remember what we talked about, but I do remember feeling awkward, and after a few minutes of benign conversation, I made an excuse that we needed to go. Being in Leilani's presence nauseated me, and I needed to get away before I said something I might regret — or threw up on her bare feet. I'm sure she was just as relieved when we left.

Later that week, she danced the hula at the party celebrating Dad, lithe and graceful in her black form-fitting muumuu with a crown of flowers in her hair. I sat stone-faced in the front row between Dad and Jimmy, missing my mother, who'd been at my father's side for nearly every one of those twenty-five years in Hawaii, and who was well-known and beloved by the two-hundred-and-fifty guests who smiled and congratulated Dad at that evening's event, then discreetly pulled me aside to inquire about Mom and send her their best wishes.

EIGHT SEPTEMBERS

***

When we weren't taking clients out to lunch, my colleagues and I usually ate in the conference room, bringing back sandwiches and chips or salads from one of the nearby delis, or on bad weather days, from the cafeteria in the basement of Chase Manhattan Plaza. We sat around the oval table and worked on the *New York Times* crossword puzzle, talking about current events and what was going on in our lives.

In December of 2001, a few days after my mother's surprise party, we were having lunch and talking about work and our holiday plans. Doug had canceled our annual client party out of fear of additional terrorist attacks, and all our nerves were on edge.

"You can't believe it," I said, rolling my eyes. Bob and Diane looked at me expectantly. "Eurobrokers won't accept responsibility, GSCC won't accept responsibility, and we're still carrying that damn overdraft, trying to find a home for the securities. It pisses me off!"

"What do the lawyers say?" Bob asked.

"Hmm," I grunted. "They're splitting hairs with each other, but the fact of the matter is, we have to strong-arm one of them into paying our interest costs. Eurobrokers' business is back up and running, and GSCC is still working on the reconciliation. It's not right that we bailed everyone out and now that the crisis has passed, we're being jerked around."

Diane smirked. "Yeah, good luck with that, Jane. I wouldn't hold my breath." I shook my head and changed the subject.

"I think we're going to spend Christmas in Hawaii with my Dad," I shared, then took a sip of Diet Snapple Peach Tea through a straw and raised my eyebrows, waiting for a reaction.

"Really," Bob said, dripping with sarcasm, exaggerated astonishment on his face. Diane looked up at me over her reading glasses, secured by a chain around her neck, her mouth open, speechless. They'd been hearing me complain for three years — first the surprise divorce announcement, then the discovery of the affair, then the affront of the remarriage, then the awkward meeting with Leilani last summer.

"Yeah, I think it will be good to get out of New York, to try to make peace with them. It will be fun for the boys, and maybe I can figure out Leilani a little bit. I really need a break from work too."

We'd spent the past three months dealing with nonstop challenges — staffing gaps created by death or the refusal to return to work, commuting difficulties, air quality conditions, terrorist false alarms, technology and communications breakdowns, reconciliation problems, compensation claims, displaced clients working from makeshift locations, and new security protocols — not to mention resuming our normal day-to-day lending and settlement activity. We were all exhausted.

"What does Jimmy think?" Diane asked, closing her empty plastic salad container and pushing it aside.

"Oh, you know Jimmy. He's all for it! Can't wait to get in there and see what the real story is." Jimmy would not be afraid to get Leilani alone to ask her a few pointed questions. He acted as my surrogate in that regard.

"I'd like to be a fly on the wall for *that* conversation," Bob commented with a shrug, crumpling his paper bag and shooting it into the wastebasket.

"Ha! I'll let you know how it goes. It feels like the right thing to do." I wasn't sure what to expect, but I knew I couldn't go on carrying around all that anger and resentment. Nothing like a terrorist attack to put things in perspective.

"Love over fear," my minister had said during the first church service after 9/11. I would try my best.

***

Dad met Jimmy, J.J., William, and me at the two-runway Hilo International Airport with colorful, sweet-smelling leis, as he had since I was fifteen years old and arriving in Hawaii from my boarding school on Long Island. Back then, he'd arrived with Mom and always wore a smartly pressed aloha shirt tucked into perfectly creased dress pants, compliments of

EIGHT SEPTEMBERS

Mom, with polished leather loafers, socks, and a coordinating belt. Bald and clean-shaven, a broad smile on his round face, he would stretch his arms wide for a hug, ceremoniously dropping leis around my neck and kissing my cheeks, my mother hanging back to take her turn at greeting me. This time, he was dressed and smiling just the same as always, but he arrived alone.

He drove us to the house in Hakalau where Jimmy and I had surprised Leilani the summer before. Dad acted like a cross between a real estate broker trying to make a sale and an errant child trying to please a disapproving parent as he showed us around.

"This room we call Janey's Room," he gushed as he opened the door to one of the first-floor bedrooms. "We named it for you."

As if I might become a regular occupant in this home...

"And this is the meditation room," he said in hushed awe as we peered into the small rectangular room filled with pillows and candles off the back of the second-floor landing. I bristled at Leilani's obvious influence over him.

"See that, boys?" he said to J.J. and Will, pointing to the outbuilding in the yard visible through the window. He let out a low whistle. "I'm going to get a big, red riding tractor to mow the lawn!"

Really, Dad? He sounded like a little kid with a new bike. I barely glanced at their bedroom, unwilling to think about the two of them in there, and scurried back downstairs as soon as I could.

That first night, we sat awkwardly around the formal dining room table in the old sugar plantation manager's house. The ceilings were high and the windows oversized, creating a spaciousness that provided shelter from the hot sun and allowed cool breezes in. The plantation-style architecture and wood-planked floors were accentuated by soft, thick Oriental rugs, an ornate antique desk, and an oversized breakfront. It all suggested a permanence and tradition that concealed the new and conflicted nature of the situation, and my resentment simmered beneath the surface.

Jimmy and I discreetly rolled our eyes at each other as Leilani purred, "A simple peasant's soup," setting down bowls of asparagus soup amidst the elegant crystal glasses, fine china, silver place settings, linen napkins, and tablecloth that were anything but peasant.

The next day, Dad pulled slowly out of the driveway with the boys and me in tow, and made a left, chuckling as he said in a conspiratorial tone, "We'll just sneak down here on the old sugar cane road. Good ole Grandfather knows a shortcut!" It reminded me of being a child and arriving late to church when he swung confidently into the parking lot, ignoring the *One Way* sign, certain the rules didn't apply to him.

He had offered to take the boys and me to swim in the local water hole. Dad hunched over the steering wheel to take in the view, his face animated as he lifted one thick squat hand to point out the ocean and the sugar mill, explaining to J.J. and William, now ten and seven years old, "The plantation workers used this road to transport the sugar cane to the mill. The water from the Hakalau Stream where I'm taking you was used for both irrigating the sugar cane and processing it after the harvest." He shook his head and scowled. "I got C. Brewer out of the sugar business in 1994." Then he turned to flash a smile at William. "That's the year you were born!"

He looked over at me. "Your mother, who is such a good worker on my board, knows the story. It was no longer a profitable enterprise." He'd gone to Washington to fight for price supports, but in the end, cheap imported beet sugar put the Hawaiian sugar cane plantations out of business. So he packaged up thousands of acres of plantation land and sold them as twenty- and forty-acre farmsteads. He was a big believer in micro agribusiness — *and* the tax advantages that came along with agricultural land zoning. Like the missionaries before him, he came to do good, and he did very well indeed.

Dad drove along the narrow road, more like a concrete path, overhung with thick tropical vines, tall trees, and wild plants that made a lush, green canopy that blocked out the bright afternoon sun. The steep road twisted along the curve of the stream. Dad occasionally got too close to the edge, and I flashed back to our childhood trip to California, Dad driving us through Big Sur in a motorhome, cackling wholeheartedly when my sisters and I wailed in fright as he careened too close to the cliffside of the highway, the wide tires kicking up gravel.

We followed the road until it brought us down to water level and drove across the stream. Water splashed under our tires as Dad navigated the Toyota Highlander to reach the parking area on the other side — the one at the end of the Old Mamalahoa Highway that we should have driven down in the first place.

The warmth and humidity hugged us when we got out of the SUV, and you could smell the heaviness of the damp earth. I held the boys' hands as we walked back toward the stream we had just driven across. It reminded me of the dam in Pennsylvania near the farm where we swam on hot days, dropping in from the knotted rope hanging high from a tree on the bank, careful to avoid rocks or being swept away by the currents. But Dad had abdicated life in Pennsylvania, so here we were in this remote corner of Hawaii, trying to meet him on his own terms.

Dad sat on the edge of the concrete path in the stream and held my sons in his lap. He laughed and encouraged them to be brave by dipping their toes into the cold water, so happy to have boys to play with. He'd told me once that I had the perfect family, confirming my suspicions that he believed two sons were better than three daughters.

The following day, Jimmy grabbed me and pulled me into the bedroom. "Well, your dad just gave me a dressing-down!" Dad had invited Jimmy to go to the store with him after breakfast to pick up a few things. I'd been playing with the boys while they were gone, and Leilani had run off to a meeting somewhere.

"What happened?" I asked, concerned.

He giggled a little bit. "It felt like a horror movie. I got in the car and he locked all the doors. I could practically hear the *da-da-da-dum*. I knew there was no getting out or going anywhere. He scolded me for speaking to Leilani, telling me I had no right to question her and warning me to stay away. But I didn't back down! I gave it right back to him!" Jimmy was quite familiar with my frustrations about my overbearing father and my inability to challenge him and prided himself on his willingness to confront Dad.

"Unbelievable," I said, empathizing with him. I appreciated Jimmy's intervention, even if it would prove as ineffective as my silent fuming.

CHRISTMAS IN HAWAII

Apparently, Jimmy had cornered Leilani while Dad and the boys and I were down at the stream. He asked her some uncomfortable questions about her relationship with Dad, trying to nail down their relationship timeline. He wanted to know why he had been excluded from her film. More importantly, he was determined to let her know *he* wasn't fooled by their cover story that they had only started dating after Dad's divorce. Leilani had reported back to Dad, who clearly found the confrontation unacceptable.

This was going to be a long trip.

Christmas morning found us all in our pajamas on the living room floor, except for Dad, who sat upright on the couch, hands folded in his lap, wearing a green-plaid bathrobe and slippers just like he always did on Christmas. His ankles were casually crossed, and he wore a relaxed smile on his face. The boys took turns opening presents from Dad and Leilani, and the ones I'd bought at the last minute at the local department store. I hadn't had the energy to think about shopping for presents before we left New York and made do with the limited choices on the island. I wrapped garlands around my neck and put ribbons from their opened presents in my hair, trying to convince the boys I felt comfortable in this intimate setting with the woman I considered to be an interloper and poor imitation of my mother kneeling at my father's feet.

After the kids had opened their gifts, Leilani got up and padded out to the kitchen in her bare feet, her straight black hair hanging down her back to her narrow waist, hidden by her blue-and-white-striped men's pajamas. She came back carrying a big box in her arms with a big grin on her face.

"Merry Christmas, Doc," she said, using the college football nickname that had followed him into business. Thankfully, she didn't call him Johnny like my mother did. She placed the box on the floor in front of him as his eyes widened and his mouth opened into an *O*.

"Oh, thank you, Leilani," Dad crooned. He invited J.J. and William to help him lift the top off the box.

Inside, they found a puppy, a black Labrador retriever, with a red bow tied around his neck — just like the one Dad had left behind at the

EIGHT SEPTEMBERS

farm in Pennsylvania. Dad enthused over the puppy, holding it close and looking into its eyes as they pressed noses together. He chuckled as he admired its big paws, in his mind an indicator of how large the dog would grow.

First the red tractor, now the puppy.

Bit by bit, it seemed to me he was replicating his life on the East Coast, where he had once planned to retire with Mom, right here in Hakalau with the new, younger substitute wife who was happily — and possibly sincerely — catering to and fawning over him.

I was so angry that I didn't see that there was something seriously wrong with Dad.

CHAPTER 8

Opportunity

"Life's too short for this shit! I'm gettin' out!" Doug blurted. A close friend of Doug's had died suddenly of a heart attack, and the pressures of the past year had culminated in the kind of clarity that informs one it's time to make some changes. It had been nearly one year since 9/11, and the financial disorder was yet to be sorted out — cash and securities positions still being reconciled, compensation claims just beginning to be negotiated, regulatory investigations about to start. Not to mention the ongoing stress of the city being constantly on high alert for possible new terrorist attacks. Doug was ready to call it a day.

As head of the Broker Dealer Division in the Financial Institutions Group (FIG) at what was now — after a series of mergers — J.P. Morgan Chase, Doug had a lot of autonomy to run the department as a stand-alone unit. Handsome, a scratch golfer, and confidante of the chairman, Doug was one of the most senior-ranking African Americans in the bank, as he made sure to mention on a regular basis. Politically adept, charming when he wanted to be, and a million-dollar earner, he was not afraid to pick a fight.

Doug had a lot of clout. And when he didn't, he just acted like he did. He decided that he would choose his successor from within the department and convinced his superiors that whomever he chose would get the job.

I had been working for Doug for about five years, but I'd been doing this kind of lending and relationship management since 1987. We ran a specialty business, lending to broker dealers and managing the day-to-day relationships across all the bank's products and services.

The department operated as a vertically integrated business, as it had been at each of our banks pre-merger. *Vertically integrated* meant that we had everything we needed to run the business under one roof, so to speak.

EIGHT SEPTEMBERS

We had our own loan operations, separate from the rest of the bank, a dedicated collateral management system different from other areas of the bank, and in-house customer service and credit due diligence teams dedicated solely to our client base. And, of course, we had client managers like me, who managed the relationships with — and evaluated the creditworthiness of — the clients. There were nearly fifty of us from three merged banks, toiling together on the twenty-first floor at Chase Manhattan Plaza.

Not just anyone could replace Doug.

I had lots of opinions about how the department should be run, but I'd never consciously aspired to the top job. Now that Doug planned to retire — early in the scheme of things, since he was in his early fifties at most — I started to consider it. I believed I would be good in the position, but I wasn't sure I had the nerve to go for it. I would need to discuss it with my husband.

With each merger, I tended to be opinionated, outspoken, resistant to change. A managing director and client manager working four days a week and refusing to work five, I made up for it by being good at my job: I had great relationships with clients, was a strong negotiator on loan terms and product pricing, had good credit and risk assessment skills, and was a cooperative partner with other areas of the bank.

By the time we'd arrived at our third merger in 2000 with J.P. Morgan, I'd told Bob proudly, "I think I'm finally getting the hang of this process. I see where the synergies are, why this is good for the bank."

Looking at me with his usual cynical smirk and rolling his eyes, he said, "Yeah, and in *this* merger your job is not being threatened!"

J.P. Morgan didn't have a broker-dealer lending group, so unlike in the mergers between MHT, Chemical, and Chase, we didn't need to consolidate our groups and lay people off. Bob and I laughed at my low-risk "merger maturity," and I was embarrassed that I hadn't connected the dots myself.

We were less than a year into the Chase/J.P. Morgan merger when the terrorist attacks occurred, and even a year later, not too much had changed for our department as a result of the merger. I knew Doug fought battles above my pay grade, and maybe that had contributed to

OPPORTUNITY

his decision to leave, but all I really knew was that Doug's announcement of his early retirement forced me to think about my own future.

Who was I? Was I a competent status-quo cog in the machine, happy to throw stones when I disagreed with the boss but never really taking any risks? Or was I someone who could grow and change, motivate my colleagues, and really own my leadership? Was I capable of solving intra-department problems, or only identifying them? Was I willing to put my hand in the air and compete for the job? Or was I going to wait in the back row until someone called on me?

Honestly, I was too conflicted to admit I wanted the top job, yet I was desperate to be designated worthy of it.

In the end, there were just three candidates: our two managing director/team leaders — one of whom was Bob, my immediate boss — and myself.

"This feels kind of weird," I told Jimmy, "reporting to Bob and competing with him for a job where he would report to me." The power dynamics made me very uncomfortable.

Bob had led the group at Chemical Bank before it merged with Manufacturers Hanover Trust in 1991, when he was pushed to the number-two spot behind Joe, my boss at MHT. Joe was the one who'd taken us out for drinks after the Black Monday stock market crash when we got stuck in the elevator, the one who hired me into the group and taught me about secured lending, the one who had my admiration and loyalty. I loved that he was patient and fair, methodical and logical, and down to earth.

I'd resisted Bob's entry into our close-knit group, wary of his unfamiliar and sometimes flippant way of doing things. But he respected Joe, and they worked together to integrate our two groups, pushing me to acclimate to the new situation. Over time, I became comfortable reporting to Bob. Plus, Bob went to bat for me, getting approval for my request to work four days a week when I came back from my first maternity leave shortly after the merger, which endeared him to me. Once I stopped resisting, I learned a lot from him, as he forced me to think more creatively.

EIGHT SEPTEMBERS

But there was nothing like a new merger to help you bond with the people from the prior merger; something about the "us versus them" mentality and a new enemy arriving on the scene. That's exactly what it felt like: intruders coming in and upsetting the dynamic we'd worked so hard to create.

When we merged with Chase in 1996, Bob disagreed with Doug getting the top job and Joe being moved to another area of the bank. We Chemical Bank people believed that we had the bigger book of business — more clients, more loans, more revenues — and that Joe had the stronger, more experienced resume to run the merged group. I had never crossed paths with Doug, but Bob had, and he clearly thought Doug was a lightweight. There was also the indelicate question of whether Doug got the job because he was Black. The industry was not known for its diversity, and there was definitely a certain passive-aggressive antagonism toward affirmative action that permeated Wall Street — not so subtly in certain circles — casting doubt on the skills of people of color, and women, too, for that matter. I didn't agree with that at all, but I loved working for Joe and didn't want to see him go, so I fought against the reality of Doug becoming the new boss, too, and cried when I went in to say goodbye and thank Joe for all he had taught me.

I would come to learn it was definitely in Doug's wheelhouse to use his race for strategic advantage; in fact, he considered it his obligation.

"C'mon, Jane!" Doug had growled at me, his voice low and serious when I had been advocating for some staffing choice or another. "You know how Wall Street is. WASPs and Jews control the front office; the Italian and Irish mobs control the back office. The rest of us gotta pick up the scraps!" He tilted his chin to eyeball me over his wire-framed reading glasses, his eyes sparkling, and raised his eyebrows. "Imma change that," he vowed with a confident nod, a cross between a smile and a snarl on his lips. I didn't dare mention the glaring gender imbalance on Wall Street.

But I immediately recognized the truth of his words, even as my heart simultaneously leapt in defense of the Italian, Irish, Jewish, and WASP men who had taught me the business and made a seat at the table for me. I was torn between my desire for social justice and loyalty to my mentors, which was further complicated by my lifelong distaste for men who used their power to dominate others. But really, it didn't matter what I thought or felt. Doug was a man on a mission to correct the imbalances and injustices he saw, and he was willing to use his power to do it. *Conceptually* I agreed with him. But *emotionally*, he presented to me as just another man with power, manipulating the world to his own desires. And I responded accordingly.

Just like I had resisted Bob, I resisted Doug. But unlike the cooperative relationship between Bob and Joe that helped smooth the Chemical/MHT merger integration, the tension between Bob and Doug permeated the newly merged Chemical/Chase group and allowed my distrust of Doug to fester.

The December after 9/11, for example, Doug refused to have our annual client holiday party. The party — a tradition started by Joe at Manufacturers Hanover Trust back in the late '80s — had grown to more than eight hundred clients who came to the headquarters building for a celebratory, alcohol-laden feast. Clients noshed on shrimp cocktail, oysters, and clams, and lined up for the pasta bar, a carving station, sushi, fruit and cheese, and a large chocolate fondue fountain surrounded by finger-size dessert pastries.

Doug said he didn't want the responsibility of gathering people in a contained space when the terrorists could attack again any minute, and it was hard to argue with that. Yet his decision was the complete opposite of my approach to my mother's party, and it made me irritated and even a little sad. Beyond believing that people desperately needed pleasure in the aftermath of tragedy, I thought Doug's decision reflected poorly on our leadership position in the market and showed an unwillingness to reward the efforts of so many people who had been working almost around the clock since 9/11.

"Doug, aren't you letting the terrorists win?" I argued, trying to sway him.

"Can't the clients make up their own minds about whether or not they want to take that risk?" someone else asked. But he was resolute in his refusal, stubborn as he could be, and I suspected it had more to do with his own fears than anything else.

I sometimes spoke disparagingly about Doug. He called me on it once, bringing me to his office and sitting me down for a "talking to," just like going to the principal's office in elementary school. He'd gotten wind of some complaint I'd made about him to one of our clients. I played dumb, denied it, refused to admit I'd said anything, and after he had sufficiently reprimanded me, he let it go, even though I suspected he knew I was lying. Chagrined, I learned my lesson about loose lips sinking ships and became more discreet. But our relationship remained strained. So strained, in fact, that I actually talked about it to my pastor, Ken, a few months before I found out Doug was throwing in the towel.

We were sitting in Ken's small office tucked into a corner at the top of a narrow staircase in the old church building on West 77th Street, overlooking West End Avenue. He'd come out from behind his wooden desk that sat in front of a wall of books to join me in one of the two comfy chairs that faced each another at an angle. The blue-gray carpeting was worn, and the paint had seen better days. But the leaded windows, wooden beams, and turn-of-the-century details made the room charming and intimate.

"Ken," I said, "that man is so infuriating, bossy, and opinionated. He inspires such anger and hatred in me."

Ken pressed his fingertips together thoughtfully and gently probed in the sonorous voice I loved. "Would you consider Doug an enemy?" he asked, looking at me with genuine curiosity and compassion.

I considered the question. "Well, not in the way that I think he's out to get me. Not at all." I realized in that moment that despite my emotional reaction to Doug, he really *wasn't* targeting me. "But yes, an enemy in that he is an obstacle to my spiritual growth, my ability to be the person I want to be. I always feel angry and irritated when I'm around him, and it makes me speak ill of him. I know I'm being disrespectful and unkind, and that's not who I want to be."

If I was being honest, I chafed under Doug's authoritarian manner — so similar to my father's — and got annoyed that he shut me down whenever I challenged him.

OPPORTUNITY

Ken took this in and weighed his words carefully. "Hmm, you know what Jesus said about our enemies?"

I'd been raised a Presbyterian, had missionary grandparents, uncles, and cousins, and went to a Christian boarding school. I was pretty sure I knew what Jesus had to say about our enemies. Still, I waited for Ken to explain.

"We are to pray for them," he said, then paused before softly asking, "Do you think you could do that?"

I'd had my quarrels with the patriarchal and hypocritical way the church ran itself, but I pretty much agreed with the actual teachings of Jesus. After all, I was the one who submitted a prayer card after 9/11 for bin Laden, asking that God would replace the hatred in his heart with love and taking Ken's breath away as he read it aloud to the congregation. My mind fully believed in the power of love, but I didn't always know how to actually live that. Especially when someone was pushing my buttons — be it my father, my boss, or my husband.

"Oh boy." I laughed nervously. "That won't be easy. Let me think about it."

Am I a lip-service Christian, or am I willing to do the hard things? I pondered.

"Yes," I decided. "I am willing to pray for Doug."

During my ten years "wandering in the wilderness" after I stopped going to church in college — except for mandatory attendance when visiting my parents — I'd explored a variety of spiritual traditions. Having tired of the rules-and-regulations branch of religion, mystical writings that spoke to my spirit particularly appealed to me. One day in the Brooklyn Public Library, somewhere between the *I Ching* and texts on Kabbalah, I stumbled upon a book called *There is a River* about Edgar Cayce, a devout Presbyterian and American clairvoyant who gained prominence in the early twentieth century.

In it, I discovered one of the most compelling concepts, which appears in nearly three hundred of the more than fourteen thousand documented Cayce readings. It relates to our ability to intentionally choose our thoughts and attitudes to alter the physical experiences of our lives: *Spirit is the Life, Mind is the Builder, Physical is the Result.*

EIGHT SEPTEMBERS

The concept appealed to me because it seemed to be a formula for changing my life. I was intrigued by the idea that our physical experience is a result of what we think and that our thoughts are influenced by our connection to the creative forces of the universe. I'd read lots of books written on the subject, including exercises to test out the theory. One of my favorites was *Experiments in the Search for God* by Mark Thurston. Mark was one of a group of scholars brought in by the Association for Research and Enlightenment to study the fourteen thousand written transcripts of Cayce's psychic readings and test them for validity and usefulness. Mark's areas of expertise were consciousness, attitudes, emotions, spiritual ideals, life purpose, and dreams. Drawing from the Cayce material, he has written a dozen books on a variety of spiritual psychology subjects, and I'd always resonated with his pragmatic approach to these somewhat esoteric topics.

After talking with Pastor Ken, I consulted Mark's book and discovered an exercise I could do in tandem with praying. Every day for seven days, I committed to finding ten positive things about the person who was challenging me, namely Doug. Day one was tough. But another Cayce passage rang in my head. When Cayce was asked, "Which version of the Bible is true?" his response was: *The version you apply* (2072-14). So I persevered.

Doug is a good dresser.

Doug is a good golfer.

What else?

It's hard to think of good things about someone when you're so set against them. Every day, though, I added to the list, finding ten different positive qualities about Doug more easily each day. I also said prayers for him.

At the end of seven days, I found that Doug was not any different.

But *I* was different. My heart had softened, and I had begun to let go of my anger and resentment and see him more objectively. Over the next few months, our relationship thawed. I never expected it might evolve into me being his potential replacement, though.

PART THREE
Adaptation

"Adapt or perish, now as ever, is nature's inexorable imperative."
—H.G. Wells

CHAPTER 9
Surprise

What would it really mean for me to be "the boss"? To run a full business unit with responsibility for both the profits and losses and all the people?

"At a minimum, I'll have to go back to working five days a week," I told Jimmy, who sat on the piano bench in front of our baby grand, tapping out a melody on the keys. Barely a few feet away, I rested on the couch with my feet up after a long day. We'd sat together many times on that piano bench over the years, composing songs, hashing out lyrics, singing and laughing.

I'd always loved the piano and dreamt of a career in music, and my childhood piano teacher had prepared me to apply to Julliard. But that all ended when my parents moved to Hawaii and the new piano teacher at boarding school only had eyes for her star pupil and couldn't be bothered with me. Still, I enjoyed writing songs and making music with Jimmy, who'd charmed all the girls in college playing the Beatles and Billy Joel on the grand piano in the dormitory lobby. Sometimes he brought out his tenor saxophone, his principal instrument, and stood beside me, blowing his horn as I played the piano part of a Vivaldi duet he'd found for us. I was always grateful that music was still part of my life.

I'd been working four days a week since J.J.'s birth ten years earlier, something Bob had gotten approved for me at a time when such things were not the norm. It troubled me to consider giving that up, even though my current role had begun to bore me and I'd taken to calling my four-day workweek my "golden handcuffs" — a great arrangement that prevented me from going anywhere.

"Doug told me I'd have to do more entertaining. Longer hours, nights out, trips to London. More pay." That last bit got Jimmy's attention, and he turned around to face me. My compensation was high on his list of priorities. He often egged me on, pointing out that the men probably made more than I did, as if my six-figure salary wasn't good enough. I depended on Jimmy's support so much that it never occurred to me he might have his own agenda.

"Sounds like a good opportunity," he encouraged. "I'll be here to take care of things."

Taking the job would vault me from the cubicle to the corner office in one fell swoop, from no direct reports to managing a group of forty-five people. I'd join the Financial Institutions Group Management Team, the first step to becoming "senior management."

Two years earlier, Jimmy and I had sat in the same room having a different conversation, about his career.

"Look, you make enough money for all of us," he'd said. "Teaching is burning me out, and I have no time to write and record my music. I can take care of things at home." For the first time in his life, Jimmy had a full-time "regular" job, yet after two years, he found it stressful. Like his father and brothers, he preferred being his own boss and was making a pitch for why he planned to quit.

"Don't you like working?" I asked, code for 'having a regular paycheck.' A musician by nature and training, over the years he'd been a taxi driver, played in a cover band, and briefly owned a pizzeria, trying to earn money to promote his songwriting career. He also tried to jumpstart the process by gambling, looking for the big score at the racetrack or betting on professional sports — something he'd been doing since he was fourteen.

After becoming a father, he'd quit gambling and gotten his master's in music education and a teaching certificate, leading to a full-time job as a music teacher at a nearby elementary school. It made me grateful to raise our two wonderful sons together, to be regular attendees and volunteers at a church we loved, and to *finally* have our financial house in order. I thought the structure of a job was good for him and kept him out of trouble. If he became financially dependent on me again and had no job, I worried about him gambling again.

"Come on, you know you'd feel better if I was around more for the kids," he added, flashing me a grin, looking for the angle that would get me to agree. "And besides, I'll have time to record our new songs." He'd already released one CD of pop rock songs he'd composed, including many with lyrics we wrote together, recording himself singing and mixing the tracks in our home studio. We enjoyed doing that together, even if we did sometimes argue in the process, and we both believed it was only a matter of time before he would be discovered.

He persisted, and I acquiesced as I often did, tired of trying to persuade him out of what he'd already decided to do.

At that point, Will and J.J. were five and nine, so we let the nanny go and hired a full-time housekeeper who did the cooking and cleaning and laundry so Jimmy could work in the studio. Jimmy took the boys back and forth to school and to play dates and doctors' appointments. The relief my working-mother guilt felt outweighed my concerns about whether or not it was a good trade.

I continued to organize the kids' lives from the office, helping them with their homework and playing with them when I got home, putting them to bed each night. Working four days a week gave me one day to take care of personal business so I could just be Mom all weekend.

It was now two years after he'd given up his job, and we walked down the block hand in hand to the Viand, our local diner, to talk about *my* career — the financial foundation of our family. We had been going to the Viand since we moved to the neighborhood in 1990, when I was pregnant with J.J., and it had become part of our regular routine. Owned by a wonderfully kind and welcoming Greek man who'd renovated the old American Diner, the space now sported beautiful blue and brown mosaic tiles and dark, gleaming wood. Having dinner together had always been a priority for me, even if we had to go out to do it, so Jimmy and the boys sometimes met me there for dinner when I finished my workday. Occasionally, like on this day, Jimmy and I would go there for breakfast on my day off after I'd dropped the kids at school.

Jimmy and I met randomly on a train on Long Island in 1977, when I was seventeen and he was eighteen, a few weeks before we both started college in Boston — a coincidence that I interpreted as fate. Tall and handsome, with brown curly hair under a baseball cap, he had an engaging smile and was full of energy and excitement. How could I resist? Three years later, still students, we were married, and by 2002, we'd been a couple longer than we'd been single, and twice as long as we'd been parents. I did not know myself as an independent adult entity.

Waiting for our food in the diner that morning, Jimmy dominated the conversation, both verbally and emotionally. He took my hands across the table and looked at me with his beautiful, soulful brown eyes, his expression sincere and contrite.

"I didn't want to tell you this before because you were so busy and stressed with work, but I went back to gambling," he confessed hurriedly. "I'm done now. I'm back in the program. Everything is okay. I love you."

Seriously? I'm running around like a crazy woman trying to restore order to the financial markets, relying on you to be there for our sons, and this is how you spend your time? Really? After twenty-two years of marriage, we're still having this fucking conversation?

I looked at Jimmy, silent. The familiar face I had loved for so long — framed between his close-cropped, reddish-brown beard and receding hairline — was now contorted, full of anxiety, and pleading. His long, slender fingers interlaced tightly with mine, telegraphing his need for reassurance.

I couldn't believe that he'd fallen off the wagon and gotten back on — and that I'd missed the whole thing. He'd been in the program for thirteen years, and I thought he had his addiction under control. Even so, I wasn't entirely shocked. An addict's partner is always waiting for the other shoe to drop on some level. I felt numb, traumatized and exhausted by the pressures of work, beyond caring and *so over this*.

Ten years earlier, I'd kicked him out after another relapse. As a new "mama bear," I did for J.J. what I couldn't do for myself: I drew a line in the sand. I absolutely refused to allow my children to grow up in an environment of addiction. But within a month he'd talked his way back home, quit yet again, and decided to get his master's degree and teaching certificate. To my knowledge, he'd been on the straight and narrow ever since.

I shook my head and took a deep breath. I couldn't change what he had done, and besides, he promised he had stopped. Maybe I even felt a little guilty for being so preoccupied that I didn't realize he had backtracked.

I suddenly decided I wanted the job. Jimmy's gambling made me feel like my life was going in circles, and this new job would be a definitive step forward — and far more appealing than facing whatever was going on here.

Look, I wanted to say, *gambling is your thing. You're either going to get with the program or not. I am not your keeper. I'm moving on with my life, and it's up to you if you come along or not.*

But after a decade of attending Gam Anon meetings, I still wasn't brave enough to say those words out loud. Instead I nodded, concentrated on eating my fried eggs, and pretended we were on the same page.

***

Back in the early 1980s, not long after I started at Manufacturers Hanover Trust, I'd called my husband in dismay.

"Jimmy, I think the bank made an error!"

"What do you mean?"

"We had two thousand dollars in our account, and now we have just one thousand. I think the bank posted a debit to the wrong account." I had just begun my entry-level job at MHT as an administrative assistant — which in those days did not mean secretary — and was learning about mispostings, backdating, errors, and remedies.

"I'm sure you'll get to the bottom of it," Jimmy assured me.

"Yeah, I'm going to the branch right now," I said, hanging up the phone.

When I got home that evening, I told him the bank claimed there was no error. "I don't know what to do! We need that money to pay the rent," I fretted.

"Don't worry. I'm sure you'll figure it out," Jimmy reassured me again.

That weekend, we met up with his parents at Jones Beach to see a Peter Allen concert. During the drive, I continued to rant and worry about the missing money and paying the bills, troubled there wasn't a quick solution. After we parked the car and were headed to the entry gate, music pulsing from the opening act, Jimmy grabbed my arm and faced me.

"It was me," he confessed, the setting sun glowing behind him.

"What do you mean?" I looked at him, puzzled. A warm wind blew across the crowded parking lot.

"The bank didn't make a mistake. I took the money. I needed it to make a bet. I didn't mean to make you worry. It's going to be okay," he said, looking sincere and contrite.

"You mean you gambled and lost it?" I asked, simultaneously processing his deceit and his apology. I didn't think a joint account meant I put money in and he took it out behind my back.

"Yes, I'm sorry. I'll pay it back. I promise!" He hugged my unresponsive body tight. "Don't worry so much. You'll see. I'll make it up to you. Let's go have some fun now!" Jimmy grinned and took my hand, and I followed him into the concert, lost in my own thoughts as he chatted away. I wanted to tell him how deceived I felt, how worried I'd been, and how much time I'd wasted on the phone and going to the bank branch trying to figure out what had happened to our money — but I didn't know how to do that in a public place. My manners and tendency to dissociate during conflict trumped my need to speak up for myself. So instead, I plastered on a smile, made pleasant conversation, and seethed inside.

***

I'll never forget the name Giocatore Benedetto, or how Jimmy's twin brother always spoke it with admiration and awe. It was Gio who'd taught the brothers how to gamble when they were fourteen, drove them back and forth to the racetrack, and, I suspect, financed their early forays. He seduced them until they were hooked, tempting them with a promised path to self-sufficiency, cajoling them into being "real men," convincing them that gambling was an honorable pastime.

Jimmy said it started innocently. He just wanted to be able to buy the things his parents couldn't afford. But during the first nine years of our marriage, Jimmy's gambling went from a quick way to earn cash to a regular way of life. Sometimes he was flush with winnings; other times he stole money and bounced checks. Sometimes he would disappear and be out of touch for hours on end, leaving me to worry that he had been in an accident. Other times he splurged on dinner and flowers, happy to be the attentive husband.

Thousands of dollars and thousands of hours had gone missing from our lives. I thought I had married a professional musician with a gambling hobby, but he fast became a professional gambler with a music hobby. But I loved him, and I'd made a vow of "for better or worse," so I intended to make things work...even though I was quickly learning I couldn't trust him.

Arguing, cajoling, shaming, logic, tears, silence. Nothing changed Jimmy's behavior. What could I do? Jimmy's sister — fearing I might leave him — encouraged me to check out Gambler's Anonymous and get some help. I didn't even know they had an "AA for gambling," but I found their info and made a call.

The woman who answered shouted at me over the phone, her heavy Brooklyn accent leaping out of the receiver I was cradling to prevent my husband from hearing. "Why are you whispering? Don't be afraid of him! He's got no business telling you what to do. Gamblers are liars. You need help. Gamblers Anonymous is the place for you."

I cringed at her words. How dare this woman boss me around and disparage Jimmy, someone she'd never met? Still, I heeded her advice and decided to go to a meeting.

Jimmy declined to come with me. "I'm a professional, not an addict," he declared. "How am I any different from a trader on Wall Street? I play the odds, just like your clients. You don't criticize them!" According to him, daily trips to the track or Off-Track Betting and his nightly sports action, monitored via two radios and two TVs so he could simultaneously track four games, shouldn't trouble me.

I kept waiting for him to agree with me that his gambling was a problem, somehow unable to act based on my own assessment.

It would be a long time before I figured out how to do that.

CHAPTER 10
Step One

It is strange that you can be schooled in social work and still be in denial about your own life. I felt bewildered at the first Gam-Anon meeting I attended in 1989, wondering why I was there and what I should say.

The group gathered in the evening in an elementary school classroom in Brooklyn, our adult bodies awkwardly wedged into the small desk chairs arranged in a circle. We were a group of disparate women, mostly wives, a few mothers. Some angry, some sad, some inspiring — and all honest with a bluntness that frightened me. I was not accustomed to talking so openly, much less in front of strangers. The gamblers met in another room at the same time; this support group was for the family members trying to cope with their loved one's addiction. I didn't realize Gam-Anon had their own twelve steps, tailored to the needs of the family members of the addicts.

Gazing into the darkness beyond the second-floor windows, I listened to the women take turns reading the twelve steps. "Step one, we admitted we were powerless over the gambling problem and that our lives had become unmanageable."

Powerless? You mean I am not in control of everything? I can't fix this myself? For some reason, I thought I could change Jimmy. I really believed I could control his behavior and make him stop. Admitting I was powerless perplexed me. I'd always assumed if I just *do this*, then things would change. If I *don't do that*, things will change. Despite a decade of failed strategies, it was incredibly painful to admit that perhaps I couldn't fix things after all.

I looked around the circle, trying to gauge the other women in the room. Rose, the woman from the phone, was older, short, large-bosomed and dark-haired, with oversized glasses on a neck chain. She was loud, bossy, and officious getting us organized as the meeting started, yet somehow welcoming and reassuring. She'd been in the program for over twenty years.

"Step two, we came to believe that a power greater than ourselves could restore us to a normal way of thinking and living."

Oh! Fighting every day about money, crying because I don't know where he is, and lying to my family is not normal? Wait — isn't Jimmy *the abnormal one?* I'd never considered that my way of thinking was not normal.

"Step three, we made a decision to turn our will and our lives over to the care of this Power of our own understanding."

This feels familiar, very Christian, something I'm always trying to do, I thought, looking at the placards on the table urging us to LET GO AND LET GOD and ACT AS IF. *I can relate.* Deciding to trust the process, to let go of control, would be a huge act of faith, but maybe it wasn't actually my responsibility to manage and control the situation.

The reader passed the booklet to a young woman, slightly overweight with big disco hair and heavy makeup, who continued reading the steps in a strong New York accent.

"Step four, we made a searching and fearless moral inventory of ourselves."

Uh oh. You mean I might have to examine my own behavior, take some responsibility? I blamed Jimmy for everything. He's the gambler, so it's all his fault, right?

I shifted uncomfortably in my chair. This was a lot to absorb, and I still questioned whether I should even be at this meeting. They'd given me some materials when I sat down so I could read along as the women passed the booklet around.

"Step five, we admitted to ourselves and to another human being the exact nature of our wrongs."

What the hell? Aren't I the victim? What am I doing wrong? How can I be at fault?

While I became increasingly angry and defensive as each step was read, I noticed the other women were taking this all in stride.

"Step six, we were entirely ready to have these defects of character removed."

Excuse me? What character defects do I have? And even if I do have a few, it's Jimmy's character defects that are the problem, not mine. My defensiveness, my sharp tongue, my righteous anger, my martyrdom — these were my tools, my armor, my protection. How could I be safe without them? And wouldn't everything be better if Jimmy just stopped gambling?

A petite, curly-haired woman around Rose's age smiled encouragingly when I glanced over at her. She took the booklet and started to read. I looked down at my feet and put my hands under my thighs, trying to disappear.

"Step seven, we humbly asked God of our understanding to remove our shortcomings."

All right, this I could handle. I'd spent my whole life asking God to do this. *Sorry I lost my temper. Sorry I yelled. Sorry I was impatient. Sorry I'm not perfect. Sorry, sorry, sorry!* Raised as a Christian — a "lowly worm," according to the hymns — I already suspected deep down that my shortcomings made me unacceptable, unlovable, and unworthy.

"Step eight, we made a list of all the people we had harmed and became willing to make amends to them all."

Hmm, how does this possibly apply to me? Who have I harmed? I was the one harmed, not the one doing harm. But as I dared to look — and did that fearless moral inventory — the list appeared: friends I had abandoned, sisters I had not trusted with the truth, a husband I had disparaged and dishonored by not holding him accountable, parents I had deceived, a self I had not valued. This was a sobering step. How would I ever set things right?

My emotions were a bubbling cauldron at this point. I felt defeated and discouraged by the work ahead of me.

"Step nine, we made direct amends to such people wherever possible, except when to do so would injure them or others."

Yeah, whatever. I don't get it. What constitutes amends? How does one gauge what harms another? How does one prepare to make amends and deal with the consequences of doing so?

I could feel my resistance hardening my body and folded my arms across my chest as the booklet was passed to another woman showing signs of wear and tear on her face. The fluorescent lights above glowed and made her look sallow. The room had grown warm, and I could smell the chalk on the blackboard.

"Step ten, we continued to take personal inventory, and when we were wrong, promptly admitted it."

Admit I am wrong, mistaken, inappropriate? Don't I always know what's best? Aren't I always right? I was pretty comfortable on my moral high horse.

Shifting again in the hard, wooden school chair, my mind wandered to what kind of children went to this school. Would Jimmy and I ever have children? Would we still be living in Brooklyn? As an uncle, Jimmy had fun goofing around and snuggling with our young nieces and nephews, and I always thought he'd be a good father — loving and affectionate, not like his own moody and often mean-spirited father.

"Step eleven, we sought through prayer and meditation to improve our conscious contact with God as we understand Him, praying only for knowledge of His will for us and the power to carry that out."

Okay, back on safe terrain. This is my Christian training, and I am constantly doing this.

Paying attention again, I thought, *Yes, maybe there is room in "God as we understand Him" for me to experience a different kind of relationship with God than the one I was raised with, something more affirming and less punitive.* The Edgar Cayce material I had just discovered gave me new language that facilitated a different entry point into my spiritual life.

"Step twelve, having made an effort to practice these principles in all our affairs, we tried to carry this message to others."

Despite my family's missionary background, I had never been comfortable as a proselytizer. Maybe I won't even come back to this meeting, so it doesn't matter anyway, I assured myself.

I looked around the room at these tired and angry women, who clearly found solace and hope in these steps and in this community, and figured I'd listen politely. That was the least I could do.

Everyone took turns telling their story. I heard the echoes of my own experience: stolen money, bounced checks, broken promises, outright

STEP ONE

lies, businesses lost, relationships ruptured, threatening bookies, Off Track Betting, illegal betting parlors, Atlantic City. I also heard about recovery and how it works: the importance of attending meetings, maintaining anonymity, and setting a budget; the need to stop any bargaining to control the gambler's behavior and hold him accountable for his actions; and finally, the cold, hard truth that the financial issues would be easier to fix than the relationship ones.

Rose pushed me to share. I reluctantly stood in front of the group, trying to introduce myself as they each had.

My tongue awkward in my mouth, my voice barely audible, I sounded meek and hesitant. "My name is Jane and... I'm...married to...a... compulsive gambler. I don't know why I'm here... other than... maybe... just to say those words out loud?" I held back tears and wanted to vomit. I felt such betrayal and shame in speaking those words.

Returning to my seat, unable to say more, I hardly registered the women affirming my courage in daring to speak the truth out loud.

***

No one in my family or professional circle knew anything about Jimmy's gambling problem. Only Jimmy's family knew. Gambling was what the men in his family *did*, so I wasn't surprised at all when I found out years later that the first time Jimmy tried to quit gambling, his twin brother called him a loser and shamed him for abandoning the pursuit. The formula was simple: The men gambled, and the women paid the bills. The men were irresponsible; the women were responsible. Trying to upset that dynamic would only result in anger, arguments, and gaslighting. Complaining to anyone outside the family was disloyal and shameful.

It never occurred to me to reach out to my own family. I assumed they would judge us harshly and I couldn't imagine admitting the scope of the problem, which I could barely acknowledge myself. My sister Ellie liked to joke that we were raised not to talk about our problems — or better yet, not to admit we had them in the first place. Denial was a pattern embedded so deeply in our WASP culture that it didn't have a name. Well, maybe it did. We called it *being polite*. And it was a hard habit to break.

I learned in the Gam-Anon program that there were three people in my marriage: me, the man, and the gambler. The man and the gambler are not the same. It is a progressive disease, and the gambler gradually takes over the man. You cannot treat the gambler the way you would treat the man. You need different strategies.

The man loves you and doesn't want to hurt you. He wants to do things together, provide for you, keep you safe, and make you proud. The gambler loves the action and doesn't care who gets hurt. He only wants to be with other gamblers. He takes from you and doesn't notice that you are scared and ashamed.

But the man and the gambler wear the same face, and it is hard to distinguish one from the other.

***

I attended weekly Gam-Anon meetings for many years, even after the kids were born. Of course, there wouldn't have been any kids if Jimmy hadn't finally joined the program a year or so after I did, so I was grateful for that. I was also grateful that I'd learned over time to focus on the ways I contributed to the problem and let Jimmy take responsibility for himself. It was finally sinking in that I couldn't change anyone except myself — and I had plenty of my own issues to face. By the time we were sitting in the diner talking about my next possible career move, I had left the program and moved on to personal therapy, but Jimmy had stayed with it.

That morning, when Jimmy confessed that he'd slipped in the midst of discussing my desire to go for Doug's job, Jimmy and I came to an uneasy agreement. He agreed to support me in my career aspirations, and I agreed to support him again in his abstinence. We'd been intertwined for decades, and I desperately wanted things to be good between us.

Still, I felt something shift ever so slightly. An emotional coldness and wariness within me that was so subtle, I wouldn't be able to acknowledge it for several years to come.

CHAPTER 11
Chosen

In less than six months after my meeting with Pastor Ken, when I'd started the prayers to soften my heart toward Doug, not only was I under consideration to replace him, but Doug *chose me* as the new head of the department! I'd still have to meet with his boss to get the formal green light, but that was a mere technicality. Doug's decision would be final. He suddenly became my strongest supporter and a wonderful mentor, both of which I had never experienced from him before. I was convinced a miracle had taken place due to the changes within my own heart.

Jimmy bought me flowers to celebrate. He did that often, always for my birthday and on Mother's Day and Valentine's Day, but also on random days when he felt good or the weather was beautiful or he thought I needed cheering up. It was always a welcome surprise when he presented me with a bunch of lilacs, daffodils, tulips, or a bouquet of colorful carnations, daisies, lilies, and greenery wrapped in paper from the local corner deli.

"Thanks!" I said, giving him a kiss.

The truth? I was petrified at the responsibilities and power that came with this new role and quickly consumed by a bout of extreme insecurity. I worried about becoming the boss, not only of my peers but especially of Bob, my former boss and mentor. I worried about public speaking. I worried about senior management's opinion of me. I worried about my competency and understanding of the industry. The more I realized the extent of the job, the more my self-confidence flew out the window.

One late fall day during the transition period, I sat next to Doug on the long blue couch in his office, our backs to the window — the same place I'd sat when he reprimanded me for talking about him behind his back. On the coffee table in front of us, he'd laid out his spreadsheets.

It was time to learn about allocating bonuses.

EIGHT SEPTEMBERS

In those days, the department got a bonus pool based on a formula that incorporated both the bank's overall performance and our individual department's performance. There were metrics, of course, but a large dose of subjectivity and politics went into the final number.

"Jane, not all revenue dollars are equal," Doug began. "You're gonna have to fight to get what we deserve." In an institution created from the mergers of many commercial banks, which now aspired to become a top-three investment bank, revenues generated from our traditional commercial banking business — loans and operating services — were not valued as much anymore, even though we earned them reliably year after year. The bank wanted fat, sexy deal fees from advising clients on mergers and acquisitions or public debt issuances, not the mundane, volume-driven fees we earned from check processing or wire transfers or even government clearance.

Once the overall bonus pool was determined, how it got allocated among the employees in the department was up to Doug. Soon, that level of autonomy and discretion would be a thing of the past as the bank moved toward more and more micromanagement of compensation, but at that moment, we still had the power to decide.

Stroking his chin, Doug watched me as I absorbed last year's numbers. For the first time in my career, I had knowledge about how much my colleagues were earning. I'd never complained about my compensation because every year I made more money than I did the year before, even after I switched to four days a week, and I had never anticipated making as much money as I did. I'd assumed I made less than my male counterparts — and I did — but age and experience could explain most of that away. I couldn't believe how much money Bob made, though, and realized why he'd never left, despite his obvious rancor toward Doug and his disillusionment with the job. Seeing his numbers, it dawned on me that his increasingly acerbic comments came from feeling trapped. I could see that Diane held her own with the male managing directors, but it challenged me to be objective about determining bonuses when I learned everyone's salaries. I was walking in a new world now.

Doug perched on the edge of the couch, his elbows resting on his knees, reading glasses in place, his compact, muscular body fully engaged in this Rubik's cube of year-end compensation.

"If we give ten thousand dollars more to one person, then we have to reduce someone else by the same amount," he said.

Again, in the not-so-distant future, the bank would micromanage this process and force certain performance levels into a zero-bonus position, but at that time we were in the last vestiges of partnership and teamwork being valued, when the bank still trusted that managers knew how to deal with their people. Bonuses were like tea leaves, though, in that they were often interpreted as carrying messages, and a slight adjustment up or down could have a big impact on morale.

Doug's philosophy — with which I wholeheartedly agreed — advocated that the department rose and fell on everyone's participation; therefore, everyone earned a bonus. The range may have been between $5,000 and $500,000, but even the most junior clerk would get a bonus.

There might be more money added to the pool over the final few weeks of the process as the numbers came in, but there was never enough, and it was always a scramble — or maybe I should say a scrimmage. Bonus allocations were a sharp-elbow game. And not just in the office.

Every year, Jimmy started lobbying me for the portion of my bonus that he felt was his due months before I actually knew how much I'd get. It started with small questions: Did I have any idea about the size of the bonus pool this year? Then came reminders of everything he did for me. Finally, it developed into full-fledged cajoling, pressuring me to give him a number. I became confused and conflicted, since I felt the need to right my father's wrongs, so to speak, and respect and compensate the non-earning spouse. I resented the concept of a woman being on an allowance, so I resisted doing that to Jimmy. Yet given the gambling problem, and my responsibility for the family's financial well-being, I probably should have exercised even more control over the money. I'd already separated our finances, cut him off from our joint account, and filed separate tax returns to protect myself from his liabilities, but

EIGHT SEPTEMBERS

I never held him fully accountable for what he did with his share of the bonus money.

Before my meeting with Doug, the game at home had already started. Jimmy had paced around the apartment one recent morning, animated and determined to make his point, then intercepted me as I tried to get out the door for work. "You owe me!"

"What do you mean, I *owe* you?" I looked up from organizing my pocketbook, a skeptical look on my face.

"I pick up your dry cleaning! I do the food shopping! I run the errands! I'm your 'step and fetch it' so you can be the big, successful banker." He counted these things off on his fingers and stood across from me, blocking my access to the door.

"Wait. That's what you said you *wanted* to do!" I put my bag on my shoulder, getting uneasy. "You didn't want to work, and you said you'd take care of things at home."

"And I do. So that means I earned a part of your bonus." He had arrived at his central point.

"But I pay for everything! I'm the one who earned that bonus, going out to work every day. I'm the one who safeguards it and makes sure we have enough to do everything we need to do. What do you need money for?" In the past, he'd talked me into spending money to fund his recording studio equipment and projects, not to mention cash that just disappeared into his gambling world — although he claimed he didn't do that anymore.

"You can't keep me on a leash like your father did to your mother! It's not right," he argued, striking a low blow that he knew would get a reaction.

"I'll think about it," I said, a delaying tactic so I could end the conversation and leave.

I slammed the door as I left the apartment, anger at Jimmy for hassling me coursing through my veins. It was the same thing every fucking year. He tried to manipulate and shame me into giving him half of my bonus. A fancy car drove by as I exited our building and I thought, *He has no idea about the type of people I work with. If one of those successful, wealthy men ever turned their attention to me, who knows what might happen.*

I shook my head. Where did that thought come from? I wasn't looking for another man. I was just becoming increasingly aware that Jimmy's sense of entitlement and lack of appreciation for me was not normal. But I didn't know what to do about it.

Who could I turn to for guidance? I didn't know any female sole breadwinners, let alone ones with a gambling-addicted husband. It would be awkward to ask my male colleagues how they managed their finances with their wives. Money wasn't really a polite topic of conversation in my family, and other than my father's admonishment to deposit checks immediately and to balance my checkbook, I didn't have much training. Honestly, even if I'd had someone to ask, I was too ashamed to form the questions.

Eventually, I couldn't stand it anymore, so we agreed to a formula: I cut Jimmy a check for 25 percent of my bonus and didn't have to deal with the haranguing anymore.

In the office with Doug that day, I felt the same sort of overwhelming pressure.

"Doug, how am I ever going to do this?" I furrowed my brow and pursed my lips. "How am I going to learn everything I need to know?"

"You'll figure it out, Jane. You're smart," Doug reassured me. "Don't be intimidated by those boys uptown. They don't know everything they think they know! And remember, *you're* the expert on the Street. You know more about this business than they *ever* will." He warmed up to his topic and added, "Trouble with those folks is they all make too much damn money! 'Fuck you' money. Any one of 'em could walk away if they wanted to. Makes 'em hard to manage, hard to control." He shook his head and grimaced, then a slow smile crept across his face, and he bit his lower lip. "They're *your* problem now," he said, arching his eyebrows and winking.

I realized that what I was missing — what those "boys uptown" had that I didn't — was hubris, something I'd avoided my whole life. I knew plenty of blowhard guys with half my abilities who would be pounding their chests and moving ahead confidently, never questioning whether they were "up to the job" of replacing Doug and allocating bonuses.

EIGHT SEPTEMBERS

That got my feminist dander up. It was high time for me to get ahold of myself and set aside my nerves.

***

When I joined the group at Manufacturers Hanover Trust in 1987, Wall Street still functioned mostly as a boys' club. Getting to know all the back-office guys, particularly in the chummy government bond market, felt like going back in time a few decades. I'd gone to a women's college and worked as a social worker in foster care before switching to banking, so all the machismo shocked my system.

In those days, we worked on the fourth floor of 40 Wall Street in a large open room filled with heavy wooden desks lined up in uneven rows. The old-fashioned black push-button telephones had recently been joined by bulky personal computers on our desks, which were still covered with ancient leather blotters. Those of us who smoked did so freely at our desks, and anyone who complained got labeled a wimp.

On Fridays in the summer back then, the guys would head off to lunch at McAnn's for burgers and beers — no women allowed. And when they got back, we would play computer golf on the PC, pushing the space bar to make the little man swing his club.

With a degree in Women's Studies and Human Services, I knew nothing about the business of Wall Street. Aside from the bank credit training program, I had never studied economics or corporate finance, had not followed the stock market, and did not understand how securities were issued, traded, cleared, and settled. Soon I would learn all of that, and more, on the job — sometimes from people who were less than thrilled about working with women. Luckily, I found more supporters than detractors over time. Still, the gender dynamics on Wall Street in the late 1980s were fairly traditional and occasionally hostile. I was determined to succeed based on competency and wanted to be taken seriously.

Eventually, I developed a theory about the four stages of being a woman on Wall Street:

1. *Invisible.* No one sees you, acknowledges you, or speaks to you. Part of this related to being female, and part of it related to being junior, since Wall Street is a very hierarchical place. But the spotlight shone on young "golden boys" much more frequently than young women, and I hated feeling dismissed and irrelevant.
2. *Visible.* You are seen — or not seen — for your physical traits only. Good or bad, they are fodder for talk. This lifelong irritant infuriated me, and I strove to be seen beyond my outward appearance, reacting angrily whenever I overheard sexist jokes, criticism or praise of other women's physical appearance.
3. *Respected.* Eventually, if you're lucky, you earn enough seniority and power to be seen and heard. I was grateful to be supported by my male bosses and colleagues to gain this level of experience and expertise, and I firmly believed that any respect I received had been earned and was warranted.
4. *In.* You bring enough to the table that you become a part of the club, regularly included and consulted. Inclusion meant being part of the conversation, whether on the golf course or in the boardroom. This was the golden ticket, and I loved it when I attained it.

The funny thing is, at any given moment someone could be trying to shove you from four back to one, or from three to two, just to see what you're made of.

Well, I wasn't the daughter of a CEO for nothing. I knew how to connect with people, honor my word, and get things done. My good reputation was merited. Now that I would be running the department, I had to step up my game, both internally and externally.

CHAPTER 12
Transitions

I sat on the brown hand-me-down couch in the small living room of our little three-room attic apartment in Woodhaven, Queens, nervously choosing my words. Dusty, our rambunctious golden setter, slept at my feet while Peeper, our tiger-striped cat, purred in my lap.

"Dad, I need your advice."

Asking for Dad's help was a rare turn of events. At a crossroads in 1982, I'd had to schedule time with my busy executive father, six hours behind me in Honolulu, for a call. To be fair, he was happy to do it.

"Janeathon! What can your dear old dad do to help you?" his voice boomed out of the telephone receiver, solicitous and cheerful. He excelled at turning on the charm.

"Well, Dad, as you know, I'm working six days a week and only making $10,500 a year as a foster care social worker. With Jimmy being a musician and all, I think I need something that pays more." I neglected to mention that my husband's earnings from his cab-driving gig usually got spent at the racetrack or the local Off-Track Betting — where he probably was at that very moment. I didn't mind being a poor college student when we were first married in 1980, but two years later, with our own apartment and monthly bills, I couldn't stand the anxiety of financial instability.

My parents had presumed that I would marry and that my husband would provide for me financially, because that is what they knew and lived. Big believers in education for its own sake, they didn't think about the economic consequences of my field of study, since I would naturally be supported by my husband. My sensitive heart wanted to make the world a better place, which is why I pursued social work, but I resisted being dependent on a man, so I didn't share my parents' expectation of being financially supported, especially since I'd gotten my degree from Simmons College, which was founded way back in 1899 to provide women with the opportunity to earn an independent livelihood. Still, having been a child of privilege, I hadn't exactly considered my earnings power, either.

"I looked into getting a master's degree in social work, but that salary seems to top out at $19,500. And while that's a big increase from where I am now, it doesn't seem like that much upside for the expense of grad school," I explained.

Dad had paid for college, but I'd be on my own for any graduate degrees. Not that he couldn't afford it; that was just his policy. He lived by the Protestant work ethic and believed we should be willing to invest in our own educations, as he had. In fact, he'd cut Becky off when she dropped out of Princeton and made her pay her own way for finishing at another college. His generosity had its limits. And its price.

I really liked the hands-on nature of working with foster kids, but I hated all the bureaucracy and paperwork, only making enough money to cover the bills, unable to afford things that might replenish me, like going to the movies or out for dinner.

"Hmm. Janey, have you considered banking?" he asked. I could imagine him in his stately downtown Honolulu office behind his big wooden desk, lush greenery visible in the courtyard through French doors and a faraway look in his eyes as he puzzled out the answer to the problem I had posed.

"Uh, no. What is that exactly?" I had taken a total of one math class — statistics — in college and written twenty-seven papers in my senior year. I'd had my own checking account and an allowance since I'd been a teenager, another policy of Dad's, so of course I was familiar with banks in the practical sense, but I didn't know what choosing a career in banking meant. I presumed it had something to do with numbers.

"The banking industry is one of the best businesses for women to get into," he said, launching into a sales pitch. "They pay for your training, and the skills you gain would be transferable — whether you move to Los Angeles for Jimmy's music career or anywhere else, for that matter. You'd learn about all different kinds of industries and meet a wide variety of people. If you get your resume together, I could write you a letter of introduction to my good friend McGoo." He was referring to one of his college football buddies from Princeton who, I would learn, was the CEO of Manufacturers Hanover Trust, one of the big money center banks in New York City.

"Thanks, Dad, that would be great. Sounds like it could be interesting, and I guess I'd have nothing to lose by considering it." Honestly, I didn't know what to expect, but I knew I needed to take control of my financial situation, and I didn't see many other options.

***

Twenty years after that conversation, here I was, taking over responsibility for a multimillion-dollar business — not just in banking, but specifically in financing Wall Street, the heart of capitalism. I often joked that my social work training helped me survive the egos and navigate the sometimes-hostile terrain I now worked in.

After two decades, I could confidently say I knew the business, but I needed to learn how to *run* the business. Advice from Doug would only take me so far, so I reached out to human resources. They offered to facilitate a "Jumpstart" session. Modeled after a military program by that name to transition new leaders, the program would allow the staff to put all their fears and concerns about me as the new boss on the table. Then HR would bring that list of concerns to me and help me develop responses to each issue. At the final stage, I would go into a meeting with all the staff members and verbally address their concerns.

Yikes! That was a lot of pressure for a woman who tended to avoid direct confrontation. But I knew I had to do it. It gave people an opportunity to speak up and allowed me to understand what they expected of me. If I didn't do it, all of those fears and concerns would be lurking around anyway, and I would be destined to fail.

The questions were predictable, I suppose.

"Can she be impartial?" Some people were concerned that I would play favorites, biased toward my relationship management peers and former Chemical/MHT colleagues. They had a point: I did tend to trust those I'd worked with longer and would need to focus on being more objective and balanced.

"Will she micromanage?" I'd been doing my job a long time and had strong opinions; maybe I wouldn't give people the space to do their jobs in their own ways. I asked a lot of questions to understand things, and I knew that sometimes it made people feel attacked.

"Will she make the tough decisions?" Account assignments, job functions, headcount reductions — there were many details around structure that would impact everyone's day-to-day experience. I couldn't make everybody happy and would have to live with their displeasure.

"Can she play with the big boys uptown?" Now we were getting closer to the heart of the matter. Could I play politics while keeping the department safe, funded, and valued? Honestly, I didn't know the answer to that myself.

"Can she get us paid?" There it was, the real concern. Would I be able to get the bonus pool and salary increases and promote my people? After all, I was their shepherd now, and it was up to me to take care of them.

***

At the same time that I was expanding into my new role, I played a part in the contraction of my father's. When Dad first nominated me to become a member of the board of directors for his company, C. Brewer, in the early 1990s, I felt honored and excited. I'd never been on a board, and I looked forward to learning more about the business that he so loved. C. Brewer grew sugar cane and macadamia nuts and was one of the oldest companies in Hawaii. Dad had taken me to the floor of the New York Stock Exchange when he'd raised some money to buy the company in 1986 by selling shares in the Mauna Loa macadamia nut farms.

Dad made it clear I needed to get the gap in my front teeth fixed before the announcement with my picture was published in the

TRANSITIONS

Honolulu papers. "I'll pay for it," he said in a tone that sounded more like an order than an offer. He considered my appearance — like all else — a reflection on him. I pushed aside my resentment at another controlling "gift" from Dad and focused instead on the opportunity.

He told me he wanted to lower the average age of his board — all of whom were in their sixties and seventies. I was in my thirties at the time, a new mother, dealing with the recent merger of Manufacturers Hanover Trust and Chemical Bank. His board feared he planned to stack the deck with a family member, but after my first meeting, they learned I did not have blind loyalty to my father as I asked probing questions and didn't accept pat answers. After ten years as a banker and five on Wall Street, I was independent-minded and knew how to execute my fiduciary responsibilities.

How would I manage going to Hawaii four times a year? Apparently, the bank considered these types of arrangements worth supporting as they helped to develop executive skills, and I easily received permission to serve on the board *and* to take the time I needed to attend meetings. Taking the nonstop from Newark to Honolulu as a board member, I learned how to incorporate the four-day trip — one day there, two days of meetings, one day back — into my packed schedule. As a busy working mother, the ten hours on the plane to read and unwind in first-class more than compensated for any jet lag. Sometimes Jimmy and the boys came with me, and we extended the trip into a vacation. Other times, Dad hosted the meetings on the East Coast to accommodate the mainland board members.

After my parents' divorce in 1998, the board meeting dynamics and interactions with my father became more complicated. Dad moved the company headquarters to Hilo, even though none of his executive team chose to relocate and were commuting by plane every day from Honolulu. The chummy spousal events Mom had hosted and the fun extracurricular activities ended. Following Dad's marriage to Leilani and the twenty-fifth anniversary CEO celebration we attended in 2000, the board's support began slipping away. They had been invested in this company for fifteen years. With most of them in their seventies, they did not want to die and leave their children with illiquid private company stock. They wanted cash.

Dad believed the marquee operating company, Mauna Loa Macadamia Nuts, was worth $1 billion, based on brand name recognition and the real estate beneath the tree orchards. That proved to be overly optimistic. He passed up several opportunities to sell and raise cash, holding out for a better offer and exposing his unwillingness to sell the business. Finally, under pressure from the board, Mauna Loa was sold to a private equity group in September of 2000 at a much more realistic price — less than 50 percent of what Dad wanted. Getting a taste of liquidity, the board pressed for a more complete solution. Dad dug in his heels, his obstinance and irrationality becoming more apparent as he began to alienate even his most ardent supporters.

The board voted unanimously to liquidate C. Brewer in its entirety in May of 2001. I was 100 percent in agreement with the sale as I understood the need to provide liquidity to investors.

Dad, however, had argued continuously and strenuously against the liquidation for months. In the end, he voted with the rest of the board, unwilling to tolerate a public defeat, but — accustomed to getting his way — this rebellion did not sit well with him. The grumpy father I knew, who pouted after losing a tennis or golf match, began to appear in front of his board and executive team, who were more accustomed to his decisive, powerful salesman persona.

Despite how he voted, Dad still did not want to sell the company and, true to form, he refused to get out of the batter's box. He loved the game and always thought he could build value, get a better deal. So the board voted to remove Dad from the process and put an oversight committee in place to manage the liquidation of the various operating subsidiaries.

Dad had always been fearful that if he stopped working, he would get sick or contract dementia or Alzheimer's like his mother and brother had. Reluctant to see the company he had built dismantled and unwilling to stop working, even at age seventy-three, he created a new company, Doc Buyers Enterprises, to purchase some of the assets being sold by C. Brewer.

TRANSITIONS

At that point, subtle changes in Dad were already apparent. He struggled with language issues, repeating himself and forgetting certain words or names, which the doctors attributed to a series of mini strokes. But he used his strong will and charisma to cover his errors.

He was forthright with me about the challenges and the "brain exercises" he used to improve his word retrieval. "Leilani is helping me every night," he said with pride during one visit as we sat by the ocean, dangling our feet off the pier in Waikiki. *Hmm, maybe Leilani wasn't so bad after all.* "The doctor says I'm making good progress." Ever the optimist, Dad believed in the power of positive thinking.

***

Nearly a year later, in the fall of 2002, during the time I was chosen and trained to take over for Doug, I headed to Hawaii for what would be a momentous board meeting.

Dad sat, tense and uncomfortable, at the head of the table, ready to chair the meeting. He had been chairman and CEO for over twenty-five years and had taken the company private through a complicated leveraged buyout fifteen years earlier, partially financed by the people in this room. He had his script tucked inside his black leather three-ring binder. He looked strained under the fluorescent lights and low-ceilinged conference room in the nondescript office building off Nimitz Highway near the Honolulu airport.

His *hui* — this board, his friends — were all in their seventies and ready to wind up this chapter, with or without my father's cooperation.

Around the rectangular Formica table — actually a few tables unevenly pushed together to make one large one — sat the other members of the management team and the board: Alan, our attorney; Kent, the CFO; Dick, Jay, and Alex — all Princeton men; Fudge and Bobby, the *kama'ainas* or local men; Jeannie, a local real estate executive and the sole female on the board until I joined; and me: daughter, banker, newest and youngest board member. Although by 2002, I'd been on the board nearly ten years.

EIGHT SEPTEMBERS

Dad opened his notebook and called the meeting to order, carefully reading the words in front of him. The agenda had been specifically orchestrated to allow my father to maintain his dignity while simultaneously taking away his power. Dad was being removed as CEO, although he'd retain a ceremonial chairmanship and his seat on the board. Such a sad day, more so because even as he stumbled over the simple task of reading his script, Dad refused to admit there was anything wrong. Everything he'd worked so hard for began to slip away.

A former investor and board member, Bill, another Princeton man, had been diagnosed with Alzheimer's not that long before. Bill acknowledged his diagnosis and resigned his positions of authority upon his doctor's advice, graciously retreating from public responsibilities just as Dad had been instructed to do.

But he didn't. In his eyes, Bill was soft, a loser, unwilling to fight. Persevere and never give up. That was Dad's way.

Maybe it had become my way too.

CHAPTER 13
Kabuki Dance

Doug had recommended me to represent J.P. Morgan Chase on a private sector working group sponsored by the Federal Reserve Bank of New York to interrogate the issue of clearing bank concentration. This happened before Jumpstart, before Doug left, even before I had been officially chosen to replace him.

J.P. Morgan Chase and Bank of New York cleared nearly 100 percent of the US government bond market. The industry reliance on only two banks for this critical function became obvious on 9/11 when the Bank of New York could not operate. As a result, there were now significant regulatory concerns about the clearing infrastructure for US government bonds. I suggested that Al, who ran the government bond clearance business, should be our representative to serve on the committee, but they wanted someone with a broader view of the industry, someone with a risk background. And Doug, I'm sure, was testing me. Eventually, both Al and I would be knee-deep in this Fed working group, but initially, it was just me.

In December of 2002, I walked alone out the side entrance of Chase Plaza and eyed the massive stone building directly across the street. The Fed looked every bit like the fortress that it was, housing 25 percent of the world's gold reserves eighty feet below ground and conducting our national monetary policy above.

It was my first time inside 33 Liberty, as Al always called it, even though my window on the twenty-first floor overlooked it. That's where I'd seen the workmen on the roof on the morning of September 11. Armed guards now blocked the entrance, checking my ID and questioning my purpose before opening the heavily armored doors and instructing me to put my things on the security conveyor belt that ran up the short staircase. Finally, I was allowed to approach the front desk, where I submitted my ID again, had my name cross-checked against the invitation list, got my picture taken, received a pass, and finally gained clearance to approach the elevator bank.

Riding up to the tenth floor, I silently hoped the elevator would not stop to let anyone else on, then breathed a sigh of relief when I got off and walked down the wide, carpeted corridor to the end of the hall. In the windowed foyer outside of the boardroom, tables draped in white linens were set up with china cups and saucers, silver urns of lukewarm coffee and tea, and breakfast pastries.

There were many people I knew and greeted as we all got settled. Ernie, head of operations at UBS Securities, who never remembered my name and referred to me as "the woman with three names" instead of Jane Buyers Russo. Paul, general counsel at the Bond Market Association and spokesman for the industry trade group. Steve, general counsel at Cantor Fitzgerald, still looking shaken by the loss of nearly seven hundred colleagues. Tom, the head repo guy at Morgan Stanley and weekend rock and roll guitarist. Frank, senior clearance guy at Merrill and one of our biggest clients. Mary from Salomon, the most senior woman in operations I knew. And, of course, Dominick from Government Securities Clearing Corporation (GSCC) and our contentious negotiations over inter-dealer broker Eurobrokers. These folks had been among the key, albeit ad hoc, decision-makers about how to manage the chaos that had erupted in the clearance world on 9/11. Most of them I'd met through Al, who was not there to lend me confidence and credibility. There were also several people I would come to know, like Ian, the future CFO of Lehman Brothers. The meeting was chaired by a former Chase executive turned consultant — and friend of Doug's.

The room was cavernous, with high ceilings and wood paneling, and portraits of old White men staring down on us. The long, wide table accommodated the full house — probably forty of us in all counting regulators and lawyers from the Board of Governors in Washington and the New York Fed, the Securities Exchange Commission, and the US Treasury. The heavy wooden chairs with worn red leather seats were uncomfortable and difficult to move gracefully.

KABUKI DANCE

Since the lion's share of the world's clearance and settlement of US government bonds went through either J.P. Morgan Chase or the Bank of New York — thousands of trades a day to the tune of more than one trillion dollars — our participation on the committee was critical. I sat next to the chair of the working group, a position I thought was befitting of the importance and stature of our bank. Brian, representing our competitor Bank of New York, sat at the other end of the table.

But what did clearing banks actually do? For a fee, they let the broker dealers use their bank accounts at the Fed to buy and sell bonds. Bonds came in; cash went out. Or bonds went out; cash came in.

Simple. Usually.

With all of that volume running through the system, the stakes were high. And as we'd found on 9/11, when one part of the system failed, the Fed was on the hook for financing the banks as a lender of last resort. Hence, this committee.

We went around the table and gave our names and roles within our organizations. There were explanations about the regulators' concerns, exhortations to find a private industry solution, implied threats about moral hazard, and speeches about maintaining the integrity of financial markets. The private industry folks demonstrated their market expertise and wariness about what the regulators might do. The regulators took notes and pushed for a private industry solution, giving veiled threats about what they might do if we didn't come up with a solution they liked.

I had a pretty straightforward, operational view of the clearance world, one where cash and government bonds were considered fungible — essentially, of equal value. *Delivery versus payment* meant bonds were delivered at the same moment cash was received to pay for them, and ownership of both transferred in real time. Most important of all, the clearing bank intermediary fulfilled the critical role of liquidity provider that kept the whole system working.

Of course, I knew the clearance world to be far more complex, but I wasn't the sort who liked to make things more complicated than they actually were. Or, at the other end of the spectrum, to pretend logistical constraints didn't exist. So when it came time for me to speak, I did so in a direct manner.

"The clearing banks aren't the only critical players in the system," I began. "The dealers, the inter-dealer brokers, the technology providers, GSCC, and the Fed... Why are we singling out the clearing banks?" It didn't make sense to me that the sole focus of the working group was on the clearing banks. If 9/11 had demonstrated anything, it was that clearance was an ecosystem connected via technology provided by unregulated vendors, and that disruption with any one of us could upset the entire system. For goodness' sake, half the industry went through Verizon, whose single building was taken out in the attacks, crippling communications on Wall Street. Our technology guru had even created a nifty diagram to demonstrate the interlinked risks in the clearance and settlement world. From the silence that met my remarks, however, I decided it was not the time to whip that out.

The Fed focused on what it could control: the banks under its regulatory purview and its completely appropriate dismay about Bank of New York's inability to function after the attacks. They weren't about to expand the universe to include the dealers, software vendors, and GSCC. And they didn't seem to be in a rush to look too closely at their *own* operations, which were dependent in many ways on the clearing banks.

Every day, Bank of New York and J.P. Morgan Chase advanced cash to the dealers to purchase and deliver bonds, taking a lien on the bonds until they had been fully paid for. To repay the banks, the dealers either sold the bonds outright or borrowed money against them. Normally, any bonds the dealers held in inventory overnight at the clearance banks would be financed by their tri-party lenders — investors seeking a safe overnight return on their money. This provided the cash to pay back the clearance banks for the intraday loan advance. In the morning, the banks released the bonds back to the dealers and returned the cash to the tri-party lenders — what we called the "unwind." The unwind effectively closed out the prior night's third-party financing and transferred the intraday financing to the clearance banks.

KABUKI DANCE

This intraday liquidity kept the whole market moving and placed the risk squarely with the clearance banks, who managed that risk tightly by monitoring the dealers' "clearance box" minute by minute. Cash, securities value, credit lines — all these were in the clearance box and taken into consideration to calculate how much the dealers owed the banks and how much collateral we had to protect the banks from being exposed beyond what had been authorized.

"The clearance banks provide billions of dollars of secured intraday financing to the dealers," I said. "The market can't function without it. Who else is willing to do that? What's the point of this task force if we don't deal with the issue of intraday financing?"

The chair cleared his throat and went on to the next agenda item, leaving my question unanswered.

Apparently, my manner was too direct, because I wasn't back in the office five minutes before Doug called me in to his office.

"You came on too strong," he said. "You're sitting in the seat now." I'd never heard that expression before, but I understood it right away. I wasn't just speaking for myself; I spoke for the bank. "You carry a big stick. Use it carefully." Of course, his buddy had already called him to complain about this "new woman" who wasn't adept at playing the game. It was Doug's job to get me in line.

Got it.

My role was to take in as much information as I could and disclose as little as possible. But in my earnestness, I'd thought my comments were constructive, helpful for figuring out the problem at hand.

Consider it a kabuki dance, one of our vice chairmen later counseled me, a choreographed process that let the regulators feel progress was being made while the banks continued doing whatever they believed was in their own best interests.

In retrospect, maybe I should have continued speaking my mind.

PART FOUR
New Reality

"Every experience and condition is a useful experience, and these are either made as stumbling-blocks or stepping-stones."
—*Edgar Cayce Reading 1424-2 (38)*

CHAPTER 14

Outside the Office

In May 2003, as we left the restaurant following my first client dinner party at an industry conference as head of the broker-dealer department at J.P. Morgan Chase, I heard Dominick from GSCC right behind me declaring, "I need a drink!"

A warm spring night in Florida provided the perfect foundation for a party. I wore a simple black dress with short sleeves, chosen specifically for the event, with gold jewelry and dressy, low-heeled strappy sandals. We had cocktails on the terrace, at the end of which I made welcoming remarks before we headed inside for dinner.

"Thank you so much for coming," I warbled, my voice sounding high and thin through the microphone. "Your business is important to us, and we appreciate your being here tonight."

How I wished I could be a relaxed, extemporaneous speaker — more like my normal personality. I knew many of the guests, and at least twenty of the seventy-five attendees, including Al, were fellow bankers who were helping to host the event, but self-consciousness about public speaking still plagued me, which is why I was surprised and pleased when Dominick came up to me to shake my hand afterward, smiling warmly. I'd expected him to be difficult, given our laborious, contentious ongoing negotiations about the IDBs. His friendliness helped put me at ease.

There were a few no-shows at my head table, which annoyed me in a way that not many things did. Did it show disrespect for the bank, or for me personally? I didn't have much experience "carrying" a table like my predecessor Doug or my colleague Al, both of whom were great storytellers. I knew that everyone at my table had been hosted by Doug or Al many times before, and I worried about measuring up. There were also a few wives at my table, which created a lopsided dynamic, as some people, including me, had no spouse at the event. Jimmy, who'd attended these events with me years ago when we were childless, stayed home with the boys. It was always tricky for me with the wives anyway. I had so much more in common with their husbands that it was easier for me to talk with the men about business and golf than to engage with the women. At the same time, the wives were quite aware that despite what I talked about, I was a woman and not really one of the guys.

After a few glasses of wine, however, everyone relaxed, and the evening progressed smoothly. Between courses, I circulated around the room, stopping at each table, greeting guests and checking in to be sure that everyone had what they needed to enjoy the night.

When the bus we'd chartered took us back to the resort, a group of us went to one of the hotel bars where conference attendees who had been at other dinner parties were starting to congregate. The dull roar of conversation, the heavy fog of smoke, clinking glasses, and bursts of laughter indicated a happy afterparty. People rotated in and out of our group as I sat in a big, comfortable chair holding court. But I eventually noticed that Dominick stayed consistently by my side. Even when I got up to go to the restroom, he showed up again, following me and heading into the men's room. It struck me as odd, but also somewhat amusing. After a while, only the two of us remained, and we moved to another bar where we sat talking and getting to know one another — sharing family backgrounds, career highlights, and industry insights.

"You're running with the big dogs now," he grunted, bragging about himself as a power broker at this Wall Street Operations Conference. Happy to be making a connection and smoothing over our rough start, I ignored his hubris and reminded myself that just staying in the male-dominated Wall Street world was my way of honoring my degree in Women's Studies and furthering the cause.

When he noticed goosebumps on my arm, Dominick offered me his sport coat, which he put around my shoulders, a chivalrous gesture I didn't give much thought to. "Know what I thought about you after that first meeting regarding the IDBs?" he asked, then paused for effect. "Cute but mean."

I rolled my eyes. "Ha! Do you only know four-letter words?" I teased, reflexively using humor to deflect his flirtation.

Eventually, I said, "I need to get some sleep." I was speaking on a panel the next afternoon regarding the Federal Reserve Bank's Working Group on US Government Securities Clearance Post 9/11.

Dominick walked with me, even accompanying me up the one flight of stairs to my floor, as my claustrophobia had me avoiding elevators whenever possible. In the hallway, I turned and shook his hand. He looked at me, holding my hand an extra beat. I looked him right in the eye, pulled my hand away, and said, "Good night. I'll see you tomorrow," then turned to go down the hall into my room.

He stood there for a moment, and I heard him call out, "Strange!" before he turned and walked away.

I didn't know what he meant, but as I thought about it, I wondered, *Did he actually think I was bringing him back to my room?* The thought was laughable. I'd been married my entire adult life. I had no intention of sleeping with him, or anyone else for that matter. I'd been faithful to my husband for the twenty-plus years we'd been together, and other men rarely crossed my mind. I'd certainly never had a one-night stand or slept with someone that I'd just met, and I had practiced stiff-arming anyone who approached me for so many years that no one bothered trying anymore. It wasn't just laughable, though. I also found it infuriating. I was still trying to find my place in the business with the senior players — the big dogs, to use his terminology — and earn their respect; did I have to constantly worry about being hit on too? I so wanted to believe that wasn't what was happening.

The message light was blinking on the room phone and there were three voicemails from Jimmy, increasingly distraught that I hadn't picked up any of his calls. I looked at my watch and saw that it was after two a.m. Oops. I'd had a really good, but long, evening.

I called him back and he lit right into me.

"Where were you? What were you doing?"

His implication of wrongdoing made me defensive. "I'm the boss now. People want to talk to me, get to know me, drink with me. It's part of the job!" I shot back. "It's no big deal, but I have to do it. Remember, we talked about that when I took this job. You don't have anything to worry about."

Jimmy had never worked in an office, never been in the corporate business world, didn't have a frame of reference.

"Come on, Jimmy, you know you're the only man I love. There's no reason to be so upset. I'm just doing my job here."

And so what if I enjoyed it? What if I liked the freedom of being away, of being important enough to be in demand? How could I talk with my suspicious husband about the complexities of navigating this male-dominated territory? Not for the first time, I wondered if my male colleagues got this kind of pushback from home, and whether this job wouldn't be easier if I were a man.

***

I was alone.

In the middle of downtown Manhattan on a warm June day at lunchtime amidst throngs of people, I was the loneliest I had been in a long while. I tried to shake the feeling as I wandered the streets toward the pier to look across the water. I'd quit smoking a few years back, but the urge to light up assailed me. I felt tears sting my eyes and blinked them back.

Jane, don't be ridiculous! I chastised myself.

I recited my blessings, but the words felt hollow, empty.

I'd never had a large group of friends, but the friends I did have had gradually fallen away — calendars out of sync, differences in lifestyles, secrets that we kept — and Jimmy had become my only confidante. Protecting his gambling addiction kept me at arm's length from friends at church who might have become closer if I'd allowed myself to breach his confidentiality. And despite my collegial relationship with my coworkers, I would never dare to share our dark secret with them.

The betrayal I felt since I'd found out that Jimmy had returned to gambling immediately after 9/11 while I had worked so frenetically had created a distance between us that kept me from confiding in him as I was accustomed to doing. Even when I did confide in him about my emotions, he offered comfort in the moment but rarely circled back to see how I was coping. Sometimes he even exposed my confidences to others without concern for my privacy, which embarrassed me.

I was wary about sharing my loneliness with him now. He'd returned to Gamblers Anonymous after his last relapse, but I'd moved on with my life and no longer attended meetings, deciding it would be up to him to manage his problem. I was too busy with my new work responsibilities, the children, Dad's declining health, and business issues. My expectation was that Jimmy would take his recovery and abstinence seriously, just like I took my therapy seriously. But it was one less thing we were doing together.

Since becoming "the boss," my relationship with my peers had changed too. Not fully comfortable in my new role yet, I believed I needed to avoid looking like I played favorites by socializing with my friends, so I didn't even hang out in the conference room for lunch anymore.

Plus, the natural griping and dissatisfaction that occurs in the workplace would now be targeted toward me, since everyone's workloads and compensation were my responsibility, and that made me apprehensive.

The truth was, I had no one to trust.

On this day, walking aimlessly downtown, I had no lunch with clients, and I didn't know what to do with myself. I figured I'd just grab something and go back to work. I'd spent enough time feeling sorry for myself.

I walked across the cobblestone triangle to a deli catty-corner from Fraunces Tavern, famous for housing George Washington and being the target of a terrorist bombing in 1975. I often bought a sandwich or salad to take back to the office and eat alone at my desk. Paper deli sack in hand, I headed up William Street and spied Dominick and one of his colleagues coming up the stairs from Harry's restaurant in matching blue blazers, their heads close in conversation. My heart contracted, longing for that kind of ease and camaraderie. Dominick stopped to light a cigarette and spotted me across the street. I hadn't seen him since the operations conference in Florida a month earlier. A smile crept across his face, and he nodded an acknowledgement. I gave him a brief wave, put my head down, and scurried back to my office.

Later that afternoon, Jeff, Dominick's general counsel, called to ask if I planned to attend the Bond Market conference in October. I'd never been before, but then again, I'd never been the head of the department before. He invited me to golf with him and Dominick, telling me how much fun the conferences were, who would be there, and all the important topics that would be discussed. It didn't take long for me to decide that I would attend.

***

Later that same summer, on a hot July Saturday, I stood on the roof deck of our new weekend house on Long Island, admiring the view across the marsh to the bay. In the distance, I could see the bridge that led to the eastern end of Fire Island and a sliver of the ocean beyond. We were the last house on the last road abutting a preserve that stretched a mile or so east to the highway and south to the water.

Jimmy and I had toyed with the idea of buying land and building a house for a few years, and after 9/11 — before I found out he'd gone back to gambling — I brought it up again. "Just get me the land." This decision was a response to the attacks, I suppose; a desire to create a refuge outside of the city, a place where the boys could run free and a haven from the turmoil of ceaseless arguments that inhabited Jimmy's childhood home nearby, where we no longer chose to stay when we visited.

We'd argued long and hard about the house over the Christmas we spent in Hawaii. Jimmy wanted to be the general contractor. I pointed out that would take him further away from his desire to compose music, believing that where we put our attention is how we spend our lives. Already frustrated that he had wasted so much time and energy on gambling, I couldn't believe that he would spend another year distracted from his goals by building the house. It's not that I thought he couldn't do it. Of course he could. But the question was: *Why?*

OUTSIDE THE OFFICE

With most of his twenties and thirties preoccupied with gambling, Jimmy's career already lagged behind schedule. During that time, I supported the family in a job I often found unfulfilling. I'd had no plans to rise up the ranks at the bank and had only worked there to kill time until his dream came true and he made it big. How was that ever going to happen if his time and energy was devoted to building a house? If he'd dropped the music dream and said construction would be his new career, that would have been different. But he still wanted to pursue music, still wanted me to spend my bonus on equipment for his recording studio, still wanted us to invest in producing CDs of his self-recorded pop songs. I loved his music, and I loved him, and I remained invested in his dream and wanted him to succeed. But why couldn't he see that building a house would only be another detour off the path to his success?

I spent so much energy trying to get him to see what I saw that I didn't pause to consider how *I* felt about what I saw. And the truth was, I felt he had squandered his time and was wasting his life. It made me both angry and sad. All I could do was what I always did: hope things would work out.

Jimmy won the argument. I had faith in his skills as a general contractor, and I didn't have the time to find an alternative, so if that was what he wanted to do with his time, so be it. Once we started building, we agreed that we wanted the process to bring us closer together, not drive us apart, so we made a concerted effort to talk things through, to be transparent, and to make our design choices together. It turned out to be fun, and we loved the end result. We built an upside-down house to take advantage of the view, with a big kitchen and great room with a vaulted ceiling and the primary bedroom upstairs, and the rest of the bedrooms downstairs. Above the garage we built a second-story sun porch, and spiral steps that led to a wooden deck. That's where I now stood, taking in the expansive view.

At the conference I'd attended in May, Dominick had made an irritating comment about *where* we'd built our house. A Southampton snob, he looked down on our less prestigious location in Brookhaven. *Who*

EIGHT SEPTEMBERS

was he to judge? I fumed, aware that I allowed his assessment to diminish my pleasure in this successful collaboration between Jimmy and me.

***

Allen B. Clark, Senior Vice President
Jane Buyers Russo, Managing Director
Cordially invite you to the annual
J.P. Morgan Securities Industry Golf Outing
Tuesday September 9th, 2003
Twin Brooks Country Club

That summer came to a close with an event I was co-hosting for the first time. Al had been doing it for years, first with Joe at MHT/Chemical and then with Doug at J.P. Morgan Chase. Now I was stepping into the role, the first woman to do so, and I wasn't much of a golfer. Then again, Joe hadn't been either, so I didn't feel too bad about that part, but given my position, I'd been assigned foursome #1A. Meaning the first tee. Playing with the big dogs.

Over the years, I'd played in our annual golf outing intermittently, but a few years before I took over the department, I'd finally given up on golf completely, as I never seemed to get any better. For several years I'd only attended the dinner and awards part of this event, joking that I was doing what I did best: eating and drinking.

My first outing was back in the late '80s. I had never played golf seriously, and I didn't think I could play with all those "good" guys. But my male colleagues convinced me that at any given outing there were only a few good foursomes, and everybody else hacked away. So I braved it, despite being the only woman out of more than one hundred golfers, and I ended up spending six hours in 95-degree weather with three guys who were even worse players than I was. My mother, an excellent athlete, gasped in horror when I told her I won the booby prize. Thus began my golfing career.

Now I ran the department and most of the clients played golf, so I'd spent the summer working on my game just to be ready for this moment.

The only thing I cared about as I stepped up to the tee was getting my drive off successfully in front of seven men. All my preparation paid off, and I hit it straight down the fairway. Phew!

Those relationships I would forge on the golf course held me in good stead during the turmoil that soon broke loose.

***

At the bond market conference in October, Al and I golfed with Dominick and Jeff from GSCC. Dominick made sure that we were in the same cart, and he went out of his way to entertain me, either with quips about golf, the industry, or comments about me.

"You have beautiful eyes," he said, smiling, his own eyes twinkling back at me. I accepted the compliment. I'd heard it many times before and agreed they were one of my best features — hazel green, with a dark rim around the edges and a lighter, almost translucent green inside flecked with brown and gold — but I avoided his gaze and hopped out of the cart to take my next shot.

At the end of the round as we were returning to the clubhouse, he changed tactics. "You need to be more arrogant," he proclaimed, which irritated me.

I rejected the advice. Why would I want to cultivate a trait I found offensive? He himself had no trouble being arrogant. In fact, he took pride in it.

"People will push you around. You need to show them you're tough. Be more arrogant."

"Okay, sensei, I'll take that under advisement," I retorted, with absolutely no such intention.

EIGHT SEPTEMBERS

***

Back in New York, Al and I had yet another meeting with Dominick and Jeff at GSCC about the dispute over Eurobrokers. After months of discussions — including over drinks at the conference — they finally indicated they were amenable to a compromise on the inter-dealer broker financing problem. GSCC wouldn't completely make us whole, but they would pay a portion of the interest expense. Victory! Lots of details to be negotiated, nondisclosure agreements to sign, and money to be collected. But I had achieved my goal. I had gotten GSCC to pay.

Am I a good negotiator, or is this personal? I wondered.

Was there even a difference?

CHAPTER 15
Inside the Office

Our department moved uptown in the spring of 2004 to join the rest of the Financial Institutions Group (FIG) at 277 Park Avenue, right across the street from the world headquarters building at 270 Park where we'd worked those first few weeks after 9/11.

The J.P. Morgan merger had finally caught up with us. As the bank continued to reorient itself, I had my third boss in two years. Senior management had determined that they wanted our department to be a more integral part of FIG, whose other clients were banks, insurance companies, credit card companies, finance companies, and government agencies.

I'd insisted that our entire department be co-located, including our non-revenue-producing staff, even though we'd be charged more for the Midtown Manhattan real estate. We needed our loan department, credit analysts, and customer service teams with us to properly manage the business. Besides earning a profit, we had to manage how much credit we extended to the Street. Keeping our department together allowed us to share critical information in real time should any problems arise, as they had in October of 1987 and again on 9/11. We had an excellent record for minimizing losses in the midst of periodic crises — something I had to remind senior management about whenever the discussion arose about the purpose and value of our department, which it did, more and more frequently.

On my first day in Midtown, I ran into Don, the new chief credit officer for the Investment Bank at J.P. Morgan, as I crossed Park Avenue. A tall, baby-faced, athletic man who walked at a bit of an angle due to a bad lower back, I had known him for more than ten years and had worked for his father back at Manufacturers Hanover Trust.

"Hey! We just moved in," I said, pointing to the building behind me with my thumb.

EIGHT SEPTEMBERS

He smiled without breaking stride. "Welcome to the Firm!" he joked. This reinforced my understanding that all the bank's power players were in Midtown, and as a result, I expected a lot more visibility and lot less autonomy than when we were working downtown. Exactly how that would play out remained to be seen.

Throughout the 1990s, deregulation allowed the commercial banks to venture into investment banking. This allowed the banks to expand from simply making loans to corporations to advising them on mergers and acquisitions and raising money to fund those transactions. In the early 2000s, this trend accelerated, despite the tech bubble bursting and a few front-page debacles like WorldCom and Enron that caused significant losses for the big banks that extended loans in order to win investment banking transactions. To make matters worse, those transactions — selling bonds to the public — led to the banks being sued and fined billions of dollars after WorldCom and Enron collapsed, far more than they had ever earned in fees.

Regardless, J.P. Morgan pressed forward with its agenda to grow its investment banking business. Bankers understood that banking was a cyclical business, and there would always be crises to offset the booms.

Our department sat in FIG, under the umbrella of the Investment Bank division of the merged company, because we oversaw relationships with large corporate clients — specifically, broker dealers and investment banks. Part of the rationale for moving uptown was so we could work more closely with the J.P. Morgan investment bankers in FIG — despite the fact that my department's activity remained 100 percent commercial banking.

J.P. Morgan had been a commercial bank like all the other banks in our previous mergers — taking deposits and making loans, clearing checks, and wiring money — but they'd refashioned themselves as an investment bank well before the merger with Chase. Their primary focus was on arranging deals between companies and only lending money to facilitate those deals. They were no longer in the stand-alone commercial loan business; they didn't have a group like ours covering the securities industry.

So while my job wasn't at risk from the merger with J.P. Morgan in 2000, as Bob and I had joked at the time, increasingly, our clients were.

Some of the J.P. Morgan investment bankers saw our top-tier investment bank/broker-dealer clients as competitors to be conquered or vanquished, and our mid-tier clients as targets to be bought or sold. They didn't have much use for our mundane — albeit profitable — lending and operating business, but they sure as heck were happy to leverage our long-standing relationships when it served their purposes. While I wanted to comply with the teamwork and partnership values espoused by the firm, as I tried to adapt to the new world, it always felt like I stayed one beat out of step.

The investment bankers were *fancy*. They rode in black luxury cars, ate at the finest restaurants, drank in the trendiest bars, flew in private jets, and summered in the Hamptons. Their world revolved around making deals, motivated by earning multimillion-dollar fees and bragging rights. Their ferocious commitment to their jobs made me wonder if they came out of the womb wanting to be investment bankers. They were both laser-focused *and* saw the big picture, and honestly, it intimidated me.

When the bank got the opportunity to bid on a deal for a mid-sized brokerage client, Refco, we faced a lot of pressure to win the business. Jimmy Lee, one of the bank's revered vice chairmen, got the call from a private equity firm that had recently purchased a stake in Refco. They offered J.P. Morgan first dibs to arrange an $800 million multi-bank loan for Refco to bridge the firm until it went public. It was understood — and becoming increasingly blatant — that the banks providing the loans would be rewarded by being paid to sell new shares of stock when it came time to list a company on the New York Stock Exchange so its stock could be publicly traded. Being paid to sell new shares of stock was the cherry-on-top prize for investment banks.

"Jane, we can earn $15 million in fees on this deal, between arranging the loan and selling the new stock," my boss Tim said, looking me squarely in the eyes. "FIG really needs this win, and so do you."

Tim was a compact, boyish-looking man whose competitive tennis-playing body had not yet fully softened from the heavy drinking and fine dining required to maintain client relationships. Raised in South Africa and educated at Princeton, he presented as the quintessential investment banker he'd been for the last twenty years — simultaneously buttoned-down and cocky. Several years younger than I, he'd been my boss for less than a year. The political ramifications of winning and losing investment banking transactions mattered to him. A lot.

"Refco doesn't have enough capital or cash flow to support such a big loan," I explained, feeling trapped between the pressure to win the deal and the reality of Refco's financial limitations. "It's going to be a tough sell to get it credit approved."

In the end, the bid we submitted, with terms to protect us from the perceived risks, did not win the deal. As a result, our department became even less aligned with J.P. Morgan's goal to become a top-three investment bank that rivaled Goldman Sachs. The fact that we considered Goldman a valued client did not improve the perception of our department within the Investment Bank, either.

But it would be the merger with another commercial bank, BankOne, in July of 2004 that eventually caused the real trouble for our department.

***

When I'd been promoted to head of the department in 2003 and got my own corner office downtown, I rewarded myself with fresh flowers every week and a bowl of candy for my team. I usually left for the office around seven a.m., mostly to avoid the rush-hour crowds, but also to get in during the quiet time of the day. Now that we were located in Midtown, I could usually grab a cab at that hour without too much trouble and avoid the subway altogether.

On Mondays, I would stop at the deli on the corner of 74th and Amsterdam to pick up flowers, an act that made me very happy. Sometimes I chose daffodils or tulips, other times red or purple exotic blooms I didn't even know the names of, but always something bright and cheery. They brought life to my office in a personal way that said, *Something is different. Something is special here.*

In my new corner office at 277 Park, I kept my papers organized in neat piles and stacks across the L-shaped desk that sat in front of the window overlooking East 48th Street. Across from the desk were a couch, a coffee table holding the candy bowl filled with Hershey's Kisses, Snickers, and Three Musketeers, and a side chair for more casual meetings. The two chairs facing my desk were for more direct conversations. Whenever I felt overwhelmed by the magnitude of tasks and calls and meetings on my plate, it helped me to organize the multiple personal and professional commitments in a big to-do list. I typed it up in Word, using categories and formatting to give me a sense of control over the dizzying number of responsibilities that threatened to engulf me, and then I put a hard copy on top of the pile. In this way, I emulated my father. But on rare occasions, I would shut my door, lie down, close my eyes, rest my feet, and "have a think," as Winnie the Pooh would say. I could never imagine Dad doing that.

One day not too long after we'd moved in, a FIG investment banker colleague named Bill — who also reported to Tim — came to see me. He wore a blue blazer, button-down shirt open at the collar, khakis, and loafers without socks. He sat in the upholstered chair next to my couch with his legs stretched out, ankles crossed.

"Jane, I'm thinking about merger opportunities in the securities industry. Which companies might buy one another, which stock exchanges are likely to partner up, how those transactions might be funded," he said, pressing his fingertips together. Bill's was a forward-looking business aimed at transforming the industry, whereas ours was simply aimed at helping clients get to the end of each day without failed transactions or overdrafts.

"Our department is focused on supporting the day-to-day activities of brokerage firms," I confessed. "We haven't spent too much time thinking about that."

We talked a little bit more about the industry, trying to help the other understand what we each did. I wasn't quite sure how we would work together, but I was willing to try, and Bill left with an agreeable handshake and friendly smile.

During this time, I'd finally come to love my job. It stimulated and interested me, made me feel important, and gave me purpose. I suppose it also satisfied something within me to be the one in charge, so I didn't feel stuck in my job like I used to. It also kept me so busy that I didn't have time for any introspection and contemplation that would cause me to make different choices. It provided just enough distraction to soothe and settle me, but not enough to change me.

***

Late that spring, I attended another industry conference. Remembering how stressed Jimmy had been by my late night at the conference the year before, I made sure to call home every day to talk to the kids and check in with him before it got too late.

One evening, after a full day of golf, cocktails, and dinner with clients, Dominick insisted on walking me back to my room, declaring he needed to keep me safe from potential predators.

Most people were drunk at that hour at these conferences. It seemed to me the fox was watching the henhouse, but I felt confident in my powers of resistance. I would not allow myself to be manipulated by this man who both infuriated and amused me.

We stood in the empty hallway, facing one another, my back to the door. He was not much taller than I, so in my heels we were eye to eye. I found myself reluctant to say goodnight, even as I knew I would never allow him to enter my room.

Leaning against the closed door, I tried unsuccessfully to remove my heels from my aching feet while standing. Surprising me, Dominick knelt and tenderly undid the ankle straps and helped me out of them. He stood and handed the shoes to me, kissing me chastely on the cheek. Then he said goodnight and walked away.

I watched him go. This gruff, powerful man voluntarily offered such a small kindness and then didn't push himself on me, respecting my boundaries so I didn't have to fend him off. It felt intimate and spacious at the same time.

***

While I'd been settling into my new role at work, things had been worsening for my father. Both Dad and Leilani made an effort to stay connected with family through letters, calls, and visits, and they'd been relatively open about Dad's challenges and their meetings with different doctors and alternative healers, assuring us the problem of simple memory retrieval would respond to treatment. Leilani was attentive to Dad and kind to my children when we were together and I began to let my guard down with her.

After Dad and Leilani visited with my sisters' families and mine on the East Coast in 2003, they stopped in San Francisco to see a renowned specialist on their way back to Hawaii. The doctor diagnosed progressive aphasia, a symptom of dementia that was most likely on its way to becoming Alzheimer's.

Dad did not tell us about the diagnosis. Instead, he tried to hide the truth and forbade Leilani from giving us any updates while also dismissing and demeaning his doctors' abilities. He seemed certain he could impose his will and alter reality, as he had done most of his adult life.

I lived far enough away and was so busy that it was tempting to put his scolding, difficult behavior on the back burner. However, I couldn't ignore what was happening as Dad continued to send me copies of the chastising letters he sent to anyone who did not do his bidding. Doctors, politicians, businessmen, lifelong friends, daughters — no one escaped his wrath.

Even with his assistant's help, he could not fully camouflage his language and reasoning problems, and I kept wondering why no one did anything about it. Finally, in September of 2004, after a year of trying to deal with Dad's condition privately, Leilani asked Ellie and me to come to Honolulu. We expected some sort of clarification about Dad's condition, but none was forthcoming.

Ellie and I swam in the pool with Dad, who grinned and showed off his water exercises with childlike delight. We tried to broach the topic of meeting with his doctor, and he dismissed us with scowl, declaring, "That guy's a turkey!"

Leilani did manage to signal us the truth, however. One day we found a box of Aricept, a new Alzheimer's medication, prominently displayed on the counter — a discreet but obvious message to tell us without betraying Dad.

Maybe Leilani would be our ally after all.

CHAPTER 16

Finding Allies

"You seem distracted," Dominick said. He was standing protectively beside me at the bar, having pulled me away from his group of colleagues who were gathered noisily around a table enjoying happy hour.

I shook my head. "You won't believe it," I said with a huff. "I was just beginning to trust that bitch. Seriously, only last week I tried convincing my dad that Leilani loved him and wasn't going to divorce him and steal his money, and today we got a letter from her saying she's leaving him!" I paused and took a sip of my wine.

Dominick listened without speaking.

"The most amazing thing is she implies she's leaving him because he's been unfaithful. *Hello!?* He cheated on my mom to marry *you*! Why did you think he wouldn't do it again? Because you're so *special?*" Shaking my head, I threw up my hands to mock her idiocy, nearly knocking over my glass.

Dominick chuckled. "Easy there, Janey girl. Take a breath." I rolled my eyes at him. "Do you have a good attorney? You're gonna have a fight on your hands now." He rested one hand on the back of my barstool and used the other to hold his drink.

"I know. I dread it. I'm going to ask Dad's company lawyer for a referral. He knows all the attorneys in Hawaii, and I can trust him." With a grimace I added, "I hope," crossing my fingers.

He touched me lightly on the back and smiled fondly, leaning in as his faint scent of cologne and cigarettes wafted between us. "Okay then. Let it go for tonight and deal with it tomorrow," he whispered close to my ear.

"Thanks," I said, looking at my watch, pretending not to be affected by his proximity. It was almost 6:30 on a dark December evening. "I've gotta get home now."

EIGHT SEPTEMBERS

He helped me with my coat. "I'll walk you to the subway, keep you safe from the bad guys," he said with an arch of his eyebrows and a sly grin.

***

Dad had led a slightly lower-profile life since our parents' divorce in 1998, his marriage to Leilani in 1999, and the liquidation of C. Brewer — his primary business — in 2001. But even in 2004, he still got recognized everywhere he went, and most perceived Doc Buyers as the "man in charge," as well as the man with the money. He'd always been a keen and exacting negotiator, but now he was an easy target for unscrupulous entrepreneurs: a Tongan fishing venture, a sandalwood forest, a maker of jewelry carousel holders. I wasn't sure about Leilani's role in all of that.

I had often wondered why no one did anything about Dad's behavior. Slowly, I realized that my sisters and I were the only ones who *could* do anything, and it was our responsibility to do so. *No one is doing anything because they're waiting for us*, I told my sisters.

But we were in the dark about Dad's financial, legal, and business affairs. Alan, the company lawyer and Dad's old friend, was our best hope.

"Well, Janey," Alan began in the deliberative tone he always used, "I recommend you call Jim. He's one of the top attorneys in Hawaii, and he's known your dad for a long time. They sit on a public board together. He and I have spoken about your dad, and he's taken some actions recently that I'll let him tell you about."

He paused as if he felt uncomfortable sharing this next bit of information. "Jim's been concerned about a series of decisions your father made, starting with moving the company from Honolulu to Hilo." I wondered if one of those concerns was the out-of-character divorce from my mother.

Alan told me that Jim had reached out to Leilani, and then to Alan himself, to confirm his suspicions that Dad might have Alzheimer's. That was news to me.

"Thanks, Alan, that's very helpful," I said, relieved to have someone close to Dad talking frankly about the situation with me, although it felt incredibly odd to be orchestrating these conversations behind my dad's back. "I will reach out to Jim. My sisters and I really appreciate the referral."

"Janey, we all love your dad. He's having a tough time. You're in a very tricky situation, and I'm happy to help in any way I can." I blinked back tears as I hung up the phone.

When I connected with Jim, he explained that he'd taken Dad out to lunch a few months earlier and suggested they should do transition planning. He proposed that Dad sell his ownership stake in the public company they both served and resign from the board.

Dad declined. "I like working and running my own company," he told Jim with a winning smile on his face. When Jim pressed, Dad said, "I do not want to sell." His smile turned to a scowl, effectively shutting down the conversation.

"Doc," Jim said the following week, attempting to broach the topic of transition planning again. "Now *I* know, and your *wife* knows, and your *assistant* knows, and your *staff* knows that your doctors have told you that you have Alzheimer's. We need to take care of this."

"Jim, you don't know what you're talking about!" Dad thundered. "They're all wrong! Everything stays as it is."

Jim forced the issue.

On December 10, 2004, at 9:30 a.m. — a week before Leilani left Dad and only a month before I called him — Jim had presented Dad with two press releases.

"We will be issuing one of these shortly. You choose which one."

The first said that Dad would retire as chair of the public board after many years of service and lauded all his successes and contributions. The second said that the board had lost confidence in him and voted him out. Dad reluctantly chose the first after extracting a promise from Jim that he and another board member, both of whom were older than Dad, would also retire in due course.

Finally! I thought. Someone *is* doing something. Someone is acknowledging the truth of the situation. I felt so relieved and grateful I wanted to hire Jim on the spot. I told him about the troubles we were having now that Leilani had left Dad. Jim was sympathetic and readily agreed that he and his firm would be willing to represent my sisters and me. He assigned his top attorneys to work with us and said he would make himself personally available as well.

Ellie, Becky, and I were united in our sorrow and resolve. We would protect our father from himself, ensure his legacy that he cared so much about, and defend his estate from unscrupulous players. We weren't sure exactly how we were going to swing it, but we were willing to take on the daily task of caring for him medically, emotionally, and physically now that Leilani had left.

Despite his dementia, Dad had different ideas.

Daughters do not tell fathers what to do.

***

J.J. and I boarded the plane at Newark Airport for the nonstop, ten-hour flight to Honolulu in the midst of a raging snowstorm at the end of January 2005. We were delayed two hours on the tarmac as they de-iced the plane before takeoff. J.J. was content to amuse himself with the personal seatback TV in coach, while I read and drank alone in business class. I'd gotten used to riding in the front of the plane when I joined Dad's board. *Hypocrite!* I thought as I recalled my own outrage when Dad traveled in first class and Mom sat in coach on the same flight, justified by the company paying for one ticket and not the other. Yet here I was doing the same thing. *Well*, I rationalized, *a son is not a spouse, and he's lucky he's even on this trip.* I'd decided to bring him along for the extended weekend trip as a fourteenth birthday present, despite missing a few days of school, since it was probably his last chance to visit with his grandfather before the dementia took over completely. Still, the parallel made me uncomfortable.

When J.J. and I arrived in Honolulu, Dad stayed at the Halekulani in Waikiki with us since Leilani had commandeered their condo in

Honolulu when she moved out of the house they'd shared the month before. Between Dad's desire to be private about his personal life and his language difficulties, I didn't have a full understanding of the situation, but it sure felt to me like she had taken advantage of him, and I resented her for it.

On the other hand, our trip came on the heels of Ellie's visit to the Big Island earlier in the month. Leilani had cooperated with her about Dad's care and arranged for Ellie to confer with his doctor, with Dad's agreement, of course. While Dad would not acknowledge his dementia diagnosis, he was sometimes open to receiving help with managing his symptoms. We wanted to leverage that openness, especially since Leilani had discovered another financial indiscretion while Ellie was visiting. Dad had cosigned for a $500,000 business loan for a young woman — she of the jewelry carousel business — who'd just filed for bankruptcy. Leilani told Ellie he'd given this woman money before and admitted that factored into why she'd left Dad — even *before* she knew about this new loan situation.

Dad, J.J., and I had breakfast together on the hotel lanai our first morning, enjoying the warm tropical breezes, bright-green manicured lawn, and oceanfront views. Small birds chirped and flitted around, trying to steal a snack from the ground or an un-bussed table. J.J. had the day to himself to explore, and he took off to walk the beach, the curving slopes of white sand contrasting beautifully with the robin's egg blue sky and his destination, the dormant volcano, Diamond Head, in the distance. I spoke with Dad alone before we headed to the board meeting.

Dad had dressed in an aloha shirt and slacks, looking crisp and clean. Although he was much thinner than he once was, his shoulders were still broad and his posture ramrod straight. He seemed happy about something he'd accomplished that morning, but his language was vague. "It was hard," he said, and "I kept trying." Finally, he raised his arms in the air like a champion, fists closed, and said, "I did it!" Something about the way he said it made me realize he meant he'd had success in the bathroom after many days of constipation, and my heart wrenched.

EIGHT SEPTEMBERS

Smiling, I congratulated him. "Dad, that's great!" Taking advantage of his good mood, I dove in. "You know how you've been having trouble retrieving words? Finding it hard to express yourself?" I plastered a positive look on my face. "I think I might know what the problem is!"

"Oh?" he responded, narrowing his eyes.

I pushed a pamphlet from the Alzheimer's Association toward him. "It looks like you might have the symptoms of dementia," I said cautiously, turning open the pages to a checklist.

He glanced at the pamphlet. I watched as he wiped his mouth with a napkin, but I didn't speak, waiting to see if he would respond. He lifted his wrist and studied the round gold watch on his hairy forearm for a moment, perplexed.

"We'd better get going if we're going to get to that thing we have to do on time," he instructed, pushing his chair back from the table and leaving the pamphlet behind.

CHAPTER 17
Turmoil

On one of the conference calls with my sisters after J.J. and I returned from Hawaii, I griped, "Dad still doesn't have anyone living on the property withc him. Leilani said she would help us find someone for in-home care, but she hasn't done a thing as far as I can tell."

Becky stubbornly believed that Leilani deserved the benefit of the doubt and would deliver on her various promises. After all, Leilani was a practitioner of yoga and meditation. "Maybe I can call her and see if she's made progress," she said.

Ellie was pragmatic and direct, dismissive even. "Becky, I've spoken to the staff at the Alzheimer's Association, and we need to get help in the house sooner rather than later. I think we need to get a recommendation from them. We can't wait for Leilani." The emerging captain of our care team had spoken.

"Look, no one's driving the bus! We need to be more hands-on," I urged.

"I agree," Ellie said. "It seems like things have gotten even more chaotic since we were there in January. It's very hard to tell what's going on with the doctors."

The three of us compared calendars and made a tentative plan for each of us to visit Dad over the coming months. I couldn't always get away from work and was grateful that I wouldn't be the only one going back and forth to Hawaii, trying to figure out the situation with Dad.

During Becky's visit in March, she tried to coordinate with Dad's assistant, the housekeeper, and Leilani, among others, to ensure the adequacy of his daily routines. Each day something new came over the transom, and we felt like firefighters, jointly responding to each development as best we could.

EIGHT SEPTEMBERS

E-mails came in from Becky every day.

The pool guy quit because Dad refused to pay him.
The housekeeper won't move in because Dad won't pay for the fence she needs for her dogs.
Dad's flying to Honolulu alone where he expects to be retired off the bank board. (After thirty years, he's taking that in stride, surprisingly.)
I'm afraid to talk to Dad about the divorce. He'll know I've been talking to Leilani. I don't want to make him angry.

There was good stuff too.

Dad had the biggest grin on his face this morning in the pool while we were doing the dumbbell exercises. He made up a move that resembled boxing. We pushed the dumbbells back and forth underwater at each other, and he laughed and smiled so hard I thought his cheeks might break. It's the little things that bring him pleasure now.

We all knew Leilani planned to file for divorce, and Dad would be served with the papers before the end of that month. Leilani said she would ask the court to name me as Dad's guardian ad litem — someone to represent his interests. We didn't know how much she communicated directly with Dad because he would often assume the divorce was off when she spoke kindly or told him she loved him. In December, for example, after Leilani left Dad and told him she wanted a divorce, he'd reached out to a divorce lawyer, but later, he'd told us they weren't getting a divorce after all because she still loved him.

When the divorce papers finally arrived, he did retain the divorce lawyer and immediately called his estate attorney to change his will. Leilani had requested a temporary financial restraining order as part of the divorce filing to prevent Dad from wasting assets. I don't know why, but there'd been no mention of me being Dad's guardian ad litem. As a result, we engaged yet another attorney — our *own* divorce attorney — to advise on divorce matters in Hawaii so we could follow the

TURMOIL

legal action between Leilani and Dad. We also began discussions about potentially becoming Dad's conservators because it was apparent that he was going downhill quickly and would soon need others to help him execute his desires.

In April, on what would have been our parents' fifty-second wedding anniversary, a family court hearing on Leilani's motion for temporary relief occurred. We did not attend but had copies of the various filings, and they did not reflect our verbal agreements with Leilani.

While being polite to our faces, behind our backs Leilani and her attorneys alleged we were greedy daughters trying to take advantage of her. Yet *she* was the one who got Dad to sign over a third of his company to her shortly after they were married — something he'd never done in forty-five years of marriage to Mom. We learned he had also deeded two properties he owned in Waimea over to her, and that she had taken whatever she wanted from the Hakalau and Honomu houses. She monopolized the condo in Waikiki and had all her expenses paid by Dad, in addition to drawing a monthly distribution from the company, and she received his monthly social security payments. The temporary relief request — meant to stabilize Dad's spending due to his illness — was really her attempt to keep the gravy train going despite dumping him and leaving us with all the responsibilities she'd abandoned. Dad's attorney fought it accordingly.

At the same time this was going on, my colleague Bob decided to retire. He'd been supportive when I got the top job instead of him and tried to help me make a smooth transition into my new position, but he'd been in the business a long time. I could see his tank had been running low for a while now. Besides, banking was fast becoming a young man's business, and Bob regularly noted the diminishing number of people with gray hair. In fact, each new boss I had was younger than the one before. My newest one, Tim, was younger than I — and *I* was almost ten years younger than Bob.

Once Bob passed fifty, the "call to the other side" looked more and more appealing. We all joked about how our retired colleagues immediately looked a decade younger as soon as they left the bank, relieved of

169

the constant stress that weighed them down. With the loss of a mentor and friend, Bob's departure marked another contraction in my professional support system.

That same spring, Dominick and I began to see and speak with each other more regularly, usually a result of business demands and often in the company of others, but sometimes not. I kept him posted on the situation with Dad and Leilani.

We had finished having lunch one day and I needed to get back to the office, yet I found myself standing on the street, frozen in place, staring at my shoes, tongue-tied. Dominick stood next to me, waiting. Why did I feel reluctant to say goodbye? Why did I feel safe with him when I knew the situation was dangerous?

I'm married. Our relationship is professional. The joking around, the repartee, the flirting... It's all part of the job, woven into the fabric of running the business, getting things done, exercising influence. It means nothing.

We were developing a professional relationship and a collegial friendship, just like all the guys had amongst themselves. They golfed and drank and went out to eat together, and why should I be excluded because I was a woman? Why should our relationship raise eyebrows when it was within my professional purview to have such a friendly connection?

"What's so interesting about your shoes?" Dominick teased. When I didn't respond, he proclaimed, "One day, we're going to have an affair. Not a sudden, passionate, 'Let's run away' kind of affair, but inch by inch, slowly, until we're so close, it's simply inevitable." He shrugged, as if adulterous affairs were nothing out of the ordinary. For him, I guess they weren't. It was rumored that he'd cheated on his wife numerous times.

As a faithful wife, a moral person who did not have affairs, I could not — *would* not — follow the trajectory of his logic. Despite my growing attachment to him, I was certain I would never break my marriage vows.

"That's not going to happen," I declared, shaking my head. "Maybe in another lifetime." "Everybody forgives a good love story," he countered, proceeding to give me examples of love triumphing over social mores.

"Yeah, I don't think so," I said. "It's just not right."

"Nobody cares," he said with disgust. He'd told me this many times before and every time he did, my mind filled with all the people who *would* care: my husband, my parents, my sisters, my pastor, my boss. In fact, I couldn't think of anybody in my life who *wouldn't* care.

***

One morning on my way to work, I slipped out of the house earlier than usual without saying where I was going, reluctant to be ridiculed or interrogated by my husband about my desire to see a psychic.

A psychic's ability to see beyond the superficial intrigued me, and seemed a lot easier than the long, torturous road of therapy I'd started and stopped a few times after I'd left Gam-Anon. I wanted to understand the dynamic with Dominick and hoped for some quick insights. Surprisingly, I'd found a business card for an intuitive in the lobby of my dentist's building. She had office hours there a few times a week, and I'd called a few days earlier to make an appointment. Now I made my way stealthily up Columbus Avenue to 79th Street, squeezing in a visit before heading to the office.

My heart pounded as the coffin-sized elevator slowly climbed to the fourth floor in the pre-war building, and I wished that access to the staircase was an option.

I still wasn't 100 percent committed to consulting a psychic. I'd never done it before, even though I'd wanted to. Was I here to tell this woman everything so she could point a way forward? Or was I here to test her, say as little as possible, and let her figure out my situation? Jimmy's voice stuck in my head, teasing me about my belief in psychics and causing me to doubt my own opinions.

Seeing the door to her office across from the elevator, I knocked lightly and turned the handle. A small, nondescript room with a desk and chair greeted me — no frills, brown walls, low light. She sat at the desk, a heavy, pleasant-looking woman, her forearms resting on the surface.

"Go ahead and have a seat over there," she said, pointing to a chair angled a few feet across from her.

I put aside my pocketbook, briefcase, and coat and sat stiffly in the chair, unsure what to do next.

"So, what brings you here today?" Her eyes were kind, but I felt them bore into me.

I hesitated. *How honest should I be?*

"Look, just say it," she urged, like a schoolteacher prodding her student. Her pragmatic manner startled me.

I glanced at my watch. *Okay, time to take the plunge.*

I told her about my husband and his history of gambling, my troubling attraction to another man at work, and my concerns about what to do.

She took it all in with equanimity. "What is it that you want from me?" she inquired.

"That's a good question." I thought for a moment. "I guess I was hoping you would have some insights into why this is all happening and how I should respond." I didn't tell her I was looking for a shortcut for therapy.

She studied me, silent, assessing my energy and what I'd told her.

"I'd say, on a scale of one to ten, that you have about a seven or eight of this other man's attention," she ventured. This both alarmed and gratified me. It was flattering to be desired but unnerving to be targeted.

"On the other hand, you have maybe a four or five of your husband's attention," she said, cocking her head to gauge my response.

I froze, unable to take in this information. Was my own husband paying less attention to me and my needs than this man I had known only a couple of years?

"You have a choice," she continued. "You can deal with that anger I see you holding in your belly and try to fix things with your husband. Or you can look elsewhere. But if you don't do *something*, that anger will eat you alive."

I wasn't sure what I would do, but my stomach roiled at the thought of telling Jimmy the truth about my unhappiness. Recently he'd asked me if I was happy, and when I tried to articulate my complicated feelings, he interrupted me and assured me that I was.

"Life is good," he said. "Great kids, great house. How could you not be happy?"

Then he'd switched on the television, and I switched off.

***

Dad traveled east for Ellie's son Alex's college graduation from Amherst. While he still functioned well enough to travel alone, Dad's conversational skills left a lot to be desired. He stayed with us in New York and got lost taking J.J. to his piano lesson a few blocks away, panicked about getting to the airport before dark, and seemed secretive about his plans. It was hard to discern what drove his behavior.

The divorce languished and Dad's health worsened, so my sisters and I filed our formal petition to become Dad's joint conservators in May. A month later, in June, the judge in Hawaii agreed to seal the hearing about our conservatorship motion, which would keep it confidential since Dad had such a public profile. But the judge did not want to decide anything right away. Instead, he ordered a *Kokua Kanawai* — meaning a "helper in the law" who acts as an investigator — to interview all parties.

Dad charmed her, his social graces and political skills hiding his mental decline, his sheer force of will controlling events as it had for most of his life. The Kokua Kanawai gave a draft of her recommendations to our attorney, and we were shocked and angered to find that she planned to recommend our petition be denied. She downplayed his disability and seemed more interested in preserving his pride, ego, and reputation. She suggested he stay engaged in making business decisions with support from others. That might have been an appropriate conclusion a year or two earlier, but Dad's level of work now consisted of opening his mail and circling his name, then leaving rambling messages on his Dictaphone for his assistant, Haidee. The Kokua Kanawai hadn't even spoken with the people dealing with him day to day. As Ellie pointed out, we were at the stage of making sure he dressed appropriately and didn't talk about his perspiration problems with random strangers.

We filed our counterargument immediately.

Ellie went out to Hawaii for Dad's birthday in July. She organized a party at the house, and when he showed people around, Dad consulted a small notebook with a handwritten list of rooms — *kitchen, living room, dining room* — so he could use the correct word. One day at the office, she tried to help him sort his mail and pay bills and he angrily turned on her, frightening her with his vehemence.

Despite the state of things, Leilani's attorney and Dad's divorce attorney both filed motions objecting to the conservatorship, although for very different reasons.

Ira, Dad's attorney, wrote, "The Respondent is a prominent and respected businessman who made substantial contributions to Hawaii's economy and society, and he rejects the suggestion that he be removed from control of his own affairs." Fair enough. Straightforward, leveraging similar language from the report of the Kokua Kanawai, and absolutely true that if Dad was in his right mind, there was no way he would let his daughters run his business. His wife either, for that matter. But he *wasn't* in his right mind. That was the whole problem in a nutshell.

Leilani's attorney focused on her share of Dad's assets: "So long as the property division issues of the divorce are not finally resolved, Petitioners are not the appropriate people to serve as the Respondent's co-conservators." Sadly, despite what she said about loving Dad and wanting to help us, when it came down to it, the legal papers always made it clear she was after the money.

***

I sat down at my beloved baby grand, my fingers striking the keys of the opening chord dramatically. Every complicated emotion flowed through my hands, running up and down the keyboard, my right foot working the pedal to blur the notes. At first, I needed to read the music, but as I began the familiar second movement of Beethoven's *Pathétique*, I closed my eyes and my body swayed in and out as the notes rose and fell with my touch. The melody soothed me. The concentration focused me. All else disappeared until there was no dad with dementia, no complicated lawsuit, no compulsive gambler husband, no Lothario trying to seduce me, no job demanding my attention. Just peace.

For a moment, I could feel my heart again.

PART FIVE
Bombardment

"It always seems impossible until it is done."
—Nelson Mandela

CHAPTER 18
Showdown

By mid-August, we were finally headed to court. I left my family in New York to go to Hawaii to stay with Dad. As I would be gone almost seven weeks, I had arranged with Tim to work remotely, telling my direct reports that I needed to go to Hawaii to care for my father, who had dementia. After so many years being strong and tough, living in the ridiculous macho bank culture where you never showed any weakness, sharing such personal details made me feel vulnerable. I cried in front of them — the one and only time I wept at work. Fortunately, both my family and my colleagues supported my decision to go, although I would have gone anyway. It was simply the right thing to do, and I wanted to do it.

It had been thirty years since our first trip to Hawaii, when Dad had accepted the job as president and CEO of C. Brewer. That had been a two-week whirlwind tour of the islands, hosted by local dignitaries. We'd gone house hunting, visited sugar plantations, toured volcanos, hiked tropical rain forests, been honored at a luau, and eaten in the finest restaurants. Everywhere we went we were welcomed with aloha, like celebrities.

And then, that was it. My sisters went back to college, I went to boarding school in Long Island, and our parents moved to Honolulu to start their new life without us. For nearly twenty years, until I joined his board, I saw my father no more than five days a year. We were not exactly estranged, but certainly not close.

The court date coincided with the beginning of my caretaking tour of duty, so Becky and I flew out together, and Ellie arrived the next morning to join us at Dad's house in Honomu.

I'd been to the 52-acre property for the first time in 1991, after J.J. was born. At that point, it was still undeveloped land, which had inflamed

EIGHT SEPTEMBERS

a passion in my father's heart. Dad and Mom gave Jimmy, newborn J.J., and me a tour as he shared his vision for the property he had earned as part of his compensation from the company. He'd already planted Norfolk pines along the upper half of the mile-long gravel driveway, and Royal palms along the lower half. He installed a green metal gate with the letter *B* at the top of the drive and envisioned a grand house at the end of the driveway overlooking the ocean, a manor reflective of his self-made success.

Dad's baseball cap shielded his eyes and protected his bald, freckled head from the sun as he strode purposefully in his steel-toed shoes, the dry cane grass crunching beneath his solid six-foot frame.

"Look at that ocean! See how steeply the land drops off? Must be thirty or forty feet down! The locals like to fish down there. We're going to plant a thicket hedge that will keep anyone from climbing up… or falling off!" His gray-blue eyes sparkled; he was never so excited as when he had a vision for a project. Mom, always the accommodating and good-natured partner, indulged Dad and his big plans.

Dad took off across the open field under the hot sun as Jimmy and I trailed behind him. I held J.J. tight against my breast in his Snugli, and Mom ambled beside us as we all headed toward the ravine on the far side of the property, the wide expanse of blue and green ocean to our left.

"And look at those trees! So tall and thick you can't see anything on the other side," he gushed, spittle forming at the corners of his mouth. "You know, it's a 365-day growing season here in Hawaii, and everything grows *fast*." Dad revered productivity and efficiency. He used his thumb and pointer finger to wipe away the spittle.

"See, right here is where we are going to have the baseball field." He pointed across the driveway behind us. "And over there is where the macadamia nut tree farm will go." Many people found his enthusiasm infectious, but I found it an overwhelming emotional invasion, since he always expected us to validate and applaud his ideas.

"Have I got a treat for you, Jimmy," Dad said with a mischievous grin beneath his high cheekbones. He reached inside his jacket pocket and produced a small machete, his eyes twinkling.

"Johnny, be careful!" my mother fretted, still looking dignified even as her wavy white hair ruffled in the breeze.

Ignoring her with a scowl and a stern, "Don't you be a killjoy," Dad and Jimmy entered the rainforest-like ravine where they climbed a tree and gleefully cut down a stalk of bananas growing wild. They emerged from the forest smiling, lofting their trophy triumphantly, as if it were big game captured on safari.

"Don't count your old man out just yet!" Dad boasted, a huge grin on his face.

Back then in 1991, that place, that plan, that dream on the Big Island was meant to be shared with my mother. Fourteen years later, Dad was completing his vision with Leilani. But she had bailed on him.

The house he once envisioned had materialized at the end of the driveway: an expansive, two-story rectangle of stucco and tile, at once gracious and ostentatious—ten thousand square feet of lifeless beauty.

Once my sisters left, I'd be alone in the big house with the man who was, and yet was not, my father.

***

North of Hilo, Dad's new headquarters building sat below the Hawaii Belt Road in Wainaku. Another green metal gate limited entry to the steep driveway leading down to the two-story building perched high above Hilo Bay, which Dad had built on the foundation of the old sugar mill. From the parking lot, we could see the decrepit concrete tunnel and overgrown train tracks that had been used to bring the sugar down to the mill from the plantations.

My sisters and I walked through the double entry doors and admired the view straight out to the emerald lawn and turquoise ocean. Our shoes clattered on the tile floor lobby, which hosted a large antique sea chest piled high with Mauna Loa Macadamia Nut brand nuts and candy and boxes of chocolates, as well as other company products, like coffee, tea, and guava juice. Dad's portrait hung on the wall above the chest, which he bragged had belonged to Captain James Hunnewell, the seafaring missionary who founded the company in 1826. In the portrait, Dad wore an aloha shirt and held a macadamia nut seedling, his squinting eyes and taut smile not quite capturing his true charisma.

We headed up the grand koa-wood staircase leading to the executive offices and boardroom to meet with Dad's loyal and efficient Hawaiian executive assistant, Haidee. After we greeted her with hugs and smiles, I walked down the hall to the office that would be mine for the next month and a half, anxious to make sure the internet connections worked so that I would have access to my J.P. Morgan desktop. The office was locked.

I rushed back to talk to Haidee. "Do you have the key? I need to get into that office as soon as possible and confirm I can access the bank's computers." It made me crazy when I didn't have the tools I needed to do my job.

Haidee looked at me with her deep-brown eyes and chose her words carefully. She had spent the better part of two years being a diplomat caught uncomfortably between the shifting dynamics. "That's Leilani's office. She locked the door and took the key with her. We don't have access."

Are you kidding me?

Furious, I stomped outside and crossed the terraced lawn toward the magnificent old monkey pod tree that graced the corner of the property. Not far away stood a seven-foot-tall bronze statue of Dad, one hand in his pocket, a winning smile on his face, and a placard: J.W.A. "DOC" BUYERS, 1986 HAWAII SALESMAN OF THE YEAR. It had been commissioned for his seventieth birthday in 2003 and was a much better likeness than the portrait. We suspected Leilani encouraged him to build the statue, assuring Dad that someone of his stature and importance deserved it, stroking his ego to ingratiate herself. Having been taught by this same man about the sin of pride, it made his daughters cringe.

I stood glaring at it and called Jimmy to complain.

"That fucking, fucking, fucking, fucking, fucking, fucking bitch! We're out here doing her job because she's running away and abandoning him, and she's making it difficult for us to boot! I hate her! I hate this!" I found myself gulping for air, shocked at my own outburst.

SHOWDOWN

Good God! Am I three or forty-three?

Jimmy chuckled a little at the extremity of my emotion. He loved the drama.

"It's going to be fine, Jane. You'll work it out. I've got your back. Call me anytime."

When my brain cooled down, I realized with chagrin that I'd been in full view — and earshot — of any employees nearby. Taking a deep breath, I went back inside, struggling to mask my emotions. Ellie, Becky, and Haidee looked up as I came in, and I could tell they had been talking about me. I forced myself back into my efficient, professional persona, and we agreed to figure it out the next day.

For now, we needed to get to court.

***

The judge had agreed in advance that my father didn't need to attend the hearing, as his interests would be represented by both the Kokua Kanawai and Dad's divorce attorney. That was a relief, as we knew he would be confused and agitated by the proceedings. Still, things were tense.

We huddled with our attorneys outside the courtroom in the hallway that could have been anywhere in America: black and white linoleum tiles, green painted walls, and fluorescent lighting typical of municipal bureaucracy. As we talked in hushed tones about testifying and potential questions from the judge, I tried to shake off my morning upset.

Leilani swept in wearing a wide-legged white pant suit belted at the waist. She wore her long black hair pulled up in a tight bun with a flowing multicolored scarf draped around her neck. Although we knew she would be there, we were caught off guard when she pranced over and greeted us theatrically with cheek kisses, her smiling face a false mask of concern and familiarity. You would have guessed that she was there to support, not thwart, our efforts.

The judge sat in his black robes at the elevated desk in the front of the courtroom, a slight man with dark hair. He was newly appointed and had to sign a conflict-of-interest waiver since his wife was Dad's accountant. Hilo was a small town. Everyone, including the judge, knew Dad and Leilani. That's why he'd agreed to seal the case and refer to Dad as "John Doe."

All our planning about testifying and worrying about what he might ask was for naught because the judge punted.

"We have the filings from your lawyers and the report from the Kokua Kanawai's investigation. The daughters are seeking joint conservatorship. The Respondent objects and is represented here today by his attorney. The Respondent's spouse also opposes the appointment, citing a conflict of interest as the daughters are potential heirs of the Respondent. The Kokua Kanawai recommends denying the broad relief sought by the daughters and suggests a narrower solution."

Why did no one see that all we wanted to do was take care of our dad?

We hoped the judge understood at least some of the issues, since we'd been told his wife's father, who suffered with dementia, had recently moved in with them.

He continued in a measured and soft-spoken tone. "This is a complicated and sensitive situation. I am not going to decide this. You are to go into that conference room and make a deal," he instructed, pointing across the room.

Really? Ugh! I so wanted the judge to give Leilani the smackdown.

We crowded into the small room, taking seats around the rectangular wooden table, my sisters and I on one side, flanked by our attorneys, and Leilani on the other side, flanked by hers. I did my best not to acknowledge her, telegraphing that she was not worthy of my attention. Ira, Dad's divorce attorney, squeezed in, as well as Diana, the Kokua Kanawai. A guardian ad litem had never been named in the divorce action. If conservatorship was granted, my sisters and I would become the de facto guardian ad litem, which meant we would control the division of marital assets in the divorce. It came out that this was Leilani's main objection to us becoming Dad's conservators.

Her attorney finally offered something doable: "If the daughters agree not to be the guardian ad litem, we will drop our opposition to the conservatorship."

Progress.

"Perhaps Doc's loyal employee and friend Alan could be the guardian ad litem," Diana suggested. "When I discussed the concept of an advisory board to help manage the company, Doc was very open to Alan's participation." She was attempting to make the conservatorship more palatable to Dad and seemed confident about his willingness to agree to Alan as his advisor. Ira, as Dad's representative in the room, concurred this would be an acceptable solution.

These were terms we could live with, and we went back to the judge with a proposal.

In the end, Alan's willingness to help saved us. The judge ruled that Leilani's argument about the daughters being conflicted since we were potential heirs was not sufficient to block our appointment.

We three sisters were formally awarded joint conservatorship on August 24, 2005.

CHAPTER 19
Conservatorship

I was nothing if not organized. Down the hall from Dad — whom I drove to work each morning since he would never in a million years agree to stay home — I sat at my desk in the office that had mysteriously been unlocked after my temper tantrum. Now that we had been awarded conservatorship, I drew up a list of all that I needed to accomplish in the next six weeks.

Of course, understanding what the conservatorship actually entailed topped the list, since we were now responsible for essentially all aspects of Dad's life. That included not only his business but also his divorce from Leilani, his estate plans, and his taxes. I had become familiar with the business as I had been on the board, but Dad always kept his personal financial affairs private.

Now I had to identify all of his assets and get them valued for the divorce mediation, then figure out his complicated will and the various amendments to his trust — the latest of which had not yet been executed as his dementia had worsened while he tried to change it. I also had to dive into the company numbers to identify any fraud involved with those dubious investments he had made. I couldn't get any help from Dad since his mind was slipping away more each day. If he understood what I was doing, he would have been furious.

1. **Conservatorship**
    1. Understand JWAB's current holdings
    2. Delegate responsibilities to Bank Trustee
    3. Consider trading orchards with co-owner (Kau/Honomu)
    4. Review brokerage and bank accounts
    5. Contact San Filipo?
    6. Make public statement?

EIGHT SEPTEMBERS

    7. Obtain formal approval of stipulation
    8. Review tax return
    9. Understand DBE responsibilities with Alan

2. **JWAB Current Holdings**
   1. DBE
   2. Trust—What does it hold?
      1. Merrill
      2. Morgan
      3. First Hawaiian
      4. Others?
         1. get account numbers
         2. get statements
   3. Real Estate—deeds?
   4. Mac Orchards (Kau, Honomu)
   5. Pennsylvania farms
   6. Waimea properties in Leilani's name
      1. Who did the paperwork?
   7. Valuation for divorce—who??

3. **DBuyers Enterprises**
   1. Review operating agreement
   2. Review amendment admitting Leilani
   3. Review operating company performance
   4. Review tax returns
   5. Obtain name of attorney who drew up papers
   6. Sandalwood investment
   7. PONO LLC (L's contribution to DBE)
   8. Prioritize what company needs us to decide upon

4. **Divorce**
   1. Determine value of assets and liabilities in 1998
      1. Tax return
      2. Estate CPA

CONSERVATORSHIP

3. Real estate
4. Brewer and BEI stock
5. Other stocks and bonds
6. Queen Victoria
7. Deferred comp and pension plans
8. Split dollar insurance
9. Other??

I finished typing the list and emailed it to my sisters, feeling relieved to have contained the riotous cauldron of my father's business in a soothing list. I knew they would pick up the slack on any "minor" missing issues, like healthcare and housing and how we were going to take care of Dad long term.

My phone rang. "It's so good to hear your voice," Dominick said. "How are you holding up?"

I'd been confiding in him throughout the spring and over the summer about Leilani and all the trouble she'd caused us, but this was the first time I had spoken to him since I'd arrived, and I was glad to hear from him.

"It's pretty stressful. We finally won conservatorship, but the paperwork is not quite complete. We're waiting for the official 'stipulation' from the judge. So I'm ready to dig in, but I'm not getting a lot of cooperation."

He cleared his throat. "I'm guessing you'll sort that out soon enough." Dominick liked to bolster my ego, confident in my capabilities.

"Yeah, well, it's hard to know where people's loyalties lie. I mean Haidee, for sure, is loyal to Dad and willing to work with me. But the president and chief financial officer? Not so much. Everyone is walking on eggshells. Leilani has some hold over them, and it's pissing me off." I cradled the phone and tried to keep my voice down, looking out the window, my back to the open door of my office.

"Well, I'm here for you, whatever you need." He paused before adding, "I miss you." It still startled me when he said things like that. I mean, we weren't a couple or anything, so why would he be missing me? Of course, I missed him, too, but I didn't have time to think about that.

"Look, if you can make the mealymouthed, spineless CFO here talk to me, I'd be very happy," I half-joked.

Dominick chuckled. "I'm quite sure you'll find a way to do that yourself."

I heard a noise behind me and turned to look. *Shit!* There stood the CFO, lurking and listening. What had he heard?

"I've gotta go," I said, hanging up abruptly.

I motioned him in, pretending I hadn't just dissed him and that he hadn't heard me do it. "Do you have the reports I requested?" I asked, trying to put a pleasant expression on my face.

He shuffled his feet. "Uh, this is what I can give you so far," he said, offering me a sheaf of papers. A quick glance confirmed it did not include the details I wanted and was simply a rehash of a typical report I'd already received as a board member.

The look on my face probably telegraphed my displeasure, but I held my tongue. I took the papers and let him go, as I needed to turn my attention back to my actual job in New York. It was time for my regular conference call with colleagues to review potential deals with our clients — the weekly "pipeline" report we had to complete for senior management.

I jumped on the call. The bankers went around the room and discussed the deals currently in motion: Therese was pitching Schwab on money transfers and leading a loan facility; Diane was trying to get an unsecured loan facility for Lehman approved. Another banker was working with the investment bankers to win a new equity transaction for Penson, and yet another was working on a pitch for MF Global. There was a possible deal with Goldman in London, and another for Salomon Smith Barney in government clearance. The team was doing well without me, and the outlook for our pipeline was promising. I hung up, relieved I could comfortably turn my attention back to my Hawaii responsibilities.

A week later, still no financial details about my father's recent investments had been provided. As I feared potential fraud and worried that management might keep stonewalling me for my entire trip, I reached out to Jim, our attorney, and asked him to pressure the judge to get the stipulation finalized.

"You can't believe it," I complained to Jimmy. "Our attorney told me that Leilani instructed both the president and the CFO not to — quote, unquote — divulge any confidential information to any 'unauthorized person,' meaning me!"

"That bitch," he sympathized.

"Well, the attorney straightened things right out. Leilani supposedly gave them authorization to speak with me, but he made it clear to her, and them, that she doesn't have any authority to instruct them one way or the other. As a minority owner, she only has the right to complain if she thinks the business is being mismanaged."

"Sounds good, Janey. Glad you're on it," Jimmy said.

"As soon as we have the final stipulation from the judge — which won't be soon enough, in my opinion — the president and CFO can only take orders from the conservators. Meaning me!" I crowed.

"You go, girl," Jimmy said before hanging up.

CHAPTER 20
Caretaking

It challenged me, waking up six hours behind New York, working a full day of banking in the morning, spending my afternoons learning Dad's business, and caring for him in the evenings. Despite that, the rhythm of the days moved along slowly.

Most days Dad allowed me to drive him back and forth to work, as long as he felt chauffeured and not babied. Once, as we were pulling out of the long, tree-lined driveway, he got his seat belt entangled in his sweater vest.

"Dad, let me help you," I said, reaching over and trying to disengage the seat belt.

He angrily pushed me away and shouted, "I am a *man!*"

I backed off and let him solve his own problem.

I cooked Dad dinner in the evenings, and we sat on the screened-in porch to eat simple childhood favorites like meatloaf and mashed potatoes or cheese omelets. He gushed his praises as if I were a four-star chef. Before my sisters and I started caring for him, after Leilani left, he'd fed himself cold food left in the refrigerator by the housekeeper, if he remembered to eat at all.

He'd lost weight but still had an athletic build and was a handsome man capable of swimming and golfing, even if he did use a fairway wood to putt or put on work boots to play tennis.

He watched the ocean and the sky and exclaimed, "There's a big one!" if he saw a cruise ship go by, or "That's a good one!" when he saw a rainbow arcing across the sky as they often did.

I bought crayons and a coloring book and, hoping to engage him, brought them onto the porch after dinner. He took pleasure in choosing which crayons I would use and watching me color, although he never chose to color himself. He complimented me for staying in the lines by saying, "You do it so well!" which became one of his stock phrases.

Sometimes after dinner I played hymns on the piano for him. He sang along lustily, stumbling over words he'd known all his life. We both pretended not to notice.

Other times we played checkers; he beat me and laughed with satisfaction when I called him *tricky* and *sneaky* and *clever*. He marveled at his win, confiding his surprise that he played so well since he'd "never played before."

Every afternoon before I left the office, I spoke with Jimmy and the boys, usually right before their bedtime. I shared some of the highlights and challenges of caring for Dad with Jimmy, then talked with the kids about school, homework assignments, issues with friends, and so on. William had just started middle school, and J.J. was a sophomore in high school. It hurt to be away from them, and I appreciated the regular contact and their support for my decision to care for Dad.

Dad was sequestered in his room by dark, one of the symptoms of his disease known as *sundowning*, reading through his papers and making lists, taking pictures of his things, and, I imagined, striving to retain his sense of self. I sat alone in the dark, too, outside on the lanai downstairs, sneaking a cigarette and letting my thoughts drift.

I often wondered about Dominick and my attraction to him. It felt like a magnet was pulling us together and I was unable to resist its force. Why did I think about him so much? What did I expect? In many ways, I didn't even like the man, and my attraction to him infuriated me. Yet there was something. It felt... fated? Where did the relationship fit into the rest of my life? How would things be if neither of us were married? Maybe it was simply a reaction to his desire for me, desire being a strong aphrodisiac. Was it simply a physical attraction that I tried to imbue with meaning to explain it away? I told myself there must be some sort of past-life connection, some karmic reason for the inexplicable magnetism between us. In the interim, what harm could come from daydreaming about him while living five thousand miles away?

CARETAKING

***

Driving remained important to Dad, and he would sometimes sneak out in the car alone. We'd been trying to hide his car and his keys, but his determination and craftiness remained strong. One afternoon, sitting in my office in Hilo, I received an email from Becky who was in Pennsylvania, helping her daughter move into her college dorm:

> *The hearing aid technician called to say Dad walked into his office this morning, without an appointment, and said he wanted the larger hearing aids. (I wondered how he got there. Did you take him, Jane? Or did he drive himself?)*

I jumped up to look for Dad, who was nowhere to be found. Apparently, he'd snuck out and driven himself into town. When he returned to the office, he dodged my questions about where he'd been. But that evening, he refused to give me the keys and insisted on driving home from the office, a winding fourteen-mile drive along the coast that could be dangerous. I tried to talk him out of it, but his trip into town alone had emboldened him.

"It's mine, and I'm going to do it! I know how to do it better than you!" He raised his fist in the air, shaking the keys at me, his face an angry mask. "Don't you tell me what to do. I have the power."

"Dad, please, let me drive. You know you shouldn't be driving anymore."

He glared at me. Eventually, I would learn that reasoning did not work with dementia, and that deception — done with love — was the way to go, but that evening we argued for several minutes, his expression shifting between fury and confusion.

"A daughter doesn't tell a father what to do!" he scolded.

Finally, desperate, inspiration struck. I crossed my arms, raised my eyebrows, shook my head, and frowned like a schoolteacher scolding *him*. "Okay, you can drive if you want to, but I am *not* going with you. You do *not* have a license," I lied, "and I do *not* feel safe with you."

EIGHT SEPTEMBERS

He raised his hands and shoved my shoulders, pushing me backwards a few steps. I stumbled but did not fall. Surrendering, he threw the keys at me, stomped over to the passenger side, and got in the car, pouting. It pained and confused me that this successful, larger-than-life, intimidating parent now acted like a kindergartner.

***

When *I* was the pouting kindergartner and *he* was the scolding adult, I remembered Dad perspiring shirtless under the hot summer sun as he leaned on his spade and instructed me on my posture as if I were a fellow Marine.

"Shoulders back, chest out, stomach in!" he growled, wiping his brow with his monogrammed white handkerchief.

We were weeding the strawberry patch behind the small stable that housed lawn, garden, and sports equipment, not horses like all our neighbors had. Wilting from the heat and hard work, I lingered in the narrow sliver of shade that hugged the edge of the stable wall. I preferred the comfort of playing "Let's Pretend" or watching TV over the manual labor Dad so loved, but I did my best to correct my posture, holding back tears and biting my lip.

Dad often told his daughters to "toughen up," whether driving a spiral football pass into our abdomens or drilling a knuckle sandwich into our deltoids with a menacing laugh. Becky, eight at the time, enjoyed getting dirty and sweaty like he did, competing hard to gain his approval. She could run the fastest and win at tennis and Ping-Pong, earning the accolades and admiration from him that eluded me, the baby. Ellie, eleven, escaped with a book to her room as often as possible, already wary of the man who reduced her to tears at the dinner table with his rapid-fire math drills.

But he also had a softer side: quick to hug, kiss us on the crowns of our heads, give over-the-top compliments. He left us heart-shaped boxes of chocolates at the breakfast table on Valentine's Day and surprised us with bunnies and baby ducks on Easter. Dad gave the best "under-runs," pushing us up so high on the swings that he could run underneath as he let us fly, his laughter deep and genuine.

***

I shook my head to clear my memories and bent over to retrieve the keys from where they'd landed on the ground. Taking a deep breath, I got into the driver's seat. We sat together in silence. It calmed me to focus on my intention to treat him the way I wished he had treated me, which was my plan to liberate myself from decades of resentment, anger, and frustration.

I gazed at his troubled face, smiled, and gently squeezed his hand. "Ready to go, Dad?" He looked at me, relieved to no longer be in the doghouse, and nodded.

As we drove home along the coast, I directed his attention outward. "Look, Dad! There's a red truck. How many more do you see?" He settled into the ride, happy to look out the window and remark on the sights he found interesting.

Eventually, we had to go to elaborate lengths to remove his car — orchestrating a visit from the chief of police, removing spark plugs, hiding keys, and finally stealing it out of the garage.

Even with dementia, opposing him remained challenging.

***

"You are going to break it off with that boy now!" Dad thundered at me. At fourteen years old — just a year before Mom and Dad decided to move to Hawaii and sent me to boarding school — I was making my first attempt to truly stand up to him.

Dad, Mom, and I were in the kitchen after supper, and he sat at the head of the table, looking tired and grumpy after a long week at the office, his dress shirt and tie off, his white short-sleeved undershirt hugging his broad shoulders. Mom sat silently at the other end of the table, sipping her coffee. Across the room, I slouched against the counter, barefoot, arms crossed, wearing my typical uniform of jeans and a T-shirt. I was as close to the door as possible without being out of the room.

I was angling to get out of a family trip to visit Ellie, then a junior in college. The date conflicted with my one-year anniversary with Aris, my junior high school boyfriend, and in my young mind, it made perfect sense that my parents would leave me home alone to celebrate this milestone. I'd gotten quite the education in racial dynamics — not just in my junior high, but in my own home as well — as I'd naively wandered outside the accepted norms of our Main Line Philadelphia suburb over the past year, and I knew my parents disapproved of our relationship. But I also knew that, at the request of our family minister, they were trying to rise above their prejudice and tolerate my puppy love for this dark-skinned, basketball-playing boy from the wrong side of town. Our relationship might not sit well with my parents' upwardly mobile, status-conscious, WASP family bloodlines worldview, but on the other hand, our Christian upbringing taught that "God loves all the little children of the world. Red and yellow, black and white, they are precious in his sight," so I was pretty sure they'd come to their senses soon.

Scowling, accustomed to his temper erupting when he didn't get his way, I shook my head at my father's attempts to control me. He couldn't tell me what to do with my heart.

"What? Are you secretly married to him? You'd better not be! Why can't you be more like your sister Becky, who loves 'em and leaves 'em?" He'd worked himself into a frenzy. I guess the word *anniversary* freaked him out. Becky, seventeen and away at boarding school, had dated many different guys for brief periods of time. She was a popular cheerleader and athlete, not a social outcast like me.

"Listen to me, young lady. You'll do as I say or face the consequences!" His face reddened and his voice turned harsh. He hated to be contradicted. The vein on the side of his bald, round head pulsed.

"That makes my blood boil!" was a favorite phrase of his when he got mad, and an apt description.

I shook my head vigorously and waved my arms back and forth in front of me as if warding off an intruder. Tentatively at first, then louder, I shouted, "No, no, no! No! *No!*" I even stamped my foot. He always called my displays of emotion "theatrics," which I resented. Is there anything more heartfelt than a teenage girl's emotions?

He slammed his palms on the table and pushed his chair back so hard it fell over as he got up to come after me. I turned and ran out of the kitchen and across the brick-floored entrance hall, stumbling on the half-staircase that led from the main floor to my bedroom, my heart pounding. I felt his hand narrowly miss grabbing my ankle.

Suddenly pressed against the ceiling, disembodied, I watched this drama play out from above as I escaped his grasp and fled down the short hallway into my room, slamming and locking the door. *Bang, snap!* I heard him hit the door with his full body weight, but it held. What would he have done if he'd caught me? It had been a long time since he'd pulled down my pants and spanked me with a hairbrush, but the memory lingered. I heard him stomp away, and relief flooded through me.

Back in my body, I sobbed in fear and frustration on my twin bed. A few minutes later, my mother came to my door, asking to come in, explaining how Daddy didn't mean it. She rubbed my back as I lay on the bed, telling me, "Your father is *sick* about this whole situation." At that moment I imagined she took my side, letting me know she agreed his response was twisted and inappropriate. Much later I realized what she *really* meant was that *my* choices and behavior made him sick, implying that if I'd only do what he wanted, he wouldn't be upset.

***

I had carried this hurt and anger — and hatred, too — in all the intervening years. It had become a heavy burden. When I arrived in Hawaii to take care of Dad, I'd decided to consider the time together a gift, a once-in-a-lifetime opportunity. Caring for him could provide a real chance for reconciliation and forgiveness, and I hoped to provide patience, comfort, and protection in ways that he should have modeled to me as a child. If I could do that for him freely and joyfully, then hopefully I would be released from the baggage I'd carried for so long. I'd be able to finally develop my own point of view and make decisions according to my own sensibilities, rather than because he would or wouldn't approve.

So while I missed my husband and children and fumed about Leilani abandoning my dad, I knew that caring for him would be part of my spiritual journey. All my years studying the Cayce readings and the Bible had left their mark. What is knowledge without application? Nothing, really. Wisdom comes from the application of knowledge. I would take this opportunity to cultivate my true self, to meet the karmic forces of our relationship, and to apply the teachings of Christ: forgiveness, love, and sacrifice. It wouldn't be easy, but at least I had set an intention and would try.

One day while outside by the pool, I found myself kneeling at Dad's feet, wielding an oversized nail clipper to cut the "Captain" — his thick, yellowed, fungus-ridden big toenail. I chuckled and shook my head.

This is what love looks like, I guess.

CHAPTER 21

Refco

A week after I returned from those seven weeks in Hawaii caring for Dad and running my department remotely, Perry, the treasurer from Refco, called me. It was Columbus Day, and my family and I were at our house on Long Island, having spent the first part of that rainy weekend in Boston at a colleague's wedding.

Refco, one of our regulated broker-dealer customers for many years, had been a client of both Chemical and Chase before those banks merged, but I'd never handled them personally. When I took over the department in 2003, I'd gone around meeting all the clients that I didn't know, including Refco. We were their main operating bank. Over the past two years, I'd gotten to know the chief executive officer, the president, the chief financial officer, and Perry, among others. But he didn't usually call me, and certainly not on a Monday bank holiday.

"Jane, we've got a problem," Perry said, sounding nervous. "We have an accounting issue," he announced, then cleared his throat. "A $430 million dollar receivable that wasn't properly recorded. Just a little accounting irregularity, but it's been repaid this morning, so we have $430 million more dollars in cash today than we did yesterday. That's a good thing, right?" He attempted a small laugh. "You can deal with that, right?"

Liquidity is king for broker dealers. Having more cash is a positive. But maybe more was going on here than he was telling me.

"We'll give it a try, Perry. Let me see what I can do, and I'll get back to you."

Two days later, the CEO of Refco was led out of his office in handcuffs, and within a week, the company filed for bankruptcy. In hindsight, I could easily imagine what Perry didn't say on that call:

And what about if they arrest our CEO for intentional fraud? And eventually the president and CFO too? Can you deal with that?

EIGHT SEPTEMBERS

Not so much.

Apparently, for the previous six years, the Refco CEO had been transferring losses to an affiliate and making them look like legitimate receivables due from a client. He'd pulled another fast one getting that cash Perry told me about, borrowing $425 million from an Austrian bank using forty-three million shares of his Refco stock as collateral — shares that became worthless pretty much as soon as he'd been arrested.

Damn. The private equity firm that had invested in Refco had taken them public only a month before the phone call from Perry. The previous Friday, I had e-mailed the Refco CEO and president offering congratulations on their well-received capital markets transactions, even though losing that deal — the deal Tim had told me I needed to win and my investment banker partner, Bill, had personally pitched — put my department in the doghouse. Bill had been so anxious to get Refco's business he'd even asked Jamie, our CEO, to call and ask for it, and when we didn't get it, he'd said that missing the new stock issuance transaction was the "whiff of the year."

That was then. Now my department looked like heroes because we didn't have any of that unsecured debt on our books. Well, okay, not exactly heroes, but at least *vindicated* in our conservative assessment of the firm's debt capacity, even if no one else acknowledged it.

But we were still Refco's lead operating bank, so we had lots of secured loans extended to the various regulated companies in New York and London, not to mention risks related to trading, clearing checks, and wiring money. I felt the pressure to make sure Refco didn't cause any losses for the bank.

Once senior management had been removed, Refco was essentially being run by a committee of managers from the private equity firm that had purchased them, not seasoned brokerage industry professionals. Said committee did not fully understand that a financial services firm only has about twenty-four hours to reassure the markets before those very same markets turn against them and put them out of business — which is exactly what happened.

By midweek, Refco was effectively done. Their clients were jumping ship as fast as they could. The industry tried to put together a mechanism to settle all the trades, but in the end, it couldn't be done, and everyone sold off their own positions.

Luckily, the markets were deep and wide enough to absorb this activity, which was possible because Refco was "only" a credit event, meaning only one company collapsed and overall markets were stable. As a result, we could focus all our attention on this one client without worrying about contagion to our other clients.

While the parent company of Refco filed for bankruptcy, we were working with regulators and the clearinghouses to do what's called an "orderly unwind" of the regulated broker dealer. That's a process where securities are sold, customer positions are returned, and debtors are repaid, all under the watchful eye of the Securities and Exchange Commission (SEC). The SEC had a team in Refco's offices overseeing things, and each day became an adventure as cash and securities and client monies moved around the Street.

We were Refco's government clearance bank. We had also issued some unsecured letters of credit — basically IOUs — on their behalf to various clearinghouses, including the Depository Trust Clearing Company (DTCC). The letters of credit served as collateral for DTCC's risk to Refco. The terms of the letters allowed us to call for collateral from Refco at any time, so we immediately held any excess securities we had from our government clearance business to cover our unsecured exposure.

Everybody in my shop already knew the rule: no collateral left the bank without my say-so. That extended to Al's shop as well. But as the week wore on and more positions were sold or returned to customers, the specific securities we were holding were needed to make deliveries.

Dominick called me and had Rick, his counterpart at DTCC, on the line. GSCC and DTCC were sister companies, but they had separate risk management processes and separate collateral pools. From his perch atop GSCC, Dominick knew that we held excess collateral.

"Jane," Dominick intoned as if expecting me to follow his instructions, "we need you to release your collateral so we can continue the process of unwinding all of Refco's security positions." GSCC and DTCC were clearinghouses, not regulators, but they played a central role in the "orderly unwind" process currently underway under the supervision of the SEC.

Does he think that tone of voice will sway me? Personal feelings aside, I didn't take my orders from him.

"I'm not releasing any collateral while you guys still have our $50-million-dollar unsecured letter of credit outstanding," I countered. "I don't know what your risk situation is with Refco, so I don't know the odds of you drawing on our letters of credit. I can't risk it."

Those unsecured letters of credit were our biggest chance of incurring a loss. If DTCC demanded payment, it meant we would have to send $50 million in cash to DTCC since that was the commitment we made when we issued the letters — which is why we had the clause that said we could demand collateral from Refco if we needed it. Current circumstances definitely warranted needing it.

Seeing I would not budge, they offered a collateral swap. They had excess government bonds at GSCC that could be moved to cover the DTCC risk, and in return they would give us back our unsecured letters of credit.

Phew! What a relief. We might just make it through without incurring any losses.

It took some time, but we managed to get out of all of our obligations related to Refco without taking a loss. I entertained a few phone calls from various members of senior management complimenting me on how well our department managed the situation.

Then I received a call from Don, the chief credit officer of J.P. Morgan's Investment Bank, who had welcomed me to "the Firm" on my first day in Midtown. "Jane, I want to let you know again how impressed we all were with you and your group."

"Thanks, Don. We're a good team and we had all hands on deck."

"I attended a senior management dinner last night and Refco came up. I thought you should know that Hilary took the credit for avoiding any losses, shutting down any discussion of your role." He added a few details describing the scene.

Hilary ran the division of the bank that housed government clearance and money transfers. She was Al's boss's boss, and I didn't have any interaction with her, although I worked closely with a lot of people in her division, and we had coordinated with them during the Refco wind down. It pissed me off that she had diminished my role, but I didn't understand the implications.

"Come and see me some time," Don offered before hanging up the phone.

***

Later that fall, I was golfing with clients at a conference in Florida. Beautiful weather, soothing green vistas, camaraderie, and deal-making were far more pleasurable than being in the office.

But the office found me wherever I went, and with increasing frequency, I missed holes to take calls, sitting on the sidelines to negotiate transactions or handle the crisis du jour.

This time it was Don, who'd complimented the way I'd handled Refco, calling about Bernie Madoff. The regulated broker dealer Madoff & Company had been a longtime client of our department. Nothing fancy or risky, just the occasional overnight secured loan and some deposit accounts. We weren't their lead bank and had never made good inroads, but the firm's CEO, Bernie Madoff, had a longstanding solid reputation as an industry titan and former chairman of NASDAQ and the financials showed regular profits and a healthy capital base, so we kept at it.

Apparently, Madoff had an investment advisory side business my team didn't interface with, placing client money in hedge funds. Our traders and hedge fund bankers wanted in on the action, but they couldn't get access to the elusive Bernie Madoff, who was shy about opening his books for this particular aspect of his business.

The guy who covered Madoff for my group could get in the door through his contacts in the back office, though. Since we were encouraged to be team players, he set up a meeting for the head of trading and one of the credit risk people to meet with Bernie for due diligence. Don called me to discuss the proposed transaction.

He went over the terms. It started with us lending $1 billion to a fund and got riskier from there.

He and I both agreed the deal didn't make any sense. If we really liked the investment opportunity that much, why wouldn't we just put the bank's own money in and earn an equity return? Being a debt provider wouldn't earn us enough return for the risk we were being asked to take.

Okay, JPM passes.

I went back to my golf game, feeling like we'd dodged a bullet.

***

Later that night, Dominick stood in the open doorway of my hotel room leaning against the door jamb, his hands in the pockets of his golf jacket. I hesitated.

He sighed. "The longer you wait to let me in, the more likely someone will see me standing here."

I motioned him in, closed the door. We stood awkwardly, silently.

"Do you know why I'm here?"

I shook my head no, my eyes locked on his.

"Because you *want* me here."

That was a truth I didn't want to hear. Couldn't admit. *Wouldn't* admit.

He took a step toward me and gently touched my arm. "May I hug you?"

I looked away, barely nodded.

His hands slid across my red silk blouse as his arms enfolded me. He stroked my back with his thick fingers and breathed me in.

How could I possibly feel such comfort from this difficult man?

I pushed him away and out the door, amazed at the intensity of my feelings and ashamed of my inability to control them.

Just this one time, I assured myself.

Yet two nights later, Dominick and I sat on the balcony of my hotel room. *Innocent enough*, I told myself. The lights were off, so I could convince myself one would see us. Yet the full moon high in the sky provided light, revealing my self-deception.

We talked in low tones. I told him about the seven weeks I'd recently spent in Hawaii caring for my father. About the mediation with Dad's soon-to-be ex-wife, my responsibilities for his business affairs, my sisters' and my plan to bring him back to the East Coast.

We then fell into comfortable silence. He reached for my hand, and we sat there quietly.

After a while, I shook off his hand and stood. "This is ridiculous. I am not going to sit here all night and hold your hand. You need to go."

Silently, we went into the room and closed the sliding glass door. He swept me into his arms and held me tight. His lips gently touched the top of my head. It felt as if a butterfly had landed.

"I'm a prick, you know," he whispered.

And I did know that. But that was not the whole truth.

He released me and left the room.

PART SIX
Inundation

*"You have power over your mind—not outside events.
Realize this, and you will find strength."*
—Marcus Aurelius

CHAPTER 22

Warning Signs

As my team and I were managing the crisis from the Refco collapse, my sisters and I were plotting the return of our father to the East Coast where we could more easily and safely care for him. The Alzheimer's Association staff warned us that if we waited too long, he would likely refuse to get on the plane.

"Dad, we're invited to the farm for Thanksgiving! You know how you love Pennsylvania. Mom and all of us will be there. On the way, Becky will take you to visit your sister Char in Kentucky! Won't that be fun?" we said, using his own strategy of exuberant enthusiasm.

Dad agreed and ended up spending two months at the farm with Mom, which of course earned her sainthood among her friends. She did it to help us, her daughters, but she also did it because, despite the divorce, she still thought of him as her husband, and he needed care.

Besides, Dad was nothing but solicitous to her — lavishing her with compliments, hugs, and admiration.

"He even compliments my driving now!" she said, giggling.

She confided that she had confronted him about their divorce. "You divorced me," she'd reminded him, showing him the papers to prove it, "and married Leilani."

"Oh no, *you're* the one! She doesn't work for me anymore." He was oblivious to the double entendre. He shook his head and smiled at her. Mom knew it was the dementia, but still, it was gratifying to hear.

Every night he still dictated to Haidee, although from Pennsylvania he could no longer give her the tape from his Dictaphone each morning to transcribe. As his language had worsened before he came to the East Coast, she attempted translation as part of the transcription.

EIGHT SEPTEMBERS

> *Haidee, you have always been my friend, and you have done a lot for our company and for me, Haidee. One thing that I have to do if you can help me is Leilani. She is down in Honolulu, and she is working down there in a great big thing there, and that belongs to me and not to her. She doesn't put any of the money there to put it upstairs with a very good person, and I had put all the money up there for her and she just can't keep doing that. She needs to pay me for all the money I gave her up there, and she is not here any longer. Haidee, you have always helped me and we will talk to Leilani. Haidee, you are the best, and we will see if we can get Leilani to change things. Thank you for what you have given me, which is Sony to get through things, and you can do it. You are the best.*

Haidee marked a comment in the margins:

> *Okay, so you want to sell the condo in Honolulu. Should we let Leilani know that we are putting the condo up for sale? Perhaps she might want to buy it?*

Dad began to call Haidee every day from the farm in Pennsylvania, haranguing her to book him a trip back to Hawaii. She collaborated with us to keep him safe on the East Coast.

"I'm so sorry, Mr. Buyers, but that flight is full," she told him gently. "No, they don't have any seats available today. Maybe tomorrow... I know, I don't understand it either. But we'll keep trying. We all miss you here! Don't you worry, though. We are working hard and taking care of everything while you are away. Please enjoy your time with your family. You earned this vacation."

When I felt guilty about deceiving him and doubted our strategy, I remembered he was not capable of making his own plans. I told myself, *If he can arrange it on his own, I'll let him go.* Sadly, he had lost that ability. We knew he could not, and should not, travel or live alone.

There is a turning point when the disease overtakes the personality, and it no longer makes sense to argue, cajole, rationalize, or explain.

WARNING SIGNS

The kindest thing is to soothe the upset and accept the reality that the child is now the responsible adult and the parent needs protection. Provide dignity where you can. Meet him where he is.

***

In early 2006, Al and I took the East Side subway up from Wall Street and got off at Grand Central Terminal, a busy hive of people no matter the time of day. The high ceilings in the cavernous main hall created a constant din of trains, subways, storefronts, restaurants, commuters, tourists, runaways, beggars, and loudspeaker announcements, all joined together in the cacophony that is New York City.

Accustomed to the bob and weave required to navigate this living beast, I moved expertly through the crowd, never breaking stride, talking all the while to Al. After so many years as colleagues, we were comfortable with each other, and our jovial camaraderie felt like the most natural thing in the world.

Three blocks up Park Avenue by way of the Helmsley walkway, J.P. Morgan's world headquarters occupied an entire block, from Park to Madison, East 47th to East 48th. We went through the revolving doors and up the two-story escalators, badges out to open the turnstiles, then up to the executive offices on the forty-eighth floor, two floors from the top.

We were on our way to meet Hilary, Al's boss's boss, the head of his division. Aside from being named one of the top fifty most powerful women in banking by *American Banker*, she came from BankOne and had been colleagues with our new CEO, Jamie, since their days at Citibank. Jamie had just been elevated to CEO and president in December 2005, a year after we'd merged with BankOne. He initially focused on the retail side of the bank — branches, ATMs, and credit cards — but I knew it wouldn't be long until he set his sights on the Investment Bank.

"She's an empty suit," I'd been told about Hilary. But you have to be careful when a man tells you that about a powerful woman.

EIGHT SEPTEMBERS

I'd never followed up with Don after our conversation about Hilary taking all the credit for not losing any money on Refco, despite the critical role my team played. I presumed this meeting would help her understand why I ran the department the way I did and how that helped us in times of crisis.

We walked into her corner office, a huge square room with wood-paneled walls, windows on two sides, and blue carpeting. A seating area with a couch, coffee table, and chairs atop an oriental rug sat across from the large wooden desk where Hilary stood talking on the phone. She looked at us over her heavy brown glasses, low on the bridge of her nose, and waved us in.

An imposing woman — tall and sturdy with a reputation for being brusque — she came out from behind the desk to say hello and shake our hands wearing slacks, a knee-length navy suit jacket, and a flowered silk neck scarf. We were there to explain how Al's department, government bond clearance, interfaced with my department, your basic commercial banking business of lending, relationship management, and selling operating services. Hilary had oversight and responsibility for all of the operating services that we sold to our broker-dealer clients, not just the government bond clearing business, so it was important to have a good connection with her. Not that I'd properly thought that part through in advance. Our clients were important to her division's profitability — more so than the Investment Bank's — so I simply assumed she would be an ally.

She joined us in the seating area, pleasant and personable but clearly busy. She leaned back and ran her hands through her short brown hair, momentarily closing her eyes. "Okay," she directed, opening her eyes, "tell me about the clearance business. I want to know how and why your two teams work together." Her tone was no-nonsense, accustomed to ready compliance with her orders.

Al and I went to a lot of meetings together. He's a funny guy, and we had a bit of a shtick going — playing off one another, trading compliments, and disseminating information in tandem.

"Jane's got all the money," Al would say, a reference to the fact that my department did all the credit review analysis for his clients, set the credit limits, approved the loan advances, determined the margin rates for the collateral, and had responsibility for the balance sheet usage.

"Al's business is my favorite product that we offer our clients," I said. I had a soft spot for his department's unique and critical function that I'd come to understand and appreciate, as well as for the people in it.

We personalized the business that way, truly believing our old bank motto: *The right relationship is everything*.

Who knows what kind of impression we made with our lighthearted rapport and sincere explanations. I didn't always see the bigger picture or have a feel for executive-level politics, so I hadn't arrived with a specific strategy or desired outcome for the meeting. Naive enough to believe that when someone asked me to explain my business, they really wanted to understand it, I helped them do just that, like the good girl I'd been trained to be. Of course, the situation with my dad and all the work I was doing to manage his affairs also distracted me.

As we left, I dared to ask Hilary, "Are you going to the senior women's tennis event?" Developing senior women was a big initiative for the chairman of the bank, so he had arranged an outing for us at the US Open, where we would play on the outdoor courts, and I looked forward to it.

"God, no!" she said with a sneer. "I wouldn't be caught dead in one of those little outfits." Her dismissal effectively killed my hopes for a collegial conversation.

It wasn't my only awkward exchange with Hilary, unfortunately. Whenever we had a client meeting that included senior management, it was standard procedure to prepare a briefing memo with all the details about the relationship: credit extended, revenues earned, trading and operating business, meeting attendees' bios, and so on. We almost always met before the meeting to review the memo and discuss what topics would be covered in the meeting, who would say what, and to strategize about our "asks." Considered best practices, it usually worked well.

Once, rushing between meetings, I bumped into Hilary in the elevator at 270 Park Avenue. We had a meeting coming up with one of our clients and were in the midst of preparing the briefing memo. "When do you want to meet to prepare for the meeting with Merrill?" I asked her.

Hilary looked at me for a moment, sizing me up, then said, "What, you don't think I know how to talk with Janice? I've known her for years."

"No," I mumbled, confused. "I just thought you might want to —"

"Forget it," she snapped. "Not necessary. I'll see you there." She got off the elevator, and I continued down to the lobby, clutching my files and wondering what I'd done wrong.

What I *should* have been wondering about? Why Hilary was so interested in my business and what I could do about it.

***

Hilary wasn't the only one who had opinions about my business. My boss Tim's boss, Douglas, was not a fan. Douglas joined the bank from Merrill in the late 1990s, one of the first senior hires brought in to make us a top three investment bank. He'd succeeded and now headed both client coverage and mergers and acquisitions for the entire Investment Bank. It was a very senior role.

After J.P. Morgan had made good inroads as an investment bank for large corporations and financial institutions, Douglas decided that we would now target mid-sized companies. This meant his definition of "the competition" expanded considerably. Already annoyed that we financed investment banking competitors like Goldman Sachs and Morgan Stanley, now the competition included even more of my clients, and Douglas was determined to cut off credit to these mid-sized investment banks.

"Why should we use our balance sheet to finance the competition when we can use it to finance clients where we are the investment banker?" he reasoned.

This put me in the position of having to fight for my department, a profitable franchise with 250 clients. The broker dealers who used our operating services and paid us millions of dollars every year looked to us to provide credit. Mostly we made short-term and secured loans, but we also did longer-term, unsecured loans.

One of the managing directors in our group had proposed such a loan for his client. It had been approved from a credit perspective, but Douglas killed it because he didn't want us providing capital to the competition.

I decided to appeal his decision and approached him at a holiday party.

"Douglas, this is a long-standing client," I said, holding a glass of wine in one hand and looking him directly in the eye. "It's a good credit; we're going to earn a good return. This is important to the franchise."

I felt confident I had a winning argument. I'd used all the important touch points for getting loan approval.

"The answer is *no*." He looked at me as if I had a comprehension problem and walked away.

Unacceptable. I followed him and started again, "Douglas..."

He eyeballed me, drew in his breath, then announced, "Jane, there is absolutely *nothing* you can say that will get me to approve this deal." He turned to walk away again, shaking his head. Apparently, I'd been dismissed. I would have to accept defeat.

He stopped and looked back, gave me a half-smile, and cocked his head. "But I kinda like how you're willing to come back at me, unafraid."

***

Douglas hosted a women's lunch, part of a program designed to improve the pipeline of senior women in the Investment Bank. We were a group of about twelve vice presidents and managing directors, sitting in a large square formation, listening to Douglas's pearls of wisdom.

He shifted somewhat uncomfortably in his chair, clearly more accustomed to running client meetings and deal teams than mentoring sessions. We were discussing self-assessments, which we were all required to do on an annual basis.

EIGHT SEPTEMBERS

The format du jour was three pluses for strengths and three minuses for weaknesses. We females — or at least *this* female — diligently reported areas for development, a sincere attempt to grow and improve.

Douglas would have none of it.

"Know what I put on my three minus? I spend too much time winning deals for the bank and don't see my family enough. My goals? Tell me what I need to do to be the highest-paid member of the Investment Bank." He looked at us like we were a different species.

Yet again, I wondered how I'd ended up in this universe where I would never truly fit in.

But he had a point. My tendency was to be transparent and literal: *I won this deal. I generated this amount of revenues. I lost that deal.* I needed to be more proactive, and more strategic and intentional about how I framed my strengths and weaknesses.

Unfortunately, self-promotion was not my strong suit.

I definitely differed from my dad in that regard.

CHAPTER 23
May Day! May Day!

Ellie resigned from her children's education job at the Awbury Arboretum in Philadelphia and devoted herself to finding appropriate arrangements for Dad. She battled on the front lines, navigating the healthcare system, educating herself on the disease, and advocating on his behalf.

On our next call, Ellie reported, "I found a nice facility with a memory care unit, and they have a space for Dad! I ordered furniture from Raymour & Flanigan for his room, and it will be here tomorrow. Mom brought him down from the farm to look around yesterday. I told him it was his new company." Her voice cracked, and I heard her take a sip of something.

"How did he like that?" I asked with a chuckle.

"Oh, he seemed a little dubious at first, but I kept repeating it and complimenting him, boasting about how everyone valued his important work and how much we all liked the new building. When we were walking around to see everything, I explained that his room was his new office! He approved of the window and the view." I could hear the exhaustion in Ellie's voice, and the relief too.

"Good thinking," Becky said. "He always did admire a view. And a nice compliment!"

"The trickiest part was the locked doors. He did not like that. But the receptionist sits right in front of the door. I introduced him to her, and she played along when I told him that she was his new executive assistant in charge of screening who could get in to see him. That she would be his Haidee on the East Coast." Ellie laughed. "He turned on the charm right away and started flirting with her."

"Oh boy. Dad is still Dad in there, I guess. Great job, Ellie," I said, impressed with her efficiency and progress.

EIGHT SEPTEMBERS

Dad's mental acuity continued to diminish, although he did have amusing moments of semi-lucidity. The staff at his facility all wore blue t-shirts, and on one of my visits, he leaned over and announced conspiratorially, "The blue ones are the best!" His physical health declined, too, and his behavior with it. He bounced from facilities to hospitals and back as he received treatment and then got rejected in various places for being disruptive. He developed bladder cancer, which accelerated his decline.

One day in early May of 2006, Ellie called me because Dad was in the hospital again. I drove down from New York and met her at Abington Hospital in Philadelphia. I parked outside the emergency room and wandered through the chaotic labyrinth of corridors and nurses' stations in a daze, feeling disoriented and out of place. I finally found Ellie. She hugged me hard.

Clutching her thick binder cataloguing Dad's medical history and visits with various doctors to her breast, she got me up to speed on his status. "His fever spiked last night. He's not able to cooperate with treatment for the bladder cancer. He has another UTI." Her voice sounded hoarse, and her lips were cracked from dehydration.

Ellie led me to the curtained cubicle where he lay strapped to the hospital bed, tubes in his arm. The small space was crammed with medical equipment, which may or may not have been necessary for Dad's condition. It smelled like the rest of the ER: antiseptic and medicinal with an undertone of recalcitrant bodily fluids.

"Janey's here, Dad!" Ellie announced loudly. Her brusque and businesslike manner surprised me. Clearly, she had taken charge.

I kissed his forehead and took his hand. He couldn't speak, but his eyes lit up when he saw me. As he struggled to communicate with me, his eyes bore into mine and began to telegraph confusion and panic. Seeing him so frail, fearful, unshaven, and disheveled alarmed me. He had always been so meticulous about his appearance, exuding strength and confidence.

"Hi, Dad! How are you feeling?" I leaned in close so we could maintain eye contact. "It's Janey, your youngest daughter."

An eager strain crossed his face as he tried to understand, like a child searching for the right answer to please his teacher.

"I'm here with Ellie, and we're going to take care of you. You don't need to worry," I said as a surge of tenderness flowed through me.

He squeezed my hand and looked up at me. His expression struck me as frightened and vulnerable. Bent awkwardly over his bed, I could not leave his side. Ellie left to deal with the doctors and nurses, negotiating next steps, and I stayed and comforted Dad. Running the back of my hand across his rough, unshaven cheek and stroking his bald head, I kept him calm with my reassuring smiles and small talk, hoping to drown out the disturbing and unpredictable sounds of an urban emergency room in action.

The previous weekend I had come down with the boys to visit Dad when he still resided in the memory care facility. It disturbed me to find him upright at a dining table, his head hanging down to his chest, eyes closed, drool slipping from the corner of his mouth. Obviously medicated, I'd tried to rouse him.

"Dad, Dad! It's Janey," I called gently. "Dad, can you hear me? It's time to wake up." His eyes slowly fluttered open, and he raised his head. As his eyes focused, a big smile came over his face. "There's two good ones," he said, sleepily pointing his finger at J.J. and Will.

But now, only a week or so later, he'd lost his ability to speak altogether, and I couldn't be sure that he even recognized me anymore.

As Dad deteriorated and we tended to his ever-changing needs, we were still in court-ordered mediation with Leilani about the divorce settlement. An agonizingly slow process, the mediator advised the best we could hope for was that both sides would be equally unhappy. Each side met separately with the mediator, who then acted as a go-between, trying to inch the sides closer together. We, of course, saw Leilani as being obstructionist and difficult — missing deadlines, going silent, refusing to agree on basic facts — and we had not made much progress. A hearing had been scheduled for early June, but that was still a month away, and the untreated cancer accelerated Dad's decline.

While the divorce mediation lingered and our focus remained on Dad's health, I was also trying to oversee his business while running

EIGHT SEPTEMBERS

my own at the bank. We had not had time to complete his estate planning. If he died before they divorced, Leilani would get far more than Dad wanted her to have. We would need to quickly amend Dad's will to reduce Leilani's share, as he had been trying to do when she initially filed for divorce. I emailed our attorneys:

> *We have received word from the doctor that Dad's condition has worsened yet again. He is moving into hospice today and may last a few days at best. Time is of the essence, and we must submit the documents to the judge as soon as possible today. Ellie is obtaining the letter from the doctor, which will state that his death is imminent, and will fax that to you. We will have to go with the documents "as is," with the few cleanups that were identified yesterday, including the ability to change the will as well as the trust amendment.*

We moved Dad to the Keystone Hospice Center, not far from Ellie. Once a personal home, it now provided hands-on care for those close to death. The care was compassionate, designed to ease suffering, and the center had a friendly and calm vibe. A guitarist came by to sing soothing songs, and a friendly golden retriever bounced freely between rooms.

Dad stayed in a private, sun-filled corner room on the second floor. It had white ruffled curtains on the three oversized windows, through which treetops and blue sky could be seen. He would have loved that, had he been able to remember his Lancaster County childhood.

He lay emaciated on the single bed, his muscular, six-foot Marine-fit body a mere 126 pounds. His shoulders were still broad, if bony; his chest was shrunken, covered in curly hair turned gray. I fed him ice chips and moistened his chapped lips with Vaseline on Q-tips, trying not to notice the blackened roof of his mouth that clearly indicated death was approaching.

Ellie and I conferred with the doctor. "He won't last much longer," he told us.

We knew the ethical thing to do was to tell Leilani about Dad's imminent death. Like it or not, technically she remained his wife, and they had once loved each other. Our attorneys alerted Leilani's attorneys to the situation, and we received an e-mail summary of that conversation:

> *I spoke to L's attorney. I told him Doc's prognosis and that Leilani could come see him if she wanted to. He was appreciative of that.*
>
> *He asked who had authority to make Doc's health care decisions, and I said I did not know. He wanted to know if someone was "hurrying" Doc into hospice, and I said that the doctor was the one who was making the suggestion. He wanted to know if keeping him in the hospital was an option and if that would keep him alive until after the hearing. I told him I couldn't answer that question, but that he had a DNR order in place and could not be tube fed.*

The suggestion that we were rushing Dad into hospice as some sort of mediation manipulation horrified and angered us. I was frustrated yet again at the misrepresentation of the role his daughters were playing. Even worse was the suggestion that we should prolong his suffering and keep him artificially alive until the hearing date.

I needed to talk to Alan.

I went outside to the parking lot in front of the hospice center. The big stone building looked like the mansion it once was, gracefully set back from the road, its circular driveway framed by two stone pillars. The spring sun had coaxed the daffodils and dogwoods into bloom, and I felt its warmth on the back of my head as I searched in my Blackberry for Alan's phone number.

Normally, he would have been in his office in Honolulu at this hour, but he was vacationing on a cruise ship in Europe and had given me specific instructions on how to reach him.

Alan's loyalty to Dad was unquestionable, and I had come to rely on him this past year. His agreement to provide his advisory services to Dad and the company had made all the difference in our being able to obtain conservatorship. He'd supported us personally as well, calling to report to me his conversation with Dad after we'd taken away his car.

Dad had reached Alan by telephone that day. "Alan, I need you to do something for me. You did that great thing last time. You do it so well!"

EIGHT SEPTEMBERS

"What is that, Doc? How can I help?" Alan always spoke deliberately and kindly.

"Well, someone's stolen my car!" Dad sounded flummoxed.

Alan knew that Becky had arranged to have the car removed following my return to New York. He also knew why we needed to do it, so he cleverly changed the subject:

"Doc, did you know you were fortunate enough to play for not just one, but *two* undefeated football teams?" He shared a Pennsylvania background and an intense love of sports with my father — baseball, basketball, and especially college football.

"Oh! I did? Yes, I did! Tell me who." Dad loved to hear stories about himself.

"Well, Coatesville, of course, the Red Devils back in high school. Remember, they honored you with a Hall of Fame award last year on the fiftieth anniversary of that undefeated season." As an attorney, Alan had a mind for details, and his memory and meticulousness had saved the company many times.

"Oh yes, that was a good one!" I could imagine Dad's big grin hearing about that accomplishment.

"And then the infamous Quantico Marine Devil Dogs." Dad still had the team jacket hanging in his closet from that undefeated season in 1947 when he trained on Parris Island and flew as far as Texas and California to compete. He wanted to hear more of Alan's stories about how he'd played in the Gator Bowl that year, and then later at Princeton University with his friend Dick, the Heisman Trophy winner.

They never did return to the topic of the stolen car.

Alan's devotion went well beyond their shared love of sports and Pennsylvania. He'd told me the story many times.

"You know, Janey," he'd begin with a gleam in his eyes, his southeastern Pennsylvania accent undiminished by the years, "your dad invited me out to Honolulu to interview for the job. Back then, International Utilities, the parent company, required a medical examination, and of course mine showed that I had cancer. You know I had leukemia. Your dad tore up that report and threw it away. He hired me anyway, and I never forgot it."

MAY DAY! MAY DAY!

Twenty-five years later, in the wake of Dad's illness, Alan continued to repay that debt. He'd taken on additional responsibilities at the company and helped us navigate the complexities of running and liquidating the business while in divorce mediation with Leilani.

"Alan," I said when I finally got through to him on the cruise ship, my throat tightening and my eyes full of tears, "Dad is about to die."

"Oh Janey, I am so sorry." Even on a boat halfway across the world in Europe, I could hear the sincerity and sorrow in his voice.

"We're doing that fifth amendment to Dad's will. We have to do it before he dies." I couldn't believe I had to deal with these legal issues while nursing my dad over to the other side. If Leilani had just done her job and stayed by his side and taken care of him, we never would have gotten involved in his marital and financial affairs or even known the terms of his will until after he was gone, and she would have all the money. But she'd walked away and filed for divorce, transferring the burden of managing his life to us. She expected to be treated as if she were still his loyal wife and an entitled victim of his dementia-related decisions. My hatred of Leilani had morphed into something even more toxic, and I could feel it beginning to strangle me.

Alan — wise, calm, articulate, and understated as always — was empathetic and pragmatic in his advice. "Yes, Janey, that seems like the smart thing to do. You know your father tried to do that amendment before he lost his abilities. Get prepared to be challenged in court, but there will be time to deal with that later. I'm so sorry about your dad. He's a good man, you know." And he launched into the story of Dad hiring him once more.

Things were unfolding so rapidly that Becky didn't have time to join us from Maine. A journalist, she raced the clock to compile Dad's obituary, which would need to be distributed to the Honolulu papers as soon as he passed.

Leilani, however, flew into town without notice and slipped into the hospice center after we had gone for the day.

That same night, May 20, 2006, Dad died.

Leilani was by his side

EIGHT SEPTEMBERS

***

Leave it to Dad to have three funerals. The first, at the family plot in rural Lancaster County, he planned years in advance, sending notes and instructions to Ellie. She had the file and knew what to do — which hymns to sing, which Bible verses to quote. He'd already taken care of the tombstone, a six-foot tall, four-sided granite structure engraved on each side with dates, locations, and activities that defined his life. One side announced his place in the seventh generation in North America and listed each son from whom he descended, going back to the John Buyers born in Ireland in 1702. Another side listed all the places he had lived. Yet another listed children and spouses. Ellie hadn't planned on having to get Leilani's name removed in a mad rush the day before the funeral, but she got that done, too, replacing it with a verse from "Now the Day Is Over," one of his favorite hymns.

Jimmy, J.J., Will, and I drove to the old church in Pequea through acres of corn fields, rolling green hills, and Amish farmsteads. We shared the narrow, winding road with Amish folk in horse-drawn buggies. The Pennsylvania air smelled fresh and reminded me of my childhood as a whiff of nostalgia tugged at my heart.

We pulled into the wide, paved parking lot behind the white clapboard and fieldstone church where Dad's father preached in his post-missionary retirement. We got out of the car and walked up the high hill through the grass, my heels sinking into the soft ground, the children running, glad to be free of the confines of the car. An ancient oak tree shaded the left side of the cemetery where seven generations of Buyers men, women, and children lay buried. I could see the headstone Dad had preordered towering above the others, a monument to his importance, his desire to do well. The open grave hungered for a coffin, which was inside the church, waiting for respects to be paid.

The church smelled old and felt cold and damp even on the warm May day. There were many people in the small space, mostly family and East Coast friends. Mom, of course, and my sisters and their families, cousins from across the country. It surprised and touched me to see that a few of my office mates made the four-hour drive to be there. God knows my struggles with Dad's illness had been anything but private.

Dad lay in the anteroom, frozen in his dark suit, 52 cents in his pocket. His classmates from Princeton showed up, reminding me of Dad's love for his alma mater, his pride in being part of the Class of 1952, hence the coins he would be buried with. Teary-eyed, I entered to say goodbye, overwhelmed by the swirl of emotions competing within me: grief, sorrow, relief, anger, fear.

Would Leilani show up and interrupt this family reunion? Bad enough Ellie ran into her face-to-face at the hospice center the morning after Dad died, Leilani having waltzed in for the final deathbed scene after we'd done all the hard work of caring for him and managing his affairs while she fought us every step of the way. Resentment blossomed in my chest, making it hard for me to breathe. Did Leilani have to invade our Pennsylvania family history as well? My heart raced and my stomach flipped when I thought I saw her across the church, but my panic was short-lived. She did not attend; apparently her sister who accompanied her east came in her stead.

Dad's funeral instructions included a family choir singing during the ceremony. We had many strong voices and lusty hymn singers amongst us. Jimmy directed the choir in "America, the Beautiful," and I kept my eyes locked on his to hold back the tears that inevitably fell.

Following the ceremony, we all trooped out to the graveyard, my male cousins carrying the coffin. A graveside 21-gun salute honored Dad's service in the Marine Corps. A soldier crisply folded the flag on his coffin and presented it to his older sister Charlotte.

At the second memorial in Honolulu, both Alan and Mayor Muffi Hannemann, Dad's protégé, spoke at the standing-room-only service in the big Presbyterian church that Mom and Dad attended for nearly twenty-five years. It was an airy space, the rafters high above painted white, the sliding doors on the side open to let in the warm, soft, fragrant Hawaiian air. An unadorned cross hung on the massive lava rock wall behind the altar. The $50,000 organ Dad had made a big show of donating a few years before he and Mom got divorced played his favorite hymns.

EIGHT SEPTEMBERS

"I learned everything — from running a small business to lobbying in Washington to carrying the principles that I carry with me — because of Doc," Muffi shared. "No matter how bleak things appeared, no matter how dark the clouds, he always preached creativity, energy, and enthusiasm. He was a corporate giant who always wanted to give back to the community."

Mom sat in the first pew on the left; Leilani in the first pew on the right. Two wives, two lives. I didn't look at Leilani, didn't acknowledge her presence. She was no one to me. As expected, she had immediately contested the amendment to Dad's will. Since the divorce had not occurred, technically she was the surviving spouse, so we were in mediation again, consuming more of my time and energy.

I sat with Mom and my sisters, with William, age eleven, by my side. J.J. had come with me when Dad started to decline; now it was Will's turn for a trip to Hawaii alone with Mom. The youngest grandchild, only four when my parents got divorced and eight when Dad got sick, he knew Dad the least.

After the service, guests greeted the former and current wives, two separate receiving lines up the center aisle. Mom may have been the ex-wife, but she was the first wife, the one everyone knew and loved, and guests warmly welcomed her back for the first time since she had left abruptly eight years before. She accepted condolences on many fronts.

Ellie and Becky went on Leilani's line to return Dad's wedding band, but I did not join them. Cold with fury and resentment, I refused to witness her grief.

Mom and Will stayed in Honolulu while we three sisters flew to Hilo for funeral number three at Dad's current church in Honomu. When I'd brought Jimmy and my sons to Hawaii to make peace with my father after 9/11, the boys had participated in the Christmas pageant at this church, the small town welcoming them with aloha, no questions asked.

The funeral was small but well-attended by the local community. The three of us swayed and cried, lips trembling as we stood together singing "Abide with Me."

MAY DAY! MAY DAY!

Leilani ambushed me as we were leaving, pulling me into an unwanted embrace, forcing her mourning onto mine without permission. Hot with anger and grief, I couldn't get away from her fast enough.

***

Months later, I walked around the Ping-Pong table in Ellie's hundred-year-old basement. Dark, cool, and musty, the limestone walls and concrete floor were reminiscent of a time when such spaces were used to keep produce and pantry items safe from the hot, humid Philadelphia summers.

The long, wide room was crowded with outgrown toys in antique dresser drawers, sports equipment tossed in wooden barrels, an old couch and TV, the end tables I'd given Ellie as a wedding gift years ago. Smack in the center of the room was the Ping-Pong table, now laden with the detritus of my father's life.

Ellie had gathered his items from the assisted living center where he'd stayed before he died. She'd also gathered them from Hawaii after funeral number three, from the house that we still needed to sell, and from the farm where he'd visited Mom for his last Christmas and still kept his things, even though they'd divorced nearly a decade before.

There were cell phones and Dictaphones, billfolds and wallets, IDs and credit cards, paperweights and pens. Watches, shoehorns, golf tees, coin sets, cameras, and magnifying glasses. Nothing valuable, just mementos for us to choose from.

How masculine the table seemed, all blacks and browns, rectangles and squares. Little of it appealed to me. It seemed to me that I already had what was worth keeping — the memory of caring for him and the reconciliation it brought. The distance, the betrayals — both real and imagined — the misunderstandings, and the resentments had melted away in the moments of unexpected intimacy that arose while tending to his daily needs.

Amidst my grief and sorrow, the ongoing struggle with Leilani, and the work I'd taken on with his business and his estate, I realized I had

EIGHT SEPTEMBERS

gained what I needed — a chance to genuinely connect with him, to forgive him, and to reclaim the love between us.

CHAPTER 24
Reorg Assault

Refco had brought a lot of attention to my department. Not a lot of people understood what we did and how or why we did it, only that the exposure numbers were very big. The close call had scared some members of senior management, and it was now obvious that the firm had gotten too large and too complex to continue running the broker-dealer department as a vertically integrated standalone unit.

For over twenty-five years and across each of the predecessor organizations, providing banking services for Wall Street clients had been structured in an almost identical way: dedicated loan department, specialized collateral system, credit analysis, operations, client service, and marketing all in one group with tight control over loan extensions, cash and securities movements, clearinghouse settlements, and overdrafts.

This structure allowed us to have the visibility and insight into the Refco situation we'd needed — to know when we should continue to lend, when we should hold or release collateral, if we should honor settlements, and how money was or was not flowing into us. This setup had served the institution well through other bankruptcies and disruptive market events.

However, as a standalone unit, we weren't well integrated into the increasingly complicated organization. Something had to change.

But I didn't want it to.

We had a profitable business — lots of net interest income generated from excess cash balances and overnight loans to our client base — and we had the number one franchise for loans, operating services, and customer relationships in the industry. We were respected on Wall Street and served as an integral part of the infrastructure that supported the financial services industry. Our department structure and depth of expertise allowed us to maintain this position.

EIGHT SEPTEMBERS

During the spring leading up to my Dad's death, Hilary had sent one of her strategy people to learn about our department structure and what each person did. Tim, the head of the Financial Institutions Group and my current boss, told me to go along with it and be as transparent as possible.

Initially presented as a best practices review, I thought it would be a good thing, since we were a successful model that could be replicated elsewhere. But the first meeting disclosed the high level of profitability embedded in our client account balances. Since all the other industry segments in the Investment Bank had their customer balances housed in Hilary's part of the world, the desire to bring our profitable client accounts under her purview, as well, became the focus of the review. Suddenly, our department was under constant analysis — our headcount, job responsibilities, profit and loss statement, and so on.

Over the summer following my Dad's death, I began to get uneasy as the process got more and more granular. I suspected that my department might get moved out of the Investment Bank and into Hilary's division. Moving the group to another area of the bank might not be so bad, but since I had a meeting with Steve, the head of the Investment Bank, on another matter, I brought it up. Steve reported directly to the CEO, three levels above me, so I was taking a risk appealing to him directly, but I hoped he would want to retain our multimillion-dollar franchise and argued that the vertically integrated business model had been proven to be the best way of monitoring and managing risk to the Wall Street firms. I reminded him that the three predecessor banks that had done business with this sector had all been organized this way, and with good reason. We had tight controls over cash accounts, credit lines, and collateral and were able to manage risks on a real-time basis.

I told Tim about the meeting afterward. "Steve understood I'm worried about Hilary's inquiries into my department and talked about being my 'wing man.'" I'd taken this as encouragement from Steve, even though he'd made no promises.

Tim grinned at me and shook his head. "Big mistake, Jane." He paused, and my adrenaline spiked. "Those guys all circle up at the end of each day and get on the same page." He meant our CEO Jamie, Hilary, and

REORG ASSAULT

Steve, among others, who had all worked together with Sandy Weill back at Citi/Salomon Smith Barney and were now in the C-suite at J.P. Morgan. "They're a tight formation that doesn't keep secrets from each other."

"What should I do?" I fretted. What had I been thinking, putting my foot into all of that without getting reinforcements first?

"Just keep cooperating with the analysis and do the best you can," Tim advised, heading off to more important matters, such as advising Jamie on acquisitions for J.P. Morgan to consider and growing his own investment banking franchise.

One afternoon in the fall of 2006, David, Hilary's chief credit officer, came into my office at 277 Park Avenue. He'd been friendly with Doug, my old boss, and we'd developed a collegial relationship over the years.

A tall, solid man with an inquisitive face, his prominent nose sat below wire-framed glasses that revealed eyes usually sparkling with curiosity and good humor. David was an optimist — sometimes to the point of selectively seeing only the good — but mainly he was an intellectual intrigued by solving problems and wondering about what might be possible.

He never failed to tell me what a joy it was to speak with me, delighting in my presence in a way that would be suspect if it hadn't been so genuine. David didn't care if people underestimated him or didn't like him, and he did not take such things personally the way I did. His enthusiasm for his priorities read as passion. Whereas I had been a reluctant banker, often feeling like a stranger in a strange land, David embraced banking wholeheartedly, believing in the importance of the job, undeterred by politics and incongruities, his faith in the better angels of humanity obscuring his view of the lesser angels.

He was the only one of Hilary's direct reports with the strength and fortitude to remain a fan of mine in the face of her growing derision toward me. He understood politics but wasn't malicious or devious like some of her other direct reports, men who took pride in describing themselves as cockroaches able to survive any hostile environment. They did her bidding behind the scenes, but David had the decency to speak with me directly.

"Jane..." The tone of his voice and dramatic pause caused me to focus. He looked me in the eyes and held my gaze. "Jane," he said again, "I don't think you're listening." He waited in silence for me to connect the dots. I knew he was implying I wasn't reading the tea leaves, unaware which direction the political winds were blowing.

I thought about it for a moment and realized I *was* listening. Listening to the silence. The kind of silence that occurs when people steer clear because they know trouble is brewing. The kind of silence I heard from the Street when Drexel went under in 1990 because they'd made so many enemies, no one wanted to bail them out, preferring instead to pick over the carcass once Drexel was dead. The "I know something is going on, and I'm going to stand back and see what happens" silence. I realized people in Hilary's world had stopped talking to me, stopped cooperating, and stopped giving me heads-up calls or including me in meetings.

"Okay, David. I get it. Finally."

I went downstairs to Tim's corner office on the thirteenth floor at 277 Park, which was filled with piles of files and paper stacked all over his desk and conference table. Lucite "tombstones" commemorating countless successfully executed deals lined the radiators on the perimeter. Aside from the conference table instead of a couch, his office setup mirrored mine — except it was a lot messier.

I sat in the chair directly across from his desk.

"We have to talk," I said, trying to hide my rising sense of panic. "I think Hilary is planning to take over my department. I need to do something, but I don't know what."

Unlike me, Tim had mastered networking and was adept at advising senior management and playing internal politics. He traded in information, like any good investment banker, and he was ambitious. Keenly intuitive, he also knew how to read people, and he'd proved to be an advocate for me. He'd supported my going to Hawaii to care for Dad, and he'd let me manage the Refco situation without interference.

He picked up the phone and called Hilary. He asked a few questions, made a few comments, and when he hung up, he said with a nervous laugh, "Yeah, you're right, Jane. A tidal wave is coming for us. A reorganization is inevitable. You can't fight this, so get out in front of it. Try to control it so the right thing gets done for your clients and your people."

It was worse than I thought. She wasn't planning on taking over my department. She was planning to *dismantle* it.

One of Hilary's lieutenants took charge of the reorganization and ran it like a military operation. Meetings and conference calls dominated my days as we painstakingly went through all the activities of the group and reassigned them elsewhere in the bank. The intention was to conform our securities industry clients with the structure used by other industry groups, moving people and jobs into "centers of excellence" that had expertise in particular functions —although zero expertise in our industry. The assumption was that if they moved people from my group into these other centers, the expertise would flow with them. I worried about my staff, I worried about my clients, and I worried about the risk to the bank. The best I could do was get my people and their functions properly aligned and hope that we could continue some sort of "virtual" version of our vertical integration.

It wouldn't be long before I was pushed out of the reorganization process and told to concentrate on my new, more focused role: generating new business.

When the dust settled, I would continue to report to Tim in FIG with a small team of client coverage bankers who would still report to me. I would also have a dotted line to the head of the new Corporate Bank being formed, but since Hilary oversaw that initiative and viewed me as uncooperative, we weren't really welcome there. The bank took away our credit authority — which meant we no longer had the ability to approve any loans to our clients — and told us we were responsible only for revenue generation and relationship management.

By the end of 2006, the dismantling was complete.

***

EIGHT SEPTEMBERS

Dominick and I stood in the early December darkness outside the bank's world headquarters as he smoked. "You're the perfect woman," he declared, confusing me. "Smart, beautiful, funny, sexy. No man would ever let you go."

He said it so definitively, I wondered if it could be true. His reputation as a womanizer made me assume he had a perspective I did not. My own self-assessment focused on my flaws, the ways I fell short. I considered pride and conceit sins, so I often minimized my positive traits. My father's outsized ego had caused enough damage to make me leery of being like him.

Dominick had arrived uptown an hour late and had been impatient in the cab, according to his colleagues, who said he was anxious to see me. I was scandalized by his blatant pursuit of me, embarrassed that he would let his feelings be known so easily. What would people think?

I couldn't believe I'd followed him outside to keep him company as he smoked when, inside, I was hosting a party for over eight hundred clients. One latecomer arrived, and I nodded and smiled at her, acting like it was perfectly normal for me to be outside on the Park Avenue sidewalk having a one-on-one chat instead of upstairs entertaining the guests.

With the lights turned down and dark velvet curtains hung against the interior walls, the cafeteria had been transformed into a party room, the twinkling lights of stores and traffic on Madison Avenue shining brightly two floors below. The annual holiday party was big enough that I had no formal presentation to make. My responsibilities were to work the room, thank existing clients for business, solicit new clients, and make sure everyone had a good time. There were at least six fully staffed bars with top-shelf liquor, beer, and wine, and waitstaff circulated frequently, clearing glasses and dishes amid the talking, laughing, well-lubricated crowd. We prided ourselves on this event, a longstanding tradition that had grown over the years, been sidelined by the 9/11 terrorist attacks, and now, under my leadership, was back on the agenda.

I did not know if it would be our last hurrah given the recent changes to my department. Nonetheless, I was inexplicably out on the sidewalk.

"Do you consider yourself a wife, mother, or woman?" Dominick asked.

"A wife," I answered immediately, knitting my eyebrows together.

He paused, then cleared his throat. "Most women would say mother or woman."

"Well, I'm not most women," I retorted.

"I think I'm falling in love with you," he blurted, as if he couldn't keep it inside any longer.

I shook my head and pushed back the rising panic. "That's not possible," I declared.

He looked at me with hangdog eyes, and I could see the pain and vulnerability there. Something honest in his gaze pulled at me, encouraged me to believe his manipulative behavior meant more than just the desire for another conquest, that I saw something in him no one else could.

"Maybe in another lifetime, when the moon and the stars are aligned," I offered as I pushed myself through the revolving doors to head back to the party, leaving him alone on the sidewalk.

***

Four months later, in April 2007, I honored Al at his retirement party in that same cafeteria, one of the few times I felt relaxed and confident speaking in public. If it had been up to Al, he never would have retired. He loved what he did and knew everyone in the business. But times were changing, and he got pushed out without even the courtesy of a formal succession plan.

The party was the kickoff for what I called the "long goodbye" — the first of several events where I would toast and celebrate Al's career. We had a big vat of golf balls imprinted with his picture to give away to the hundreds of people who were there — employees, clients, and, given his forty years at the bank, lots of previously retired folks too.

EIGHT SEPTEMBERS

Jimmy came with me and as we entered the lobby through the revolving doors, we ran into various men in the industry who came up to greet me with handshakes and kisses.

Riding up the escalator, Jimmy said, "I get it now. You're the gazelle."

"Meaning?" I asked as I turned to look at him.

"Pack of lions," he responded with a smirk.

I rolled my eyes and shook my head, turning my back to him. I needed to focus on my speech, not the gender dynamics on Wall Street.

I wanted to give Al a good send-off. Not only had he been a mentor and long-time partner for me, but I also felt he'd been disrespected by his own senior management — the same senior management that had destroyed my department and discredited the value of our business model. Of course, my affection for him played a role as well.

In any event, I took a page from my father's book and created an acrostic poem using all the letters from his full name to articulate the attributes that made him special and beloved by his team — things like loyalty and commitment. His employees ate it up, and I got a big round of applause. I ignored the drunken idiot who shouted, "Get a room!"

At conferences and industry gatherings over the next few months, I continued to gather Al's clients and colleagues to give him the send-off I thought he deserved.

Life at the bank would be very different for me after he left.

***

"Just relax," Dominick told me with enough authority for me to comply, yet not so much as to make me rebel. It was a balm to give up being in charge of everything.

We were at another conference in the spring of 2007. We had been sitting in two chairs in front of the hotel room window, talking, and he had gotten onto his knees and sidled over to where I sat. "If you won't come to me, I'll come to you," he said, then rested his head in my lap. I tentatively touched his closely cropped graying hair for the first time, my fingers trembling, electrified. That moment of intimacy had progressed to the bed.

"Lie back. I'll do everything." His manner was gentle and tender.

I scooted up from the foot of the bed where I had been sitting demurely until my head rested on the pillows and my legs, firmly closed, were stretched out. I let my heels drop off and smoothed my mid-calf skirt primly around my panty-hosed legs. I stared up at the hotel ceiling, hands on my belly, wondering exactly who I was at that moment.

"Lucky for you, I am not intimidated by a woman's anatomy," Dominick announced.

Seriously? I winced at his arrogance.

"Like we're all the same," I spat back, propping myself on my elbows so I could see him. I hated any reminder that I was not singular in the universe. I hated myself for my own duplicity.

He sighed, biting his tongue, holding back a retort. I realized he wanted to make me relax, bragging about his competence. But it wasn't his experience with women that annoyed me. I had already capitulated to my inexplicable attraction to this serial adulterer. It was the fact that I hated being a cliche. Ever. In any circumstance. And here I was, willingly participating in the biggest cliche of all: a career woman cheating on her husband during a business trip.

I put my head back down and closed my eyes. *Technically, I'm not cheating*, I told myself. There had been no sex, no orgasms, no nakedness.

On the other hand, we had friendship, emotional intimacy, hugs, handholding...and soon fondling. Business meetings, lunch, dinner, golf.

A distinction without a difference as they say.

I let Dominick hold me tenderly for a few moments before I sent him on his way.

I put my head back down and closed my eyes. *Technically, I wasn't cheating*, I told myself.

CHAPTER 25
Shadow Banking

In August 2007, Steve, head of the Investment Bank, called me on my cell when Jimmy, the kids, and I were driving home from a two-week vacation in Maine. Alarm bells should have been going off. He'd never called me before, and since when did he have my cell phone number anyway? But I took it in stride, acting as if this was an everyday occurrence. He was calling about a trade dispute with Bear Stearns Asset Management that wouldn't go away.

Time to problem solve. My specialty.

After the dismantling of my department, my title didn't change, but my job description had narrowed significantly. My focus was now solely on new business development and winning investment banking transactions with my partner Bill. Tim and Bill were counting on us landing a big deal from one of our clients, and we'd been spending our time putting together a pitch for why we should win what Tim was calling "the deal of the year."

But I had a long history of putting out fires with clients when disputes arose, and this seemed to be why Steve was calling.

"Sure, Steve," I said, my pulse racing. "I can look into that and report directly back to you."

As usual, I put my head down and got to work. Unfortunately, I forgot about the three layers of management between Steve and me. Apparently, I should have kept all those people informed about the work I did for him. No one likes to be blindsided, and in my rush to get Steve what he needed, I neglected to update the chain of command.

I would continue to make that political gaffe as the credit crisis escalated and my new role — ostensibly marketing and new revenue generation for securities firms and hedge funds — morphed into full-time crisis management. Because the regulators were involved and we had so many client problems, senior management was instructing me directly, cutting out those three layers of management that I should have kept in the loop. I barely had time to breathe, let alone keep people updated.

Bear, Lehman, Merrill, Morgan, Goldman, MF Global, Royal Bank of Scotland, Credit Suisse First Boston, United Bank of Switzerland, Cantor Fitzgerald, Bernie Madoff. Who had a more challenging client list than I did? Well, maybe the guys covering the largest mortgage company in the country: Countrywide.

One evening a few days later, I sat perched on the arm of our couch, my Blackberry pressed to one ear and my finger in the other, my back to the kitchen where my family was eating dinner.

"Can they really do that?" Tim asked in a low voice, incredulous, as conversations were going on around him. He and his colleague were calling from the Federal Reserve Bank where they had been attending an emergency meeting trying to restructure Countrywide's $11.5 billion loan. As the largest mortgage company in America, their cash-flow crisis was bound to trigger an industry-wide problem, so the investment bankers were trying to work their magic with a debt restructuring.

But Bank of New York, Countrywide's government securities clearance bank, had thrown a monkey wrench into the process. They'd burst in and announced they were not going to do the tri-party "unwind" unless they got $2 billion in cash — basically, making a margin call to protect themselves against the declining value of the securities in Countrywide's account.

"Yeah, absolutely, they can do that," I said to Tim, who wanted to find out if Bank of New York had a legitimate stance in refusing to advance credit to Countrywide without an additional deposit of cash. I'd been steeped in the logistics and legalese of the clearing and tri-party business for a long time and knew all about our rights and remedies. Certainly, Bank of New York had the same rights we did.

Tim did not like that answer. "What? Why?"

"Well, what happens in the unwind is this: Every morning the clearance bank extends a loan to the dealer, so they have cash to pay back the tri-party lenders. At the same time, the bank takes the securities back from the tri-party lender and returns those securities to the dealer so they can do their trading," I explained. "In exchange for making the unwind loan, the bank gets a lien on the securities to protect itself against losses if the dealer doesn't repay the loan. Typically, at the end of the day, the dealer does pay back the loan, usually by booking another tri-party loan. But the bank isn't *required* to do the unwind by extending a loan. So if it chooses to make a loan, it has the right to demand additional collateral."

Bank of New York's demand for cash would force Countrywide to borrow under its credit facility — its prearranged loan agreement — because Countrywide didn't have a few extra billion dollars of cash just sitting around to meet Bank of New York's margin call. And that's the last thing the investment bankers wanted.

This reliance on intraday secured credit from the clearance banks was not widely understood. That had been the main point I tried to make at that first Fed Working Group meeting I'd attended so many years ago, but even now, the key issue remained unresolved: Like blood to the heart, or oil to an engine, the provision of secured intraday credit by the clearance banks kept the whole system running, and there weren't any viable alternatives when that dried up.

To compound matters, an operational process that had been built for US government Securities — a safe and sound, low-risk investment — was now being applied to riskier assets using the same mechanics.

As homeownership exploded and housing prices kept rising, the dealers grew their inventory of mortgages and mortgage-backed securities to keep the housing market humming. And they were able to do so by increasing their reliance on the tri-party market — borrowing cash from non-bank lenders to fund mortgages and mortgage-backed securities, then using the clearing banks' operating infrastructure to facilitate the movement of collateral and cash between parties.

But then housing prices plummeted. The value of mortgage-backed securities fell in tandem, and investors grew less interested in owning them. Those securities were getting riskier by the day.

"Tim, you know better than anybody that mortgage-backed securities are getting toxic. What if Countrywide can't find anyone to make them a tri-party loan tonight? Bank of New York would be stuck financing them. And the securities may well be worth even less tomorrow. That's why they want the extra cash collateral."

Countrywide was still underwriting new mortgage loans, but they were unable to sell them due to market conditions and had been forced to stockpile mortgage inventory. Instead, they financed them with third-party lenders using Bank of New York's clearance infrastructure. But those third-party lenders didn't want to get stuck with the mortgage securities any more than Bank of New York did. It was just like a game of hot potato.

"Hang on, Jane. I'm patching in Jamie."

Tim brought our CEO onto the line.

"That's how the clearing banks get comfortable doing the daily unwind," I continued confidently, even as I became aware of my heart thumping now that Jamie was listening in. "But our documentation specifically says we do not have an obligation to lend. If we think the dealer won't be able to refinance their overnight positions, or that we won't be able to sell them to cover our intraday loan, we absolutely have the right to give the securities to the lender instead of fronting them the cash. In fact, that's the bank's real obligation — to give the dealer's collateral to the tri-party lender if the dealer doesn't pay them back." I loved it when I could explain things to the investment bankers, since they usually acted like they knew everything.

Tim started to argue the point with me, hoping for a different outcome, but Jamie interrupted him. "Jane's right. Bank of New York is doing *exactly* what we'd do in that situation. Find a way to work around it."

I'd known I was on solid ground in my explanation to Tim, but still it was a huge relief to have the CEO confirm my position. I appreciated his deep understanding of the many facets of the bank's business. So many of us only understood our own silos.

Now Bank of New York had set the precedent, moving the theoretical concept into the realm of action: To protect itself, the clearance bank could demand additional collateral or refuse to do the unwind.

All of a sudden, this dark corner of the world — known as the shadow banking system — surfaced under bright lights.

It became evident that the third-party lenders, who were perfectly happy to earn a return and take a lien against the collateral when it looked like a safe, investment-grade transaction, had *no* interest in actually taking possession of the mortgage-backed securities or having to sell them in the open market to get their cash back. Not only did they not have any interest in doing it, they also had no operational ability to do so.

Wall Street's dirty little secret was out: It depended completely on secured financing from entities who could withdraw it on a moment's notice. Imagine your mortgage or car loan suddenly becoming due one day, and you are required to return the collateral — your house or car — immediately or be thrown into bankruptcy. All that leverage built up like a Jenga tower. Removing one or two blocks might be sustainable, but if everyone withdrew their blocks at once, disaster would ensue.

Truth: The industry would collapse the minute the tri-party market stopped functioning. As I hung up the phone and joined my family at the dinner table, I wondered who else beyond our insular Wall Street financing world understood that.

PART SEVEN

Frenzy

"That which we hide from ourselves and others has power over us and robs us of our true power."
Spiritual Energy Principle #5
Personal Transformation and Courage Institute (PTCI)

CHAPTER 26
The Fall

"Why are we hearing about this just now?" Ellie demanded. It was late September of 2007, and Mom had called Ellie from the hospital near the farm in Pennsylvania, telling her she'd had emergency surgery. Ellie, Becky, and I were not pleased.

"I had a little indigestion that wouldn't go away, so I called my friends Chuck and Kay. They insisted I go to the hospital," Mom said defensively, minimizing the severity of her situation.

She hadn't thought it necessary to inform her daughters, likely to keep us from worrying. Not that any of us lived close enough that we could have taken her ourselves, but still. It was serious and unusual enough that we should have been notified, at least in our opinion.

Mom often had indigestion and ate Tums regularly. She attributed it to her coffee and ice cream habit, but it turned out she had gallstones — more than five hundred of them. The doctors cut out her gallbladder, which was so enlarged they had to take it out in pieces.

"I'll be fine," she insisted. "You don't need to scold me."

No one bothered to check if the gallbladder was cancerous before they sliced it open. That omission released the damaged cells into our mother's abdomen, where they wreaked havoc. We were later told by one insensitive jackass of a doctor that no one knew much about gallbladder cancer because "only little old ladies get it."

Now she needed to heal from the first operation so she could have a second one to remove the cancer.

Ever since Mom had moved back to the farm from Hawaii, she'd been involved in getting a community center off the ground to provide a safe environment for the local kids, some of whom were getting into trouble with drugs and guns. It had been her vision, her community-organizing skills, her financial contributions, and her optimistic enthusiasm that had kept the project moving forward over nine years, bulldozing past community pessimism, political maneuvering, and petty in-fighting. She enjoyed using her executive function and being the one whose opinion people sought after so many years playing the supporting role for Dad. She'd always been happy to be a corporate wife, homemaker, and volunteer, but as Dad's self-importance and public persona ballooned, it had become increasingly difficult for her to remain in that box. I began to see that her "acquiescence" to the divorce might have been a cover for her unarticulated desire to exit the marriage, and I was happy to see her flourishing in her new life.

The groundbreaking for the Northern Columbia Community & Cultural Center had been scheduled for October, and Mom refused to miss it, so the second surgery would have to be delayed.

Meanwhile, back in New York, Jimmy and I argued about her treatment.

I sat on the couch and watched Jimmy pace the floor, animated and agitated. The boys were nearby, in earshot but not part of the conversation. "Janey, she needs to get a second opinion! New York has the best hospitals, and she's got to beat this cancer!"

"I don't disagree with you, Jimmy, but it's not our decision," I said evenly.

"We have to convince her! *You* have to convince her! Geisinger sucks compared to Sloan Kettering! She has to come to New York and get a second opinion!" He was practically shouting, which made me nervous.

"I get it," I said, hoping to calm him. "But she doesn't want to. She feels safe at Geisinger. She trusts the doctors. They cured her breast cancer, after all." She'd developed that not long after her surprise seventieth birthday party, but they'd caught it at stage 0 and she'd responded well to treatment.

"Not good enough! That's crazy. She has to get a second opinion!" I knew Jimmy loved her and advocated for what he thought was best, but his shouting rankled me, and it annoyed me that he wouldn't let it go. I agreed with him about second opinions and New York hospitals, but I also respected Mom's right to make her own decisions.

"What do you want me to say? It's not like making decisions for my Dad because of his dementia. She's a grown woman in charge of her own health care."

Like a dog with a bone, he pointed a finger in my face and said, "You have to convince her to get a second opinion. It's stupid not to!"

Frustrated at our inability to have a rational conversation, I shook my head and walked away. Mom would make her own decisions and live — or not — with the consequences.

***

Jimmy, the boys, and I headed out to Long Island for the weekend late on a Friday night in October 2007, after the city traffic had died down, to spend the weekend at our summer house. The following afternoon was the thirtieth reunion of my high school class at my Christian boarding school, which I planned to attend. Jimmy was not interested in going with me, his reason being that at the ten-year reunion, my high school boyfriend gave him such a tight Christian bear hug that it made him uncomfortable and suspicious. Maybe it was just as well.

After I got the boys settled in their rooms, I sat with Jimmy to watch TV.

My Blackberry dinged and I looked at the incoming text. It was from Dominick. *I'm all alone this weekend. Come see me.*

Shocked, I felt heat rise to my face and looked up. Jimmy was intently watching TV.

I texted back: *I'm here with my family.*

Dominick texted back: *So? Find time for me.*

I'd never seen him outside of our professional sphere, and it both petrified and intrigued me.

Jimmy looked at me with suspicion. "Who are you texting? It's so late."

"Work," I told him. "What else?"

He gave me a doubtful look. "You're always on that Blackberry. Maybe you're having an affair."

EIGHT SEPTEMBERS

"Don't be ridiculous, Jimmy. You know those investment bankers. They work twenty-four seven and don't care about anyone's personal lives."

I texted Dominick: *We're both MARRIED, remember??*

I turned the phone off and went over to Jimmy and gave him a kiss. "Come on, let's go to bed," I said, taking his hand and pulling him behind me. I still loved him and didn't want to be the kind of person who would betray their spouse. I thought my affection could ease his mind... and maybe mine.

The next morning, I fixed bacon and eggs while Jimmy and the boys sat at the breakfast bar. We loved having a big breakfast together, the one meal I felt confident cooking.

When I went to shower and dress for the reunion, I checked my phone. There was another text from Dominick: *I will wait for you.*

My heart lurched and I texted back: *I can't.*

He texted back immediately: *Please make me the happiest man in the world.*

I knew the right thing to do was go to the reunion and stay faithful to my husband. But my emotional attachment to Dominick made me not want to disappoint him. Plus, it was hard to resist being so desired.

I texted back, offering a bone: *MAYBE.*

He texted me his address.

While I put on my skirt and blouse, I decided that I needed to try harder with my marriage. I went looking for Jimmy, hoping for... Well, I didn't know what. Maybe a sign of some sort.

Jimmy was working in the kitchen, fixing something under the sink. I tried to get his attention, but his project preoccupied him and he kept complaining about what he needed to do, dismissing me. I felt tired of being ignored and talked over.

"I guess I'll see you later then," I said, shrugging my shoulders in frustration.

I got into the car, still unsure where I'd go. Thinking about the reunion, I felt a weariness and weight on my heart. Why did I want to spend my time with people from my past I barely knew anymore, in a place that would make me hyperaware of my hypocrisy and remind me that I had become duplicitous, just like Dad? When I thought about visiting Dominick, I felt magnetized, not only because of his desire for me, but because of the way he made me feel: like a rare and precious gemstone to be valued, admired, and protected. Even if it was an illusion, I needed that illusion.

Before I even realized I had decided, the car headed east, and I started to worry about what would happen if Jimmy checked the odometer when I got home and figured out I hadn't gone where I was supposed to go. I wasn't sure if I was just being paranoid or if that was something he might really do.

Dominick's home was not what I expected. When he told me he had a house in *the Hamptons*, I'd had certain expectations. But the house was small and shingled and sat tucked away on a side road with a gravel semicircle driveway in front. As I pulled my car into the driveway, I saw Dominick sitting on the front stoop, barefoot, wearing a sleeveless white tank top and gray sweat shorts, smoking the ever-present Marlboro. I realized I had never seen him in anything other than business clothes or golf attire, and I felt nervous about this next step in familiarity.

He stood and flicked away his cigarette, clearing his throat and walking toward me. "I feel like a little kid on Christmas Day!"

His boldness frightened me. I wondered how a married man could talk to another woman like that.

We hugged hello. I wanted to rush inside, self-conscious about being seen by neighbors or anyone who would know I was somewhere I didn't belong.

Inside, my eyes adjusted to the darkness and took in a small rectangular room with hardwood floors and an open floor plan. I sat awkwardly on a barstool at the L-shaped kitchen counter and put my bag down beside me, taking in the ordinary furnishings and finishes of a regular home, trying to reconcile what I saw with the reverential references he had made to "his castle" and my own expectations — sprawling estates like we saw in Maine and Hawaii. My critique embarrassed me, knowing the emotional significance of the place for him, a self-made man like my father. What was I even doing in another woman's home, let alone assessing her decor?

EIGHT SEPTEMBERS

God, I was an awful person.

If he hadn't told me a million times that it didn't matter and no one cared, maybe I would have been able to activate my own moral compass. But as it was, I couldn't. I didn't. I take full responsibility for that.

I stood and looked out the sliding glass doors to the built-in pool that was glistening in the sun, protected from prying eyes by tall evergreen trees swaying in the breeze. It was so peaceful and pretty, a perfect place to hide from the world, which is all I really wanted to do.

It wasn't long before Dominick took my hand and led me upstairs.

***

Mom's second surgery was a success, all margins clear of cancer. Not long after her seventy- sixth birthday, she was able to travel to Philadelphia to celebrate Christmas of 2007 at Ellie's house, frail and thin but in good spirits. She wanted to hear all about the new project my sisters and I had embarked on: building a family house together in Maine. Mom loved building and renovation projects and especially loved Maine, where her grandfather had bought a summer home in 1919. We poured over the blueprints and shared the decisions we had made with her, and I told her I'd drive her up in February. The boys had a brief President's week school vacation, and Jimmy was going to take J.J. to look at some colleges while I took Will with me to Maine to check on the progress of construction, a task my sisters and I alternated doing.

Before that, however, we sisters met in Portland over Martin Luther King weekend to purchase bathroom fixtures and door hardware. We were in Becky's car, driving to yet another store, when Ellie's cell phone rang.

Ellie put the phone on speaker and Becky found a place to pull over so we could focus.

"Hi, girls! It's Mom." We held our breath. We knew she'd recently had a checkup with the doctor and was waiting for results.

"We're all here, Mom," Ellie assured. I leaned forward and we all stared at the phone.

"I don't want to ruin your fun weekend together, but I have another spot on my liver," Mom said, her voice quivering.

"Oh no!" Ellie said. "What does the doctor say?"

We looked at each other, fighting back tears. How could this be? She was first diagnosed in September; the cancer was removed in October and gone by Christmas. How could that have changed in just one month?

"I need to start chemo and radiation again. This time with the Fox Chase Cancer Center in Philadelphia."

Mom had recently purchased a two-bedroom unit in a new luxury life care community near Ellie and was transitioning from living full time at the farm to apartment living. She'd had a ball meeting new friends, eating in the dining room every night, and participating in group activities. Luckily, she'd still be able to live there while getting this new treatment, and Ellie would be nearby to help out. If things got worse, she could transition to the assisted living wing, even just temporarily. It sounded like a good plan.

"Okay, Mom," Ellie began. "We'll be home soon —"

"We'll get through it together," I interrupted.

"We love you!" Becky chimed in over us.

I stared out the car window and wondered how I would do this again, working full time and caring for a sick parent. We still had our hands full dealing with the fallout from Dad's death. In fact, that very day, we had finally gotten Leilani's signature on the estate settlement agreement — twenty months after Dad died and three years after we began mediation.

I couldn't bear to think about losing another parent. So, I didn't think about it.

EIGHT SEPTEMBERS

***

Bonus season again.

We were having yet another argument. Jimmy wanted more money; I wanted more accountability.

"Stop being so controlling and greedy. We had a deal," he said, using a line that had worked on me before.

"Are you fucking kidding me? How can you expect me to honor that when you have nothing to show for it? I work hard for that money."

"So do I! I don't have to report back to you about how I spend my money."

I bit my tongue. I was prepared. I had calculated all the money I'd given him since we'd struck our bonus arrangement deal more than five years before. What I'd given him amounted to well over half a million dollars, and all of it was gone without any tangible return for the family. Gambled away, put into his music career, or otherwise consumed — I could never be quite sure which.

Still, after all these years, I held out hope that I could shock some sense into him.

I called out the total, daring him to take the paper with the numbers written down. Jimmy stood at the top of the spiral stairs and turned around to face me.

"Don't make me look," he begged, tears in his eyes. Then he turned away.

CHAPTER 27
Valentine's Day

Ellie called me the next month, in February. "Janey, Mom's like a wilting flower. When they give her fluids, she perks right up. But something is wrong. It's not just the gall bladder cancer. Can you come?" I heard the strain in her voice. She told me Mom had been hospitalized because she couldn't stand on her own.

I drove down immediately and met her at Fox Chase Cancer Center, a four-story, glass-walled building on a hill in Philadelphia. I planned to stay with Ellie for the weekend, as I frequently did after we moved Dad back from Hawaii. We worked well together — she on the front lines coordinating medical care, me providing emotional support and tactical backup as needed. Becky remained physically distant in Maine, on call and hoping for the best.

"Mom, I'm here. How are you?" I kissed her hello as she lay in her hospital bed, weakened and lethargic, a far cry from her normal athletic, can-do, optimistic self. She smiled and nodded, patting my hand.

"This is for the birds," she said, arching her eyebrows and rolling her eyes. This woman played golf and tennis and traveled; she didn't lie around in bed. I kicked into caretaking mode, brushing her white hair and putting ChapStick on her dry lips.

"Gotta have kissable lips," I joked.

Our extroverted and optimistic middle sister, Becky, always held out hope that things could be different than they were, but Ellie and I delivered the hard truth that the time had come, and she flew in from Maine the next day. Mom grinned ear to ear to see her.

"Now I have all three daughters with me," she said to anyone who would listen.

Jimmy and the boys arrived the following day, a cold and rainy Sunday. They had planned to come the next weekend, but after I saw

EIGHT SEPTEMBERS

Mom's condition, I told them to come immediately. J.J. and Will took turns massaging Mom's sore and swollen feet while Jimmy put on the Super Bowl to watch with her. He and Mom rooted for the Giants, but his money was on the Patriots, although I didn't know that then. When Jimmy took the boys home in the late afternoon, I told them I'd be leaving soon myself and would meet them at the apartment. I had meetings in New York in the morning.

Later, I sat by the bed and helped my mother eat her dinner.

My mind went back to one of my earliest memories, sitting on her lap at our kitchen table when I was four and still loved to snuggle with my "Mommy." We always had lunch together after she picked me up from kindergarten, and she'd make my favorite: baked beans and franks right out of the can. We ate from one bowl, using one spoon, alternating bites. Years later, when I was eleven, I'd awoken one night in pain, bleeding, not knowing why. Even with two older sisters, I'd had no warning about the coming "transition to womanhood." Mom had explained, showed me how to use the belt and pad, and then taken me downstairs, where we sat at that same table eating graham crackers and milk. The same table where Dad had ordered me to break up with my boyfriend while Mom sat there, silent.

So many meals, so many memories.

Now she was too weak to lift the utensils, so I spoon-fed her. Chewing tired her, so I waited patiently between bites. "Do you want any more, Mama?" She shook her head and frowned in disgust.

I'd always called her Mom or Mommy; she called her own mom Mother. But now I was the tenderhearted caretaker, not the obedient child, and "Mama" slipped out of my mouth as easily as holding her hand and stroking her cheek. I found I needed to touch her frequently.

I put her dinner tray to the side and fluffed the pillows behind her, using the remote to slightly lower the bed. I petted her head and smiled, looking into her eyes. "Why don't you rest now? Get some sleep. I'm going back to Ellie's for dinner, then I have to drive home to New York." I made sure she was warm under the handmade blue-and-maroon afghan, a gift from her friend, and tucked her stuffed hospital kitty, a gift from Becky's daughter Marisa, into the crook of her arm, then kissed her forehead.

"Thank you," she croaked, her voice barely audible. She blinked her eyes slowly and without raising her arm gave me a weak waggle of her fingers before nodding off.

That night, I couldn't bring myself to drive home to New York. It was cold, dark, and rainy outside and so cozy and comforting in Ellie's house — bright lights, soft seating, warm food, good wine. I felt the tug to stay.

Ever dutiful and driven, I told my husband and sisters, "I'll head home in the morning and go straight to the office."

Early the next morning, Becky called to say Mom wanted to see me. She had spent the night at Mom's apartment, taking care of the cat, and had arrived at the hospital to find Mom agitated.

"Okay, I'll come by the hospital now before I get on the road," I said.

When I got there, Becky met me in the hallway. "Mom had a bad dream. She dreamt she needed you and you couldn't hear her calling because you were in your house on Long Island. She'll be glad to see you."

She turned abruptly and went into the room. I could tell my competitive sister's feelings were hurt that even though she'd been right there, Mom had asked for me.

"I'll stay," I said after I kissed Mom hello, relieved to see her knitted brow replaced with a crooked smile as I looked into her eyes. I glanced at my watch; it was too late to make it to New York anyway. "I can do my meetings by conference call and head back this afternoon after the cousins come to visit Mom."

Our cousins arrived late morning in a cloud of perfume, presents, and energy. The hospital room became a dorm room, full of laughter and tears, stories and hugs.

Mom beamed as she introduced us to the nurse. "Meet my three daughters and my three nieces. Aren't I the lucky one?"

Monday afternoon, after skipping my calls to focus on my mom, I said goodbye to my mother for the second time in two days. "Feel better, Mom. You're in good hands here. I've got to get back to the boys and work. I'll come see you again soon." I hugged my sisters and cousins and headed out, scrolling through my Blackberry as I maneuvered my way through the hallways and down the stairs to the exit.

I got behind the wheel and began to start the car, but I couldn't bring myself to do it. I couldn't move. Something squeezed my heart and I couldn't breathe. Tears ran down my face, and I sat there in my car in the parking lot, frozen in place. I texted Dominick.

Me: *I don't think I can leave her.*

Dominick: *I understand. I'm here for whatever you need.*

Me: *I'm not sure I can go through this again.*

Dominick: *You can do anything you set your mind to. I'm proud just to know you.*

Me: *My heart hurts!*

Dominick: *Because it is so big.*

Me: *I guess...Talk later. Thanks!* I tossed my phone on the seat.

After a few minutes of deliberation, I called Becky. When she picked up, I started sobbing.

"What are you saying, Janey? I can't understand you; you're crying too hard. Where are you?" Her concern only made me feel more tender.

My voice trembled. "I'm in the parking lot. I haven't left. I can't. I just can't."

"Oh, good! Come back in then. We're in the cafeteria." She and Ellie and the cousins were visiting over a late lunch.

Becky rushed over to greet me when I got inside and hugged me hard. I felt relieved, settled. I knew I was where I needed to be, doing what I needed to do.

Mom looked surprised and happy to see me when I got back upstairs, giving me a smile and patting my hand. I accompanied her as the orderlies wheeled her gurney to her next test. I held her hand the whole way and promised to stay with her, keeping a lid on my panic as we all crowded into the tiny elevator taking us down to the basement.

Results of the CAT scan showed the tumor had quadrupled in size.

The doctors told us Mom had weakened too much for chemo and her cancer would be fatal, and that we should meet with the hospice people to understand our options before telling Mom the prognosis. In a daze, Ellie and I did. Becky stayed with Mom.

The next day we went with the doctor to break the news to Mom, who was sleeping heavily in her room.

Ellie put her hand gently on Mom's shoulder and said, "Mom, wake up."

Mom's blue eyes slowly fluttered open, and she smiled to see the three of us there: Ellie on one side of the bed, me on the other, and Becky at the foot, rubbing Mom's swollen feet.

The doctor spoke loudly. "Mrs. Buyers, we've figured out what's making you sick." She leaned over Mom to be sure she understood.

Mom's face lit up with hope. "Oh, goody! You can make me better!" She flashed us a quick grin.

"I'm sorry," the doctor continued, "but there's nothing more we can do. You are too weak for treatments. We don't have any more options. No more bullets in our gun." We glanced at each other, grimacing at the doctor's poor choice of words.

Mom's face deflated as the implication of the words sank in. "Oh, so fast!" At just seventy-six, she expected to live a lot longer. Then, as it sank in further, she added, "Oh, I'm going to ruin Sara's wedding!"

Ellie's daughter Sara, her oldest grandchild, had plans to be married in May.

"Mom!" Ellie cried. "Of course not!" Tears in our eyes, we assured her we loved her and would do whatever she wanted. Once she realized that the doctors were unable to keep her alive, we asked her if she wanted to stay in the hospital or go home to die.

"I want to go home," she said decisively. Caring for a parent with all her mental faculties was such a relief as she could make her own choices. We wouldn't bear the burden of deciding for her like we had to for Dad.

"Is there anything special that you want?"

"Home movies," she said and closed her eyes.

EIGHT SEPTEMBERS

***

Although her complex had a full care unit she could use, we were able to set Mom up in her own apartment with the addition of a hospital bed and visiting hospice care nurses. The first night back at Mom's, though, Becky and I were her nurses. I slept in Mom's room, Becky stayed in the guest room, and we took shifts looking after her. In the middle of the night, I knocked on Becky's door.

"Mom needs to go to the bathroom. I need help." At this point, Mom found it very difficult to move and could not walk on her own. In fact, she had been provided with adult diapers. But at her age, she could not allow herself to urinate or defecate in bed. We had to help her to the bathroom.

The two of us struggled to get her upright and then off the bed and into the wheelchair.

"Be careful of your back!" Becky warned as she tried to singlehandedly shoulder Mom's weight when we slid her off the hospital bed and into the chair. I suffered from chronic weakness in my lower back, and sometimes it spasmed. I nodded and grunted as we let go of her, and Mom landed hard on the seat.

"Hurrah!" Mom said, weakly raising her arms and giving us a thumbs-up. We all giggled at the ludicrous effort required to move her.

I pushed the wheelchair toward the bathroom and maneuvered it in, pulling her backwards and turning it so that she was parallel with the toilet. Becky and I looked at each other skeptically and I widened my eyes, wondering how on earth we were going to get her out of the chair and onto the throne. When we put our hands under her armpits to lift her 150-pound, five-seven body, she was limp, heavy, and uncooperative. She'd always been self-conscious about her weight — no doubt influenced by Dad's unflattering comments about the size of her arms — but she simply had a normal, athletic woman's body.

I leaned against the shower door to rest my back and caught a glimpse of myself in the mirror: pink camisole, maroon silk pajama bottoms, wisps falling from my pinned-up hair.

"Maybe we need professional help," I said, ready to declare defeat.

"I think we can do this," Becky said, wanting to spare Mom the indignity of yet another stranger doing this intimate task. She'd already witnessed our prudish mother endure the open-door bathroom attempts in front of various nurses and the full-body shower given by a male attendant at the hospital.

Shorter and stronger, with muscular thighs from years of gymnastics and yoga, Becky gathered her strength and encouraged me to work with her.

"One, two, *three*!" With an inelegant, lopsided shove, we got Mom out of the chair and on top of the toilet.

"All right, Mom, we'll give you some privacy now," I said, panting, and Becky and I left the bathroom. I checked my watch. It had been an hour since I had awakened Becky.

"Oh my God! I don't think I can do that again," I admitted. "That was fucking nuts."

"I know. How are we going to get her back into bed?" Becky wondered.

"Professional help," I declared.

Twenty minutes later, we went to check on Mom.

"Any luck?"

"No," she said, shaking her head. "Nothing."

"Maybe we should get you back to bed now?"

She nodded, defeated and exhausted from the effort, and discouraged the trip had been unsuccessful.

We tried to lift her, but it was nearly impossible. We had no room to maneuver around the toilet.

"Becky, that's it! We need to call for help. I know Mom doesn't live in the assisted living part of this facility, but there have to be nurses on call, someone who can come and help us." It was three a.m., and I was tired and frustrated. I had reached my physical capacity.

"Okay," Becky said reluctantly, still wanting to help Mom and hating to fail at anything.

We waited another forty-five minutes, then two big male attendants came and were able to finally rescue Mom and get her back into bed.

Three hours, all our efforts, and nothing to show for it.

EIGHT SEPTEMBERS

***

The next day was Valentine's Day. Pink and white balloons filled the large room and a basket of red and white carnations sat in the middle of the wooden dining table that doubled as a game table, with a bowl of Hershey's Kisses beside it and a red heart-shaped Mylar balloon tied to one of the chairs. Instrumental music from the forties played softly, welcoming visitors into the cozy room. The blue paisley couch in front of the window held three guests, who were sipping soda from plastic cups and eating potato chips and baby carrots. Two more sat in the oversized blue swivel armchairs, watching the black-and-white home movies playing silently on the TV screen that rested inside the large wall unit.

Picture perfect. Except for the hospital bed in the corner where Mom lay dying. We were holding a living wake for friends and family while Mom could still greet them, a tribute to her popularity. An act of love, a kiss goodbye.

"Things are unraveling quickly here," I told Jimmy over the phone that evening. "Do you want to bring the boys down to say goodbye?"

"I don't think so," he said. Jimmy had some old-fashioned ideas about death. He hadn't let the boys say goodbye to his own father when he was dying of cancer. Of course, they were a lot younger then. But I didn't share such taboos about it, and plus, it would be comforting to have them with me, so I pushed.

"Did you ask them what they want?"

"Will says no, and J.J. says yes," Jimmy said. "But we had a nice visit with her at the hospital last weekend, so I think that's enough."

"Well, I'll leave it up to you. My hands are full here. I don't think she has much time left."

"Give your mom a hug from us," Jimmy said, holding back tears. "Love you."

"Love you too. Goodnight."

I lay down on Mom's bed and had myself a good cry.

VALENTINE'S DAY

***

On Friday, I arranged flowers that had been delivered to Mom in the tiny galley kitchen. I welcomed the creative and peaceful respite from the task of caring for her and gave it my full attention.

I could see my mother on the other side of the pass-through, her head lolling on the pillow of the hospital bed. Becky hovered over her even though the morphine had reduced her agitation. There were people constantly coming in and out of the room, which still sported Valentine's Day decorations, dropping in to say goodbye or pray for a miracle, talking quietly, sharing memories. At the "party" the day before, Mom had been able to acknowledge them, but now she had entered the active dying stage; she was unable to speak, and her eyes were closed most of the time.

She often groaned, and the hospice nurse told us she was making peace before she passed. I knew from Dad's time in hospice care that soon the inside of her mouth would turn black, and the death rattle would come.

Becky looked over at me, her nose red and her eyes swollen. "Come over here and take care of Mom!"

I glared at her. "I'm happy doing this." *Don't fucking tell me what to do.*

Becky hadn't slept in days, refusing to take care of herself, running on adrenaline. She'd even slept at the hospital in a chair in Mom's room the night before we brought her home so she could help with the early morning transport. She'd refused to leave Mom's side to go to the funeral home with Ellie and me to make arrangements, forcing us to face the inevitable while she clung to hope.

"I want to tell the hospice nurse what happened last night, how the night nurse treated Mom. I don't want to leave Mom alone!"

After that first night, we'd gotten smart and hired a night nurse, but she wasn't very good, and she'd woken up Becky instead of me when she needed help with Mom, and she'd also been rough turning Mom over. Becky teared up, and her lips quivered.

The hospice nurse was barely ten feet away on the couch across the room, talking with Ellie.

EIGHT SEPTEMBERS

I felt stubborn. And mean. Becky wasn't the only one running on fumes. "Go ahead. Who's stopping you? I can see Mom from here. She's fine." Her bed sat on the other side of the little window opening in the kitchen, literally three feet away. I continued fixing the flowers and refreshing the trays of food for guests. Mom liked things done properly, and I knew how to do it the way she would want.

I remembered back to when I smoked and still hid it from my mother. We were at the farm, and she brought an ashtray into the living room so her brother's wife could smoke — in a house where no one ever had. My eyes popped out of my head. My mother glanced at me sheepishly, and suddenly I understood. Like me, her training in "being polite" outweighed all other considerations. She would be a good hostess, hypocrisy and health be damned. Her mother, long dead and an anti-smoker herself, would be pleased. Well, I would be a good hostess too.

I watched Becky approach the couch and begin to tell her story to the hospice nurse. She quickly became overwrought with emotion and broke down in sobs, exhaustion and worry finally taking over. I felt satisfied that I'd pushed her over the edge.

My energy softening, I came out of the kitchen and bent over the side of the bed to kiss my mother's cheek, stroke her hair, and hold her hand. I looked over at my sisters. Becky was on the floor, spent. Ellie had her notebook full of medical details and funeral arrangements in her lap. Sadness and gratitude flooded my heart. I lifted my mother's hand and kissed it. I realized we were all doing the best we could.

It had been a week since I'd arrived in town and only three days since the doctors gave her the terminal diagnosis.

She died peacefully the next afternoon, when I left the apartment briefly in search of solitude and a breath of fresh air.

CHAPTER 28
Bear

I could barely hear my cell phone ring in the noisy restaurant. It was close to nine p.m., and Jimmy and I were out to dinner with the boys and their cousins — Becky's daughter Marisa, who was visiting from college, and Ellie's youngest son Mark, who lived in the city. It had been less than a month since Mom died, and family connections felt more important than ever.

"Wait, Donna. Let me go outside so I can hear what you're saying." Donna headed up Credit Risk for Financial Institutions, never a good call to get late at night.

"Jane, there's an issue with Bear Stearns, and I'm giving you a heads-up should we have to address it. I'm not going over there without you." Donna's background was capital markets trading risk, and mine was loan and operating risk, and we had worked together to ensure the bank didn't lose any money when Refco suddenly went bankrupt as a result of fraud. But that was two years earlier, and a lot had changed since then — not least of all the dismantling of my department. My credit risk team had been transferred to Donna's department, causing tension between us. Nonetheless, she respected me enough to demand that I be part of the team — even though managing credit risk no longer constituted an official part of my job description.

"Okay, Donna, let me know what you need and I'll be there."

It was a fluke that I was in town, as I had intended to go to a conference in Florida. In early March 2008, we'd held Mom's funeral in Pennsylvania. She'd been cremated, but her ashes were buried in the cemetery where her parents and siblings lay, near the town where she grew up. The service, held on a cold and snowy day, was family only, and afterward we all caravanned to the new Northern Columbia Community & Cultural Center in Benton that Mom had founded. Over three hundred people showed up to celebrate her life. When we returned to New York, I'd gotten sick and stayed under the covers all week instead of going to Florida. The trip to the restaurant with Jimmy and the boys was my first day out of the apartment.

Just after I got in bed at eleven p.m., my cell rang once more. It was Donna again, saying she needed me over at Bear's offices in midtown. Having been through 9/11 and Refco, I knew it might be a long time before I would be home again, so I made sure to take a shower, wash my hair, and put on a fresh set of work clothes before I stepped out the door at midnight.

It felt eerie arriving at an office building in the middle of the night, a first-time occurrence for me that would be repeated many times over the next two years. The marble floors in the lobby of 383 Madison echoed with my footsteps, and the elevators were mercifully empty. Arriving upstairs, I found the corridors abandoned, offices dark. Outside the large windows, the streetlamps far below glittered against the black sky. I found my way to the conference room, where the exhausted treasurer and CFO were meeting with Donna and a few others from the bank, and joined the group reviewing the numbers. We were getting increasingly concerned that Bear had a cash flow problem—the kiss of death for a broker dealer.

Then Matt, our head trader, arrived. Shaved head, intense and opinionated, he took one look at the numbers and said, "They're toast!" What else could be said? We got up and went over to our offices across the street at 270 Park to figure out next steps.

By three a.m., we were on a conference call with Jamie, our CEO, and the president of the NY Fed, discussing options. I'd never worked with Matt before, but he and I were on the same page; it was very clear to both of us that the entire tri-party market was at risk, not just Bear Stearns.

"Look," Matt began, "all the dealers use tri-party repo to fund themselves. It's one thing if the collateral is US government bonds; it's quite another when it's mortgage-backed securities." His eyes practically bulged out of his head as he leaned his taut body in toward the speaker phone.

"We can't do the unwind," I blurted. "With Bear's lenders backing away and no new lenders to replace them, we need to exercise our right as their clearing bank to give the lenders the collateral they were financing instead of advancing the cash."

It was obvious now that Bear would not have the cash to repay an intraday loan if we made it, and we did not want to get stuck holding their mortgage-backed securities collateral.

"It would be irresponsible to do the unwind knowing that they have no way to repay us," I said, glad that Bank of New York had paved the way with Countrywide and everyone knew what I meant.

"And once we do that, every tri-party lender is going to pull their money out of the tri-party market," Matt declared.

I nodded my head vigorously. Thank God for having someone in the room who understood the situation and apparently had the credibility to be heard.

Bear, like Countrywide, had a cash-flow problem because it had created a lot of securities backed by commercial and residential mortgages that it could not sell. And those securities were fast becoming worthless as the underlying real estate fell in value and mortgage repayments were at risk. However, if we didn't do the unwind and simply returned the securities to the lenders financing those securities, the lenders would become the new owners of those securities, causing regulatory and cash-flow problems for themselves.

"If the tri-party lenders get the collateral back instead of cash, there is going to be enormous pressure to sell those securities, which will further drive down the price of the securities," Matt explained. The lenders didn't mind financing mortgage-backed securities, but they certainly didn't want to own them. In some cases, regulations even prohibited them from directly owning such securities, which would cause them to dump those securities into the open market as fast as they could.

Matt was right. There would be a rush to sell.

What he didn't say, but what the Fed well understood, was that the massive selling would cause prices to go down, and that would require other owners of those securities to revalue what *they* owned at the new lower price. That revaluation would likely trigger cash-flow and regulatory issues for *those* entities, and suddenly the Bear Stearns problem would become an industry-wide problem.

The contagion risk was real. The Fed needed to contain that.

With Refco, "all" we'd had was a single bankruptcy that did not infect the overall market. But with Bear, the credit problem could swiftly become a market problem, which could create additional credit problems. The circle of life would become the spiral of death — not only for Bear, but for other broker dealers, banks, the markets, the economy, the country, and the world.

It was Thursday night — actually Friday morning by now — and the Fed did not want to face the possible financial Armageddon that Matt and I described. They wanted us to support Bear through to the weekend so there could be a more thoughtful response to the crisis. That would require us to do the unwind for one more day, advancing the cash to the tri-party lenders so that Bear could trade or sell the securities Friday. But we couldn't. Even though Bear was one of the smaller players with a $37 billion tri-party book — J.P. Morgan had a $100 billion tri-party book, and Lehman's tri-party book was well over $200 billion — it was a sum we were unwilling to gamble. In a worst-case scenario, we would be left with a $37 billion overdraft, and trying to sell securities no one wanted into a declining market.

Jamie finally proposed to do what the Fed wanted, but *only* if the Fed guaranteed us for the full amount.

The Fed agreed to provide a $37 billion one-day guarantee to get us through Friday, and then the industry and regulators would have the weekend to explore alternatives.

Since no one else from the clearance operations side of the house had been involved in the midnight negotiations, it fell on me to prevent the unwind from happening until we got the guarantee in hand. The documentation process went down to the wire, and we barely got the guarantee inked with the Fed before markets opened in the morning.

We managed to make it through close of business Friday, and then the real fun began.

***

All weekend, teams of bankers gathered at 383 Madison and 270 Park to go over Bear's books and figure out how to value the company. Could we, *should we*, buy it? If nobody came to the rescue and purchased them, the regulators would put Bear into bankruptcy Monday morning and begin to liquidate the company.

Douglas, Tim's boss and the Global Head of Mergers and Acquisitions, led the due diligence process. A thick, squat man, Douglas had the build of someone who had been a wrestler in school. He was aggressive like that, too, always moving, circling, looking for his opponent's weakness. He led the regular client coverage meetings every Monday morning at eight o'clock and once, after Goldman reported their earnings — and had, as usual, beaten us — he remarked with a smirk that was part admiration, part admonition: "Somehow they've figured out the right mixture of fear and greed to motivate their people." His laugh was caustic and the Sunday school teacher inside me had cringed. *What am I doing here?* I'd wondered for the millionth time.

Now I found myself sitting at the table with Douglas, who was clearly in his element running this massive emergency due diligence session on Bear Stearns, with the added satisfaction of a competitor on its knees.

Every two hours the deal team would meet with Jamie and Douglas in a conference room, with people dialing in from overseas. We went around the room and each person shared what they had learned in their respective due diligence area. The first time we tried it, people were going into lengthy detail about what they were finding and what their concerns were, as if this were a regular due diligence exercise.

Douglas quickly put a stop to that. "Hey! Everybody, cut to the chase. We don't have time for this. Just put your number on the table. What's the maximum downside risk you estimate for your book?" Douglas wanted to figure out how to value Bear Stearns so we could determine what to pay if we were going to buy them.

We tried again. Equities, mortgage-backed securities, governments, repo, prime brokerage, foreign exchange: We went through every business unit and every trading desk across the globe essentially asking, what are the assets worth? What is the quality of the people and clients? What is the worst thing that could happen if we own them? My area of responsibility was liquidity. And Bear Stearns didn't have any. Without sufficient cash flow, they could not survive. They would either have to be bought by someone or declare bankruptcy.

I spent all day Saturday at the bank. In addition to doing the due diligence, I had to consider what to do about the rest of our client base. What would happen if we did a deal to buy Bear? Worse yet, what would happen if we didn't do a deal? We were the only ones looking at buying them; the alternative was bankruptcy. Bankruptcy would risk creating contagion that would extend to the rest of the market and, specifically, to the rest of our client base. But J.P. Morgan buying them would risk that contagion spreading directly to us.

On Saturday night, J.J. was directing Junior Sing, a highly anticipated and competitive event at Stuyvesant High School where he was in the eleventh grade. I told my colleagues earlier in the day that I had a hard stop at 6:30 but would come back after the show if needed. I had to pull myself away because it seemed my contributions at work were critical. But honestly, there were plenty of competent people there, and I had only this one opportunity to see the show directed by my son, so off I went, leaving in the middle of a conference call with the Fed. Such are the choices a working parent must make.

Jimmy, William, Marisa, and Mark were all seated in the dark auditorium, saving a seat for me, when I arrived toward the end of the prior class's performance. It was a competition between grades, and the juniors were up next. J.J. ran around behind the scenes making final adjustments before his class went on, and the overheated state-of-the-art performance hall buzzed with excitement. I felt proud of J.J. and his friends and kept my Blackberry off in honor of their efforts. I never did go back to the office that night, choosing instead the comfort of being with my family.

By Sunday morning, it was a binary decision: either J.P. Morgan would buy Bear, or they would declare bankruptcy; there wasn't time for any other potential buyer to appear. It became clear to me that I had to bring the rest of my team "over the wall" to prepare for whatever might happen. Those of us working on the Bear due diligence were on a confidential team walled off from the rest of the bank. People were added to the team — brought over the wall — on a need-to-know basis. Now my team needed to know.

When I came back from a meeting and told my team we were buying Bear for $2 per share, they thought I was delirious from working around the clock. A year before, the stock had been trading in excess of $150 per share, and even earlier in the month it had been in the $60 range. Their doubt had me questioning myself. But the rapid due diligence required we take a worst-case scenario approach to the potential losses in Bear's assets and the possibility of the markets getting even worse. Senior management believed that if we got the Bear Stearns headquarters building at 383 Madison and their prime brokerage business, then we got our money's worth. Nearly everything else Bear owned had been valued at zero.

To be very honest, I wasn't convinced that the deal wouldn't take J.P. Morgan down as well. It posed a big risk for J.P. Morgan, which is something everyone discounts in hindsight.

Monday morning started another wild roller-coaster ride. While we'd guaranteed all of Bear's activities — except its unsecured public debt — as part of the deal, there was a problem: The entire transaction hinged on Bear's shareholders' approval, and *no one* liked the $2 per share price.

I spent the week assuring everyone: "Yes, we are guaranteeing all trades, all settlements, all deliveries. Yes, we mean it. *Yes, I was in the room when Jamie said it!* Yes, you are facing J.P. Morgan now." Our creditworthiness would be sufficient to calm fears until the sale was completed.

On May 31, 2008, J.P. Morgan completed its purchase of Bear Stearns after negotiating a higher, but still exceedingly low, price of $10 per share, temporarily soothing a market just waiting to implode.

CHAPTER 29
Sabbatical

It required a certain suspension in my brain to hold back the moral question and focus on the logistics of having an affair. Once the line had been crossed to enter the relationship with Dominick, it was best not to probe the reasons why and just tune out the recriminations and inner reprobation. If I blurred my vision just enough, I wouldn't have to acknowledge my hypocrisy and shame. If I pushed away my awareness of the tawdry nature of the situation, I could enjoy the benefits of being doted on by this man

Jimmy had noticed I was feeling happier and told me, "I don't know what you're doing, but keep on doing it!" I felt like he'd given me permission to continue the affair — and to withhold that information. He didn't really want to know what caused the change in my mood. His life was easier when he didn't have to deal with my emotions. Eventually, though, dealing with the grief of Mom's death, the intense stress at work, and the secret of the affair got to be too much to carry alone.

I found the brochure for PSI, the Psychotherapy and Spirituality Institute, in the back of the church. I'd tried therapy before, and it was time to try again, but with someone new. This offering incorporated my spiritual life, and that appealed to me. I decided to make an appointment.

The therapist, also named Jane, had her office on the first floor in the back of Saint Bart's, the Episcopal church on Park Avenue. Sometimes I walked up the broad concrete steps where people sat eating their lunch, watching the crowds go by, and pulled open the main wooden door, immediately feeling the cool, quiet refuge of the stained-glass and stone-walled sanctuary. Occasionally, the organist was practicing, and I sat for a moment on a hard pew in the darkened room, drinking in the private concert, a balm for my overheated brain. Other times I slipped

EIGHT SEPTEMBERS

in on 50th Street between Park and Lex, where the security guard sat behind a high metal desk to screen visitors, then wound my way through the strollers that belonged to the children upstairs at preschool, where artwork was taped to the walls in the fluorescent-lit corridor.

Jane's office was small and old-fashioned with high ceilings, ornate wood trim, and a window overlooking the courtyard that she opened and closed frequently, trying to moderate heat and noise. She had a couch where I sat with my shoes off, one pillow behind my back, another clutched in my lap, and a box of tissues nearby.

To nearly every question she asked, I began my response with "Jimmy thinks" or "Jimmy says," reporting his assessment and critiques of me.

"It sounds like maybe Jimmy is taking up all of the oxygen in the apartment," Jane observed gently as she shifted gingerly in her chair. "We can create some space here for you to hear your own thoughts." She bent down and lifted her injured leg up onto the footstool.

I blinked, afraid to acknowledge this truth.

After few moments of silence, she quietly offered a suggestion. "Let's make this a guilt- and shame-free zone. How does that sound?"

Relief washed over me as tears of recognition met this unfamiliar concept. Suddenly, the corrosive nature of my guilt and shame revealed their power to negate all other thoughts and feelings before they even had a chance to emerge. No wonder I always felt exhausted.

She created an environment where I could tell her everything, and in this way, I began to know myself and see my situation more honestly.

I had three things I wanted from therapy: to grieve my mother, to get clarity on my marriage, and figure out if I should leave my job.

***

The close call with Bear's unwind caused Hilary's risk world to kick into gear and start reassessing the collateral they were financing intraday through the clearance operations. Suddenly, dealers who were getting 98 cents on the dollar against all their bonds were now only getting 95 cents on the highest rated government bonds, and as little as 50 cents against some of the riskier mortgage loans. What did that mean for the dealers? It meant that in order to clear and finance their positions, they had to put up millions — and in some cases billions — of dollars of additional collateral.

Under the old department structure, Al's clearance operations team would have coordinated with the credit risk team in my department to help determine how to value the collateral, how much to lend against the different types of securities, and how much credit to extend to each client.

But with the new setup — wherein I was a client coverage person with no credit authority and no official connection to the clearance operation — I was not part of the conversation, and separate groups in different parts of the bank made recommendations and decisions about how to proceed. When it was time for the policy to be rolled out to the clients, however, it fell to me and my remaining team to use our contacts and relationships to explain it and justify the changes, even if we knew the changes would be difficult for the clients to implement and would likely kill the business.

Those meetings were tense and exhausting, and I used all my political goodwill with the clients to be the face of this new stance toward the Street.

***

"I need a break, Tim. I want to talk about taking a sabbatical," I said, wondering if I looked as burnt out as I felt.

I'd finally pinned him down in May. We sat in his fourteenth-floor corner office overlooking Park Avenue, his L-shaped desk covered with stacks of files, dual flat-screen monitors between us.

It was the same place I'd been two years earlier when I told him my concerns about the future of my department.

Tim oversaw FIG's portfolio of banks, broker dealers, insurance companies, mortgage companies, and hedge funds, who were all stumbling under the pressure of rapidly deteriorating market conditions. We'd been in crisis mode for more than a year. After the dismantling of my department in 2006, Tim had asked me to take on client coverage responsibility for hedge funds as well as the broker dealers, hoping I could build as successful a franchise as we had for the broker dealers. No one seemed to understand that part of building that franchise was due to two things: first, our willingness to lend; and second, the way our department had been structured to cover the industry. I lost access to both under the reorganization, so I didn't know how to meet Tim's mandate. But I set about meeting the clients and tried to develop a strategy.

Due to the rapidly escalating market problems, however, instead of drumming up new business, I'd been dropped into one credit problem after another, once flying back and forth to San Francisco on the same day for a single meeting with a large hedge fund.

William, thirteen at the time, declared the trip "ridiculous."

Meanwhile, I'd been making the rounds, telling clients we were requiring more collateral to continue clearing for them.

A sabbatical had been on my mind for some time. I'd been running nonstop for a good three years, dealing with Dad's dementia, the lawsuits and mediation with Leilani, Dad's death, Mom's unexpected illness and sudden demise, trying to settle two separate estates, running my department, managing the reorganization I opposed, dealing with the financial crisis ... I was sick of my litany of woes and often wondered at what point my world had turned into a bad Lifetime movie.

Tim stopped checking emails and sifting through pink phone message slips and turned his full attention to me.

"I need to reset and regroup. I'm exhausted. I'd like to take the summer off."

It wasn't unheard of. Other senior folks who'd worked more than twenty-five years at the bank had taken sabbaticals. I even had one client, Spear Leeds & Kellogg, who *required* their partners to take a sabbatical after twenty-five years.

Tim looked at me, both sympathetic and curious, elbows perched on his desk.

"That's not the full story, is it?" His blue eyes peered at me pointedly, one eyebrow arched under his thinning sandy hair.

I answered cautiously. "Well, I really want to spend quality time with my kids, and all the hours at the office and traveling are hard on my marriage. We're still trying to sell my dad's house in Hawaii —"

"You're in love with someone besides your husband, aren't you?" he interrupted. His voice contained a bit of glee, and his pale eyes sparkled above his coy smile. It felt like he'd pointed an épée at me and shouted, "*En garde!*"

It shocked me. First, that Tim had said such a thing. Then, that he'd figured it out.

Or had he? Aside from being ashamed, I was paranoid. The bank had an email monitoring system, and questionable emails were flagged and sent to your boss for review. Had he been reading my personal emails? Running all my emails through my work account for simplicity's sake probably wasn't the best decision I'd ever made.

Desperate not to give any facial or body language cues, I wondered how I could ever command respect if the affair was discovered. I'd excoriated my father for the same behavior, spoken derogatorily about powerful men cheating on their wives. Wasn't I guilty of the same?

"Tim, even if that were so, I wouldn't discuss it with you." There I sat, Little Miss Prim and Proper. I could practically see my lips purse as I attempted to neutralize my features.

"Why not?" Tim was fully engaged now, impish in his delight to have something juicy to discuss. I remained silent and avoided his gaze, feeling like a specimen under a microscope.

He leaned back and tried the philosophical angle. "You know, marriage isn't easy, Jane. You do what you have to do to survive. Everybody cheats at one point or another." His own marriage was falling apart, too, although I didn't know the details. It happened to a lot of us during the financial crisis, working around the clock like we did, relieving stress by self-medicating with alcohol and affairs. But I wasn't about to discuss my private business with my boss.

I wouldn't give in. No love-life discussion.

EIGHT SEPTEMBERS

Tim had already made one major accommodation for me in 2005, when he let me work remotely from Hawaii for seven weeks while I cared for Dad. Now, he once again had mercy on me. No, I didn't have to confess my sins. Yes, I could take a sabbatical. Yes, they would hold my job for me. Yes, he wanted the best for me. I could start on July first and come back after Labor Day.

I wanted to cry with relief and give him a hug. Instead, I maintained my professional protective armor.

"Thank you, Tim. I really appreciate it." I shook his hand firmly without making eye contact and quickly left his office.

I felt liberated already.

PART EIGHT
Calamity

"Calamity is the perfect glass wherein we truly see and know ourselves."
—*William Davenant*

CHAPTER 30
Summer

I sat in the blue swivel chair in the living room of our new house in Maine, staring out across Saco Bay, finding solace in the gentle flow of the incoming tide. Only five months before, the chair had still been in my mother's apartment in Philadelphia, and I'd sat in it, watching her die. Now, partially because of her death, I had the summer off for the first time in twenty-five years.

My sisters and I were building this house when Mom got sick. After the pinball years of Dad's illness and death, the mediation with Leilani, operating his business, and trying to settle his estate from afar, we were happy to take on a fun project. We purchased the vacant lot not far from where our mother's grandfather had purchased a summer cottage one hundred years before, a small coastal community where Winslow Homer had painted and we'd spent many happy summers. There were fewer hotels and more private homes now, but the rocks, bird sanctuary, and bathing beach all remained the same.

We hired an architect and builder and drew up plans designed around the rotation of the sun and views of the water. Three sisters might not seem to be the ideal clients, but we had honed our consensus decision-making process through the years of dealing with Dad's problems. The house came in under budget and ahead of schedule.

We named it Eventide. In addition to being a reference to our view of the nightly sunset, it was also the tune to "Abide with Me," the hymn we sang together at Dad's funeral in Hilo. We loved the lyrics: *"Abide with me, fast falls the eventide, the darkness deepens, Lord with me abide, when other helpers fail and comforts flee, Help of the Helpless O abide with me."*

Mom got so excited when we purchased the land, but she didn't live to see the house built, never occupied the first-floor bedroom we designed for her to use.

283

EIGHT SEPTEMBERS

I hadn't been exaggerating when I told Tim we still had work to do to settle Dad's affairs. After ten days of relaxation, my brief refuge in the new house ended, and Jimmy, the kids and I left Maine and flew directly to Hawaii. We had the good fortune of selling Dad's house for 100 percent of the asking price, all cash. But it required a thirty-day close, and the 10,000-square-foot house had to be emptied out quickly. Everything had been packed up by Haidee, whom we still employed, and First Hawaiian Bank, the trustee of Dad's estate, since none of us could get there. Now we needed to sort through his stuff. Furniture, housewares, silver, sports trophies, business awards, clothes, personal effects — a lifetime of memories crammed into a storage unit the size of a one-car garage.

***

By the end of July 2008, we were back in New York. A month with Jimmy had frayed my already stressed nerves. Being so busy with work and my parents' issues had shielded me from his nervous energy and incessant talking, and I'd forgotten how irritating his argumentative "know-it-all-despite-not-knowing the-facts" attitude could be. Our frequent disagreements ranged from low-stakes skirmishes about travel logistics to full-on marriage-threatening battles. I didn't fully understand that his gambling was a symptom of an impulse control disorder, and that the disorder manifested in different ways beyond the gambling.

"You!" Jimmy bent over me, his angry face inches from mine as I cowered back on the bed, his eyes wild, his arms gesticulating.

He shouted, and I cried.

He pointed an accusatory finger close to my face, bringing his rambling and somewhat confusing and paranoid argument to a climax. "You're probably having an affair and in love with someone else!" His instincts were good, even if his logic was not. Truth was, I had been dodging him for a while, avoiding this very confrontation, although his accusations had begun long before reality caught up.

I was so tired of lying and hiding and arguing. I looked into his eyes and said tentatively, "What if it's true?"

He rocked back on his heels, uncharacteristically silent. "*What?*" He looked as if I'd thrown boiling water in his face.

I repeated my response with a little more strength. "I said, what if it's true that I love someone else?"

We had been married for our entire adult lives, longer than we'd been single. We met at seventeen, married at twenty. We had grown up together. Or, more accurately, we had grown apart together. Somewhere in the back of my head, I thought, *If he really loves me, he'll want to figure out how this happened.* After nearly thirty years of marriage, how long should I wait for him to assume some responsibility? I was deeply saddened by what our marriage had become, but I also realized my sorrow masked my burning fury. Child that I was, I had refused to acknowledge both feelings for years.

Jimmy was supposed to save me. We were going to leave our overbearing, emotionally immature fathers and fucked-up family dynamics behind us and create something new, something special, unique, healthy, and good. And in many ways, we had. We had created a full life with our sons, our music, our church. Ultimately, Jimmy's gambling and our inability to deal with its impact on us stole what we had built.

Jimmy was angry and hurt. Stunned. The stunned part gave me hope. He didn't argue, and he didn't attack. Surprisingly, he had no words — for once. *Maybe he's awake now,* I thought. *Maybe we can work this out and get back on track.* I felt relieved that I no longer had a secret. Guilty as hell, but relieved.

A few days later, he sat at the bottom of the spiral stairs that led to our bedroom. He put his hand on his heart and let out a nervous giggle.

"You're like Zorro," he said with a measure of awe, reaching out his arm and making an exaggerated *Z* with an imaginary sword. "You cut my heart out in one fell swoop." His eyes teared up. We'd both been invested in our "happy marriage/great family" story, unwilling to reconcile the facts of addiction, codependence, and our temperamental incompatibility.

"I love you," I said, unable to bear the sight of his anguish, or my role in causing it.

He was unaccustomed to betrayal and took my loyalty for granted. I, on the other hand, had decades of experience of being betrayed by him, putting my suffering aside, and offering him second chances. Was Jimmy finally acknowledging the cost of his gambling addiction, the many financial and emotional betrayals I'd endured over the years? Saying I'd somehow evened the scales in an unexpectedly elegant way? *Is that what I'm actually doing?* Or had I unconsciously identified the one thing — an affair — that would ultimately sever us? Maybe this had been the real reason I couldn't resist another man. It was easier to let Jimmy throw me away than to put my foot down and end it myself.

The hurt and resentment I carried from Jimmy's years of gambling — which I had considered forgiven — were, in fact, only buried alive. The more I pushed them down and away, the more they struggled to get out. They clawed their way to the surface in the form of my affair, and now that they had burst through to see the light of day, they raged with venomous abandon.

Jimmy's shock only lasted a few days. Then he went on the offensive.

"I knew when you started teaching Sunday school and stopped staying in the service for the sermons that your morals were going to slip. I gave up my job so you could be the big money-making banker. Look what happened. You turned out just like your father, you big hypocrite! I do everything to make your life easier, and this is how you repay me?" My guilt prevented me from launching a defense. Carrying the weight of the affair, how could I dare to correct his misrepresentations of the past?

"*Character before Career*, my ass!" he spat, throwing my high school's motto in my face. "Who the fuck have you been sleeping with? No wonder you got promoted! I bet you spread your legs for Doug! For Al! For Tim! You fucking cunt! Tell me who it is!"

The longer I refused to tell him, the angrier he became.

Then he pushed me. I fell back onto the couch and he raised his hands to hit me, something he'd never done before. He managed to stop himself from following through.

I knew we should get outside help. Gone were my hopes he might want to know why, might want to find a way to a reconciliation that included some level of shared responsibility for the mess our marriage had become. According to him, everything was perfect until I ruined it with my ambitious and immoral behavior. Never mind the decades of gambling and deceptions on his part, never mind the reality of *my* pain and suffering.

He forced himself to walk away, and I went upstairs to cry. That night, we decided to separate, taking turns staying in Mom's apartment upstairs, which had remained vacant since her death.

In the weeks that followed, Jimmy went on a rampage. The investigative skills that he used so effectively to ferret out Leilani's existence were now supercharged by his hurt and anger at being betrayed, and he started calling my colleagues, badgering them about who I was having an affair with. Since he had known them for a long time, he felt they owed him the duty of loyalty — like the one he tried to impose on J.J. and Will — with no regard for the lack of professionalism or the fact that their primary relationship was with me.

I am sure there are those who sympathized with him, or who suspected and disapproved of my behavior, but those closest to me, like Al, were kind enough to set boundaries and try to allow my personal life to remain private.

Truth: This was not the behavior of a man who wanted to reconcile.

***

Two weeks later, August 16, 2008, was our twenty-eighth wedding anniversary. I sat alone outside on the restaurant terrace overlooking the Atlantic Ocean in Virginia Beach, drinking a glass of wine and looking at the full moon reflecting off the water. At forty-eight years old, it might have been the first time I ever ate alone in a restaurant. I was happy. For that moment, I was at peace, enjoying the silence and beauty.

For years — ever since I found my first book on the topic in the Brooklyn Public Library in 1987 — I had wanted to come to the ARE,

EIGHT SEPTEMBERS

the Association for Research and Enlightenment, in Virginia Beach to take classes and study the Edgar Cayce readings. Work, kids, and marriage always got in the way. We'd come down once or twice to vacation at the beach, but I'd never had the time to take a course.

I took advantage of my sabbatical and signed up for a conference on life purpose. Maybe I could finally figure out what I really wanted to do with my life. Since it was our anniversary, I'd gotten Jimmy's permission to attend. At first, he'd offered to come with me. After finding out about the affair, though, he refused to come, which was a relief and certainly not the punishment he intended.

I'd arranged to meet with the author and longtime ARE employee, Mark, whose work I admired. Even though we'd never met, I felt like I already knew him through his books. Since I was a member and financial donor to the Association, Mark knew of me, and had sent me a copy of his book, *Willing to Change: The Journey of Personal Transformation*, in 2007 as a thank you for being a donor. A slim volume, it was deep and challenging but offered me hope that I could change my life.

During a break in the conference, I met with him for fifteen minutes outside his office on the second floor above the auditorium, the ocean visible through the window at the end of the hallway. He smiled as he shook my hand, reminding me at once of my missionary uncles — understated, sincere, old-fashioned. Even his black rubber-soled shoes, gray slacks, and white short-sleeved dress shirt felt familiar.

He asked how he could be helpful. I told him I was struggling under the weight of my job, my family obligations, and the death of my parents.

"How do I decide what to do?" I lamented. "I have so many priorities — husband, kids, work, family, church, personal interests — that I've neglected for years. I feel so lost and confused. I'm torn in so many directions."

I neglected to mention the additional complicating factor of another man.

He considered my words thoughtfully in his kind and professorial manner, not at all put off by this sudden rush of personal information in a first meeting. "Well, you know, Jane, we work with this concept that when you know who you are — really and truly know at your core — then what to do becomes self-evident. In fact, several courses of action may become available, all of which are appropriate or interesting, that you might want to pursue. But it starts with knowing who we are, what motivates us, what inspires us, what makes us unique."

I nodded, tearing up. This sounded right to me. Beautiful even.

And totally unattainable.

"How does one go about figuring that out?" I asked.

"Well," he said, a smile creeping across his face, "my wife just so happens to teach some workshops that help people with that very thing. There's one coming up in December that might be something you'd like to attend. I can send you the information."

"That would be great," I responded, wondering how on earth I would manage to get away for another three days at Virginia Beach, especially around the holidays. Wasn't I supposed to be going back to work full time at the end of the summer? Not for the first time, I considered making the sabbatical a permanent retirement. What would I do if I didn't work? According to Mark's theory, if I could figure out who I wanted to *be*, then what to *do* would follow naturally.

Maybe, I thought, the first step was figuring out who I *didn't* want to be.

CHAPTER 31
Margin Call

By the end of my sabbatical, I had decided that I would tell my bosses I planned to leave the bank. Like Doug, my predecessor, I would give a year's notice, find a replacement, and make a graceful exit to a new life.

I was scheduled to return to the office right after Labor Day, and figured all I had to do that first week was move into my new office at 383 Madison, the old Bear Stearns building that I referred to as the "spoils of war" since J.P. Morgan had obtained the billion-dollar office tower in the deal to bail out Bear earlier in the year. Then I would talk with Tim about an exit strategy.

I was wrong.

Maybe I should have paid a little more attention over the summer, but my personal problems had prevented me from tracking current events.

"I don't think my marriage is going to survive," I confessed to Becky, who was in town with friends to attend the US Open over Labor Day weekend. I burst into tears. I'd used the same line a week or so earlier when I'd gone to visit Ellie for an overnight at the farm. I'd wanted to tell them each in person, not over the phone like our parents had done.

"What? Why?" It was not hard to understand why they were confused. I hadn't ever shared anything about our problems.

"Well, it's a long story. In a nutshell, Jimmy has a longtime gambling problem, and I got involved with someone else." Jimmy had made it very clear that if I disclosed his gambling, then I also needed to fess up to my own sins. He'd insisted we tell the boys, too. I didn't think they were the right age for all the intimate details, but I knew he would tell them anyway, so I did it with him to control the narrative in an age-appropriate way — if that was even possible.

EIGHT SEPTEMBERS

My sisters were shocked, of course, and yet completely supportive.

"Oh no! Janey, I am so sorry," Ellie said.

"I'm here for whatever you need," Becky volunteered, and I wondered why I had waited so long to tell them the truth.

Personal crisis notwithstanding, back to work I went, as scheduled. The week was dominated by meetings with, or about, our client Lehman Brothers. By Friday morning I was in front of the Investment Bank Risk Committee with Donna, the cool, calculating Teflon-like head of the financial institutions credit team I worked with during the Refco and Bear crises. We were going through the broker-dealer portfolio, answering questions about Lehman, Merrill, Morgan, and Goldman — but especially Lehman.

While my attention had been elsewhere, things had deteriorated badly over the summer. I quickly learned that Lehman was in the crosshairs. There would be no more advocating on behalf of my broker-dealer customers. Nobody trusted any of my clients, and nobody cared about anything other than J.P. Morgan protecting itself.

One day, I was instructed to attend a meeting with Hilary and Lehman's new CFO, Ian. Ian had served on the Fed working committee on clearance and settlement of government bonds, so we had gotten to know each other in that context. He'd come up with a brainstorm to create a "New Bank" to centralize the clearance and settlement process, although the key question of intraday liquidity still remained unsolved. In my opinion, his plan was a sleight-of-hand initiative, another one of those collective delusions that allowed business as usual to continue without making substantive change. I also thought maybe Ian was a little too clever for his own good. A previous meeting between Ian and Hilary that I'd organized had not gone well; each tried to be the smartest person in the room and let me know afterward they were unimpressed with one another.

At this meeting, Erin, the former CFO, joined Ian. She had come from the hedge fund side of the business and looked more like a model than a banker — spiky blonde hair, black fingernails, Jimmy Choos, short skirts. She was smart and articulate, but she had been tossed into the deep end as a Hail Mary pass by Fuld, Lehman's CEO. Ian and Erin tried to sell us on their plan to separate the firm into Good Lehman and Bad Lehman, explaining how they were going to raise money and why we should be comfortable remaining their banker and government clearance bank. We took it all under advisement, but it struck me as yet another sleight of hand.

Walking back to 270 Park, Hilary — lumbering along in her flats, pantsuit, and oversized raincoat — raised her eyebrows and smirked about Erin, "Don't put *her* in front of Jamie. She'll get whatever she wants." I kept my mouth shut.

The operating committee met three times a day, at seven a.m., noon, and five p.m., and twice a day on weekends. Just like we did with Bear, people called in from every trading desk around the globe, sharing commentary on what markets were doing, what was happening with clients, and how meetings with regulators were going. While not senior enough to be on the operating committee, as point person for the broker dealers, I was expected to be at all the meetings, sharing — but mostly receiving — information.

As a member of the DTCC risk committee, as well, I attended multiple calls every day to discuss real-time member and industry problems. Constantly moving with my notebook in hand, ricocheting between meetings, conference calls, buildings, and rooms, I didn't have much time to think, only to react. Efficiency and multitasking were my hallmarks.

***

On the morning of September 11, 2008, I sat at the oval conference table in the boardroom on the forty-eighth floor at 270 Park Avenue. All the seats at the table were full. Jamie, our chief executive officer, sat at the head of the table, in full command, his thick head of hair starting to gray. Next to him sat Steve, the head of the Investment Bank, the one who'd called me on my cell the previous summer about the Bear Stearns trade dispute. He had kind brown eyes and a thick white mustache that made him look a bit like Sam Elliott. Douglas, the aggressive head of client coverage, attended, his dark-brown eyes and round face serious beneath his closely cropped hair. With them at the table were the chief risk officer, the head of the Private Bank, the chief financial officer, and the treasurer. The heads of every trading desk were either in the room or on the teleconference phone, which sat in the middle of the table with microphone tentacles spreading in all directions like a big spider. Senior credit officers from London and Tokyo were on the line as well.

They were almost all men — maybe there were two other women in the room — and every single person was senior in rank to me.

The topic at hand was Lehman Brothers, but it could have been one of several other entities, since investment banks, broker dealers, insurance companies, finance companies, hedge funds, and money market funds were all under duress across the globe, and under scrutiny by this same group. The credit crunch spiraled out of control, feeding on itself, squeezing more and more participants to death.

How much exposure did we have to Lehman? How much collateral did we have? What kind of documentation existed? What kinds of legal risks were involved? What did we need to keep banking them? Why *should* we keep banking them? What were the chances of them filing for bankruptcy? What would their bankruptcy do to the rest of the market?

My decades of customer focus urged me to find a solution to save my client, but it became very clear that the goal — the first, foremost, and only goal — was to protect the bank.

Through some combination of analysis, debate, and self-protection, we determined that we needed $5 billion more in collateral, and this time it needed to be cash.

Jamie leaned back in his chair and looked around the room. He said to the head of the Investment Bank, "Steve, call Fuld," the Lehman CEO. Then he pointed at me. "You, call your contact in the treasurer's office. Let them know we mean business."

Ignoring the sense of dread and reluctance that seized my chest, I got up and went to my office to do as I was told.

MARGIN CALL

***

"Paolo, it's Jane."

I first met Paolo, the global treasurer of Lehman Brothers, in 2003 when I went to London to meet with clients after becoming head of the broker-dealer division. The bank hosted an annual party for European clients as part of a weeklong set of meetings to talk about existing business, new business opportunities, relationship issues, current market conditions, and organizational changes. Our man on the ground, Bryn, was their primary contact, and he organized the meeting schedule and coordinated the dinner. Previous dinners had been held at the Tower of London and the Victoria and Albert Museum, but in 2003 we were at The Ivy, a trendy restaurant popular with famous musicians and movie stars as well as investment bankers. A lot had happened in the five years since that dinner.

"The situation has changed, Paolo. We need more collateral." With my elbows on my desk, I hunched over my phone and spoke intently into the receiver pressed tightly to my left ear.

I could hear his pen scratching furiously across his notepad. I knew he was writing down my every word, anticipating the day when the tables were turned and he could use them against me.

"How much more?" He sounded wary.

"Five billion. Cash. Before the open tomorrow." The number had been determined less than an hour before. I knew it was a big ask — too big for them, yet not big enough for us — but I had no choice but to make the call.

I could almost hear his gasp. His pen stopped. Then there was silence. I held my breath.

"We've already given you a significant amount of collateral," he said stiffly, his British accent clipped. By Lehman's count, they already had pledged more than $10 billion in additional collateral.

"Well, we don't agree with your valuations," I retorted evenly.

They'd given us $3 billion worth of bonds that were highly rated, but the rating was based on a guarantee from themselves. We valued that collateral at zero; they claimed it was still worth $3 billion.

"And markets keep deteriorating," I continued. "We want to continue operating for you and trading with you. We don't want to take any actions that will be visible to the market. The cash collateral will allow us to continue to do business as usual with you in the market and settle your trades. Like we always do."

I tried to sell him on the upside of giving us the collateral. In order to avoid panic and contagion in the marketplace, appearances mattered, and getting more collateral would allow us to hedge the multibillion dollar risks we took every day by trading with, lending to, and clearing for Lehman — a rapidly declining credit counterpart, and one whose explanations and strategies seemed more far-fetched every day.

I wasn't explicit about what would happen if Lehman didn't provide the collateral, but I didn't need to be. Paolo knew how dependent they were on us and how the dominoes would fall if J.P. Morgan backed away from Lehman.

It was a tense conversation, difficult for both of us. Our normal relationship — me the banker, he the valued client — was usually collegial and respectful, but it had been taken over by the masters of the universe, and forces were out of our control.

What neither of us said but both of us knew?

Game Over.

Without an eleventh-hour rescue, this margin call would put Lehman, the fourth-largest investment bank in the world, permanently out of business.

CHAPTER 32
Lehman Weekend

Sunday, September 14, 2008, I told everyone at the bank I would be out of pocket between eleven a.m. and noon. It marked the first day of the new church year, and another "Welcome Back Sunday" at West End Collegiate Church. I taught Sunday school to second through fourth graders and wanted to honor my obligation to be there for them.

At 12:15, I left the church, pushing the heavy wooden side doors of the church open with my shoulder. I pulled my Blackberry out of my pocketbook and was bombarded with voicemails and emails. Everyone had been working around the clock, scrambling, putting out fires, trying to figure out what might happen next. It felt surreal to be contemplating how to manage the possibility of multiple clients going belly up simultaneously.

Tim: *Call me!*
Barry: *Come to the Fed. Here's my cell.*
Susan: *Hilary wants you at 270 Park. Now!*
Bill: *We need you!*

I thought for a moment, then decided to call Barry, the chief risk officer. I considered him a grownup, meaning someone you could have a rational conversation with. He'd arrived at J.P. Morgan from Goldman recently, filling a position that had been vacant for over a year.

"Barry, it's Jane." I stood on the street, wondering what I'd missed in the hour I'd been at church.

"Oh good! Been praying for us?" He chuckled. "We need you down here at the Fed."

"Um, Hilary wants me to come to 270."

"This thing is unfolding in real time. *She* doesn't know what's happening!" His voice was harsh. "Jamie wants you down here now."

EIGHT SEPTEMBERS

Far be it for me to ignore a directive from the CEO. "Understood, Barry. I'm leaving now."

I got to the corner of Broadway and 77th and hailed a cab. I kicked off my sandals and tucked my legs under me as I started to read my Blackberry in earnest, my black shift riding up my thighs. So many emails and updates to catch up on.

I emailed Tim: *Spoke with Barry. I'm on my way.*

Next, I emailed Susan, taking petty satisfaction in what I sent: *Sorry, tell Hilary that Barry & Jamie want me at the Fed.*

It slowly dawned on me that the cab wasn't moving. I looked up and saw we were pulled over near Times Square. "What are we doing?" I shrieked at the cabbie. "I need to be downtown!"

He looked thoroughly unimpressed. "We've been in an accident," he said, tipping his head slightly toward the curb.

Seriously? I looked and saw another cab pulled over behind us. Must have been a fender-bender and I'd been too absorbed in my work to notice it.

I shook my head and gathered my things. *Un-fucking-believable.* "I can't deal with this," I said. "I'm in a hurry." I slammed the door and walked away without paying, then found another cab going down 5th Avenue. "Thirty-Three Liberty Street, as fast as you can, please."

I faced the armed guards outside the Fed once again, a familiar experience by now. I showed my ID, put my bag through the X-ray machine, and approached the security desk for my pass. I expected to head up the elevators to the left as I always did when I had meetings at the Fed, but instead, the guard escorted me off to the right, walking me down an unfamiliar hallway on the ground floor. At the entrance to the Fed's dining room — more like a ballroom, replete with high ceilings, crystal chandeliers, and wainscoting — I found Barry waiting for me. Blue button-down open at the collar, sleeves turned up to the forearm, khakis belted tightly around his bulging waistline, he wore a smile of relief on his face. Unexpectedly, he gave me a friendly bear hug, which I returned.

"You're needed in there," he said, pointing to a door off to the side. I noticed the main room was set up with large round tables covered in white tablecloths, each with the name of a different firm on a placard in the middle: *J.P. Morgan, Morgan Stanley, Merrill Lynch, Bank of America, Credit Suisse, Goldman Sachs, UBS, Citi, Barclays, Lehman.* The room bustled with activity.

Not your typical Sunday... unless, of course, you were an investment banker closing a deal.

I started to walk to the room where Barry had pointed me but was intercepted by Jamie. Black button-down untucked, blue jeans, cowboy boots. Just another day at the rodeo.

"We're working on putting an industry backstop together," Jamie informed me. I understood that to mean some sort of agreement where the different banks would agree to finance one another to ensure everyone could continue to operate even if other non-bank lenders backed away. He looked me in the eye. "I need you to get this right. Don't commit us to anything before talking to me."

In other words, *Don't Fuck Up.* Sometimes I wished I worked for Jamie directly. He was intimidating and knowledgeable about almost everything, but he was also direct, no BS, and I appreciated that. It didn't seem to me like he played politics, but he must have. You can't be CEO of a place like JPM without knowing how to work the system. Still, when I was in the room with him, I usually understood his questions and perspective, and his pragmatism, which was sorely lacking in some other members of his team who were always trying to prove how smart they were. So what if he wanted everything summarized in bullet points? That's efficient — and sufficient — if you're smart. Some people use too many words to say nothing.

I looked him back squarely in the eye and nodded. "Okay, Jamie, I understand. I'll do my best and circle back to you before I sign anything." He walked away and I headed toward the door Barry had indicated.

I pushed open the door, surprised to see the windowless room so crowded. At least fifteen people sat in executive-style black chairs on all sides of a large table in the center of the room, with others leaning or sitting against the walls. I saw Tim right away, but the biggest surprise was how many other people I knew — at least half the people in the room. Not just from J.P. Morgan, although Bill and Tim's other investment bankers were there, but from across the Street — CFOs, treasurers, repo traders. Someone stood to make a place for me, the guest of honor, at the table. As I took my seat, I kept nodding at people I recognized, saying a silent hello and trying to take stock of the situation.

"Jaaaane!" Tim smiled while he spoke, leaning back in his chair, genuinely glad to see me.

"What's going on?" I asked as I got settled and took out my notebook.

"We're putting together an industry credit facility where we all agree to finance one another's collateral in case the tri-party repo market dries up. A loan agreement among the companies here in this room."

I nodded my head. Made sense so far. Basically, the top-tier players in the industry would have one another's backs to keep the system from collapsing in on itself.

"Turns out, we need *you* to structure it. Now." He winked at me. He always counseled me that I needed to do things to make myself indispensable to stay relevant in the investment bank. The Lehman shit show gave me yet another chance. My expertise structuring secured credit facilities was about to be tested.

All eyes were on me. I took a deep breath and scanned the room. No corporate banking colleagues. I was on my own. Good thing I had fifteen years of experience honing my skills on these kinds of loans.

I started asking questions. "How many banks? What kinds of collateral? How long of a commitment? How big of a credit line? What is the purpose? Who has what rights and responsibilities as the lender? As the borrower?"

We went around the room, hashing out details, taking note of who might be willing to do what. There were eleven banks in the room, all primary dealers, and we each agreed that we would seek approval to commit $7 billion to the deal for a total of $77 billion — $70 billion of which would be available to any one firm at a given time.

"Okay," I said a few hours later, "looks like we might have a basic outline here. Let's all see if we can get it approved by our respective teams."

Thus, the Primary Dealer Liquidity Facility was born. One of many emergency solutions devised on the fly in the wake of Lehman.

Barry poked his head in. "Jamie needs you." Apparently, all the CEOs were heading into a meeting with New York Federal Reserve Bank President Tim Geithner and US Treasury Secretary Hank Paulson, and I would have a back-row seat.

Oh, God! This is getting crazy.

CHAPTER 33
Immediate Aftermath

Throughout that weekend, Lehman still expected to be bailed out in some form or fashion, essentially playing a game of chicken with the regulators who had never before allowed a firm of that size and importance to go under. But the best they could get out of the Fed was an agreement to step in and finance Lehman's assets in the tri-party market, since all the other lenders were disappearing.

By Monday morning, Lehman's parent company filed for bankruptcy, without much of a plan in place for how they would unwind the company. Immediate chaos in the markets ensued.

Our clearance client, Lehman's regulated US broker dealer, had ponied up the $5 billion in cash we'd asked for and had not filed for bankruptcy, so we continued to clear for them, as we had for Refco. This was not unusual. The parent company would file for bankruptcy and allow the operating subsidiaries to keep functioning, then the regulators would oversee an "orderly unwind" in lieu of a formal bankruptcy for the regulated broker dealer in order to return cash and securities to their clients — just like they did with Refco in 2005. In this case, though, there were a lot of mixed messages coming out of Washington, the New York Fed, and the Securities and Exchange Commission, plus a lack of coordination with critical non-US regulators like the Financial Services Authority in London. No one knew whether there would be a bankruptcy, or an orderly unwind, or some other type of liquidation, or sale to a third party.

On Tuesday, Lehman — whose eleventh-hour acquisition by Barclays Bank had been denied by the UK regulators — struck a deal to sell only their assets to Barclays instead. This absolved Barclays from any risk associated with Lehman's debts.

We were told on Wednesday — specifically, *I* was told — that Barclays would be taking over Lehman's remaining tri-party book — all $54 billion of it — which was owned by the regulated US broker dealer. Art from Bank of New York and Gerard from Barclays — people I had known for years in the business and thought I had reason to trust — called to tell me their intentions. We'd worked together on industry committees and spoken on panels at conferences, competing with and soliciting business from each other, as financial institutions do.

"Jane, Barclays is going to buy Lehman's assets. They're going to take over the entire tri-party book." Art had been dodging my calls for days, and now he was reaching out to me.

"Really?" Barclays, the only firm in discussion to bail out Lehman, refused to take responsibility for Lehman's liabilities; they only wanted to buy the broker dealer's assets. As a creditor, this was distressing. But as the operating agent for the tri-party book, we'd be happy to transfer the assets to Barclays' clearing bank and be done with it.

"Yes. We're going to send you the cash, and once you get it, you send us the securities."

Gerard confirmed what Art had said.

"You mean you'll pay us *first*?" It astounded me that they would release the cash before receiving the securities. I assumed they knew someone had to "go first" to get the transaction started, and we certainly would never agree to release securities without payment. I wouldn't, anyway.

"Yes. Absolutely. Barclays will send the money to Bank of New York, who will send it to J.P. Morgan. Once you get it, send the securities to BONY's account at DTCC."

"All $54 billion?" As far as I knew, the securities were a mixture of US government bonds and structured debt instruments that cleared at DTCC.

"Yes."

What a relief. And ...? What weren't they telling me?

I didn't have time to think about that.

"Okay, I'll let the clearance team know. Thanks!"

I called Ed right away. Ed oversaw the clearance department, having taken over from Al a few years earlier. He'd been placed in Al's group without it being expressly stated that he would become Al's replacement, and originally I'd considered him a spy, someone to be wary of. But he'd taken to the business and tried hard to satisfy his many masters.

The clearance and tri-party business did not report to me — never had — and its current senior management discouraged the close coordination with our department that had existed for decades when Al ran the business. However, although I'd been boxed out of the clearance business since the reorganization of my department and Al's retirement in 2007, people on the Street still considered me the point person. Dominick could take some responsibility for that. When I'd been promoted to lead my department, he went around telling everyone on the Street that I was Al's new boss, which was not true. Indicative of the type of mischief Dominick liked to stir up, it served the double purpose of yanking Al's chain and elevating my profile. The impression had lasted over the years, which is why Art and Gerard called me, not Ed.

"Barclays said they'll send over cash first and then we can send them Lehman's collateral. That seems like a good deal, and easy enough. $50 billion of cash in and $54 billion of securities out. I confirmed with Art and Gerard. Cash in free. Then securities out free. No delivery versus payment," I blurted everything out in one breathless rush. "Ed, can your guys figure out the logistics?" I asked. I didn't get involved with the day-to-day operations.

"You got it, Jane. We'll take it from here." I knew his team had been through many crises before, and I trusted them.

***

The transfer of the tri-party book was scheduled for Thursday, the next day.

David and I and a few others were gathered in Hilary's office, now on the forty-sixth floor at 270 Park. We sat around the expansive, elegant conference table across from her massive desk.

Tensions were running high. There was a problem with the Lehman unwind.

EIGHT SEPTEMBERS

Barclays had sent the first $5 billion payment of cash, and we released the first lot of securities, but a number of those securities got kicked back to us instead of being accepted as agreed. This didn't make sense given the deal we'd struck. Barclays was supposed to be taking *everything*. Lehman employees blamed a problem at DTCC. We brought everything to a halt and now were meeting in Hilary's office.

Hilary was yelling on the phone at Gerard from Barclays, who was trying to get her to restart the transfer process for the tri-party book. She put her hand in my face to stop me from talking as I weighed in on why that wasn't a good idea.

I bristled. I thought I deserved some respect for my years of experience, specifically for my knowledge of how tri-party operations worked and what risks should be considered. I had protected us in the Bear crisis and demonstrated repeatedly that I knew what I was talking about. We were, after all, in the middle of the largest transfer of a tri-party book *ever* — $50 billion plus, the sum total of all their third-party loans and related collateral.

But since the BankOne merger, I'd been facing an environment that considered experience suspect and assumed that people and businesses that had been operating a certain way for a long time only did so because they were afraid of change and innovation and unwilling to cede fiefdoms, not because there was a particular logic or functional reality that made those operating procedures continuously appropriate. It was one of the reasons I'd lost the battle to keep my department intact.

I didn't always understand the nuances of this complicated business, but I certainly understood the big things. Like you don't give away your leverage. Meaning, when you've got collateral, you don't let it go unless you get something of equal or better value first. We had control of $54 billion of securities, and it was our only leverage. How could I explain twenty years of experience about clearance and tri-party operations to someone who put her hand in my face and didn't want to be slowed down by the details?

Like I always said, in the absence of information, *the one thing you don't do is release collateral.* But that's exactly what Hilary did.

IMMEDIATE AFTERMATH

Why? I don't know. I wasn't privy to that decision.

Guess it was above my pay grade.

***

When I came in the next morning, Friday, September 19, someone told me Lehman had a $50 billion overdraft. I said, "No way. That's not possible. Must be a mistake."

Because of the chaos of the day before, all transactions and settlements had been delayed, causing inaccurate reporting. When the dust settled, however, we had an actual overdraft of $28 billion. Still unacceptably high. What a shit show. We did, of course, have collateral. We just didn't know whether it had any value.

Turns out, most of it was garbage. We now had the distinction of being the largest secured creditor in a bankruptcy *ever*. That's when the hunt for people to blame commenced.

I went downtown to Ed's office at 4 New York Plaza to help figure out what happened. I walked into a conference room filled with auditors and controllers and lawyers and clearance guys. Ed saw me, got up, and gave me the tightest hug of my life, one that nearly broke my ribs.

"Thank God!" he said. "A friendly face." Ironic, for someone who'd been playing both sides of the fence, keeping his distance to make his bosses happy yet staying close enough to capitalize on my credibility on the Street.

It was an inquisition. Someone at the top of the house fucked up, and now heads were going to roll, bodies were going to get buried.

We spent hours trying to reconcile journal entries and understand what had happened. Then Ed and I were summoned to attend a meeting up at Lehman's bankruptcy law firm, Weil Gotshal.

Riding uptown in the cab, Ed's cell rang. Hilary gave him orders: We were not to speak. We were there as subject matter experts only to advise senior management behind the scenes. Ed and I looked at each other and shrugged. Again, above our pay grade.

EIGHT SEPTEMBERS

We arrived and joined Hilary, Barry, and a few other senior executives from J.P. Morgan at the rectangular table in the conference room. There were representatives from Lehman, Barclays, various regulators and DTCC, including lawyers for each of those entities. Each firm had a breakout room for confidential strategy discussions. The all-hands meeting was to sort out the conflict around the debacle arising from the transfer of assets from Lehman to Barclays, and J.P. Morgan's resultant overdraft and collateral.

It shocked me to see Ian, Lehman's CFO — unshaven, fly of his green corduroy pants undone, glassy eyes that did not recognize me — roaming around aimlessly, leafing through a stack of papers.

Late that afternoon during the big powwow, I learned about a hearing scheduled at the bankruptcy court regarding the liquidation of the US broker dealer. Hilary and Barry were in the thick of negotiations and my input was no longer needed, so I rushed downtown to the courthouse that sat at the foot of Broadway, recognizable from the movie *Ghostbusters*.

By the time I got there, the courtroom was packed, despite the late hour. I wedged myself onto a wooden bench as Paolo testified on the stand about the deal between Lehman and Barclays. As I caught up with the questioning and his answers, I gradually realized that Lehman and Barclays had intentionally stuck us with the crap collateral; it wasn't some random operating problem at DTCC like they tried to pass off. They absolutely knew — down to the specific, individual level — exactly which securities they were transferring to Barclays. But those were not the instructions they gave us.

Instead, they had us deliver everything over to Barclays' account at Bank of New York on the assurance that Barclays was taking over Lehman's entire portfolio. The securities that were kicked back were the dregs that Barclays didn't want; securities that we now held as collateral for our $28 billion overdraft. Barclays, Lehman, and Bank of New York had taken advantage of the government clearance back-office operations procedures. J.P. Morgan was left holding the bag.

I was furious. I gathered my things and rushed out into the hallway to call Ed.

While I fumed, I tried to alert the lawyers to the fact that allowing the Lehman broker dealer to file for bankruptcy would cause their bank

IMMEDIATE AFTERMATH

accounts to be frozen immediately. The new owner of Lehman's assets, Barclays, would not have access to the accounts until they gave proper banking authorizations.

All of my warnings were to no avail.

They had far more important issues to handle than mundane bank accounts.

Monday morning, all activity in Lehman's account came to a standstill. The existing authorizations no longer applied as the company was out of business. Some Lehman employees were now Barclays employees, some were still Lehman employees, and some were now unemployed. How would J.P. Morgan know who had authorization to give instructions to move cash or securities? We needed new corporate resolutions, new signature cards, new online access.

Were these *Banking 101* intricacies understood by anyone outside the bank? They were not.

My phone rang off the hook. Lehman clients who wanted their money. Regulators who wanted securities. Barclays employees. Lehman employees.

I was berated. I was yelled at. I was accused of seizing assets inappropriately. But there was nothing I could do. Everyone had to wait until we got the proper authorizations in place.

This went on for weeks.

***

During the same time, Jimmy and I started seeing a marriage counselor as we decided we wanted to salvage our relationship and keep the family intact. We managed to wedge it in during the early evening whenever I could leave work to spend an hour talking and crying. It broke my heart to think about divorce. I worried about what it would do to the kids. I'd had a hard enough time with my own parents' divorce, and I was a grown woman when it happened.

The therapist was tough. My therapist had recommended her for that reason. She knew we needed someone strong enough to manage Jimmy's personality. She tried to make room for me to express my feelings, but Jimmy still talked over me — and her. Even as I said, "He doesn't listen to me or validate my feelings. He won't acknowledge —" he interrupted me and demonstrated the very behavior he denied.

"She owes me! I'm the victim here. She needs to break off this other relationship." He lurched forward off the couch toward the therapist, elegant and calm in her oversized chair across the room. Her office had a purple velvet couch and beaded lamps — a cross between a French salon and an Art Deco parlor.

The therapist noticed I shrank back, tears silently falling. "I think you're misreading the situation," she said to Jimmy. "Your wife is hanging on by a thread. I'm not sure you're in a position to make demands. She's asking you to notice her pain and suffering, to recognize the toll of your gambling."

"Well, I'm not coming back to therapy if she doesn't end things! She's making me look like a fool." In all our years together, I'd noticed that Jimmy would do many things for me. But if we ever got too close to the subject of his gambling, it seemed as if his very manhood was threatened, and he veered away from any close examination of the causes of his addiction or taking true responsibility for the consequences of his actions.

Still, if Jimmy was willing to change, if he demonstrated that things would be different, I'd end things with Dominick because it would mean that Jimmy was finally ready to take responsibility for his actions. And I'd waited a long time for that to happen.

But it felt to me like the same old story of my making accommodations for Jimmy without sufficient reciprocity. I feared isolating myself further by giving up my companionship with Dominick prematurely. The realization dawned on me that if the "happy family" story we projected depended on my continuing to keep my mouth shut about my unhappiness, I couldn't do it anymore.

That was our last trip to the marriage counselor.

CHAPTER 34

The Year Finally Ends

Jimmy and I finally separated at the end of 2008, J.J.'s senior year in high school. He threw himself into school and friends and after-school activities, naturally involved but also turning away from the parental drama and tension. William was a freshman at Brooklyn Tech High School, angry and aggravated by this change in his family's status.

Jimmy and I were taking turns living with the kids downstairs and staying alone in Mom's apartment upstairs until we decided on a more permanent solution. One night when it was my turn to stay in Mom's apartment — she'd died only six months earlier — J.J. came up to stay with me, unable to handle his father's wrath and outbursts about me. I had decided I would not defend myself to my children, that I had put "money in the bank" long ago when I bathed them and read them bedtime stories every night, planned and delivered their birthday parties and happy Christmas mornings, taught their Sunday school classes, and attended their school outings.

They either knew who I was or they didn't. Badmouthing their father or justifying my actions would not be in their best interests, so I didn't do it.

I climbed up the ladder to the small sleeping loft above the closet where he rested, my head nearly touching the ceiling, and looked him in the eye.

"Look, J.J., I understand you are angry and upset. I understand this is difficult for you. I will give you a long rope to process this and let you do whatever you have to do to cope. But I intend to have a lifelong relationship with you. Over time, sometimes I'll do things that you don't like, and sometimes you'll do things that I don't like. We'll figure it out. Just know this. If you ever get too far away from me, I will come and find you. I will not let you get lost. I will give you plenty of space,

EIGHT SEPTEMBERS

but I have no intention of losing you or letting this situation define our relationship or your life. Do you understand what I am saying to you?" I had never been more serious.

He paused, looked away, then let out a sigh. "Yes, Mom, I do."

I climbed back down the ladder, satisfied I had made my point, but concerned for my sons. I was determined to help them get through their parents' divorce. What I wasn't tempted to do was change my mind.

***

In the immediate aftermath of the Lehman Brothers collapse in September of 2008, more than twenty-five thousand Lehman employees around the world lost their jobs. Just one day after it became obvious Lehman Brothers would not survive, the federal government, in an effort to prevent further damage, loaned $85 billion to keep insurance giant AIG — which was drowning in a sea of credit default swaps it could not cover — afloat. The American economy, already heading for a recession, went into a tailspin.

Despite the US government's efforts to contain the damage through bailouts and emergency legislation, however, both General Motors and Chrysler — two iconic American institutions — declared bankruptcy in the month after Lehman's collapse. Banks cut back sharply on their consumer lending and thousands of American homes went into foreclosure as the Dow Jones plummeted, retirement accounts disappeared, unemployment rose, loan defaults skyrocketed, consumer spending declined sharply, and financial markets and institutions faced losses and credit freezes that hampered their ability to do business. The knock-on effects weren't unique to the United States, of course. Just as the 9/11 attacks on America sent ripple effects around the globe, the impact of the 2008 financial crisis was felt in all corners of the world, spurring debt crises in Greece, Spain, Cyprus, Portugal, and Ireland.

THE YEAR FINALLY ENDS

***

In early December 2008, in the midst of the insanity, I made my way back to the ARE in Virginia Beach. I attended a three-day personal development workshop called "Vision and Courage," two things I sorely lacked at the moment.

A group of about twenty people were sitting in a circle, sharing their reasons for attending.

"I am hollowed out, burned out, trying to find my way in the darkness and confusion," I said. My voice seemed tentative, my heart tight. I recited my litany of losses: parents, marriage, career. I didn't know how to be fully present, to listen as others shared, to allow myself to see myself.

We spent the day "priming the pump," doing small introspective exercises, meditations, and reveries to prepare us for the upcoming exercise: The Power Line.

Our workshop leaders — Mark, the author, and his wife, Mary Elizabeth — explained it to us. "Each one of you will have the chance to go down the power line. A group of you will stand, one behind the other, while the person whose turn it is will start at the front of the line. She or he will face the first person and tell them to move," Mark explained. "At the end of the line is something that you want very badly, maybe even your heart's desire. You cannot have it until you move each person, or obstacle, out of the way."

"Make sense?" Mary Elizabeth, Mark's wife and the co-leader of the workshop, asked.

Sure. Easy enough. So why did my heart start to pound?

"Okay, those of you standing in the power line will not move unless there is a clear, authentic instruction to do so. If she meekly says, 'Please, can you move?' do not move. If he cries or pleads or manipulates, do not move. It's only when you hear something with energy and conviction that you believe is sincere, then you can move out of the line."

First step: Choose the prize at the end of the line. That was easy for me. *The freedom to be myself.* I desperately wanted that. I was so tired of being externally defined: wife, daughter, mother, lover, banker, teacher.

We broke into two groups. I began to get nervous.

I watched as others went down the line. I participated in other people's lines. My trepidation grew. Sweaty palms, thumping heart.

When my turn to go down the line arrived, I found I could not start. My tears turned into sobs, and I panicked, paralyzed with fear. Unable to move, the room closed in on me.

Mark attempted to settle me. "Okay, let's not collapse here. You can do this, Jane. How much do you want the freedom to be yourself? Take a deep breath. Come back to yourself. I'm right here, standing in support of you. I know you can stand in support of yourself too." His voice was firm yet compassionate.

Out of the corner of my eye, I saw the other group. The woman going down the line — long brown hair flowing, tight jeans, high-heeled black boots — easily ordered people out of her way, swift and commanding, like a military officer.

Sniveling and unsure, feeling broken, I agreed to start.

I looked at the first woman in my line. Her expression was a mixture of compassion and sternness, and she struggled to hold her ground in the face of my instability.

"Okay, power line people, remember to resist Jane if you don't believe her. This is not a time for compassion or mercy. You need to hold onto your intention to really listen for her sincerity and strength." Mark was clear about the rules and was not about to let me off the hook.

I whispered as I avoided her eyes. "Please move."

She did not.

My eyes welled up. "Please, can't you move?"

She would not.

Mark encouraged me kindly. "Look her in the eyes, Jane. Say it more firmly."

"Move."

She held her ground.

"NOW!"

She stepped aside slowly, reluctantly, not convinced she believed me, holding her eyes on mine.

THE YEAR FINALLY ENDS

I was exhausted, terrified. Six more women to go.

When I finally made it through and could see the scarf on the floor that represented my heart's desire, Mark suddenly jumped in front of me.

"I think you need to stand up to some male energy!" He towered over me, blocked my way, almost menacing.

Already wretched from this exercise, now I felt myself tumbling toward defeat.

"You are in my way."

Nothing.

I closed my eyes. Took a long, deep breath. Gathered my courage. Opened my eyes and looked at him.

In the strongest voice I could muster, I managed, "You are in my way! Move!"

He stepped aside. I grabbed the scarf and went into the corner of the room, where I sat on the floor and cried heartily with relief and despair.

How could such a simple exercise be so difficult? Had I really become so powerless?

***

Upon my return to New York, yet another crisis burst onto the scene: the confession by Bernie Madoff that he'd been running a $50 billion Ponzi scheme. I was flabbergasted. The man's reputation preceded him, and the only part of his firm I had familiarity with was its successful NASDAQ market maker business. I recalled that I had been brought into the conversation when one of the traders in the bank wanted to make an investment in Madoff's investment advisory business, but we had passed on that transaction. From my perspective, we were in the clear on Madoff — no operating exposure to work out like we had with Refco in 2005, and certainly no exposure on par with what we were dealing with in the Lehman bankruptcy.

By chance, I was over at 270 Park on the executive floor when a meeting convened to discuss the bank's exposure to Madoff. I joined

EIGHT SEPTEMBERS

in, taking a seat in a chair against the wall to observe, not a principal player at the conference table. Imagine my shock upon learning that the bank had a $250 million exposure in the transaction I had been told we passed on.

How did that happen? Apparently, some high-earning trader had countermanded the credit decision — not unusual, unfortunately.

Worse yet, from the sheepish glances and muttered asides, I realized there were people at the table trying to blame it on *me*, since my group had provided the introduction to Bernie for the due diligence meeting. My presence mitigated that effort, but not so much that I couldn't see that was the plan. It would not be the last time someone tried to throw me under the bus.

The knives were coming out.

***

I spent Christmas Day of 2008 alone with the dog at our house on Long Island. I'd celebrated Christmas the night before with the boys up in my mother's apartment, savoring our time together. After they'd left with their father in the morning for a visit with his family, I'd driven out to the house to spend the day.

It was the first Christmas I'd ever been alone, and I appreciated the peace and quiet. No talking, no arguing, no guilt, no remorse, no equivocating.

I took the dog for a long walk on the beach. The sun was bright, the sky blue, the air crisp. I stopped to gaze at the ocean and inhaled deeply, then let it out slowly.

Out of the blue, a smile broke out on my face, and I knew that I would be fine. Better than fine.

Whatever is coming next, it won't be what was.

CHAPTER 35
Performance Review

"You should have had a plan. Like Jimmy Lee. Like he did for GMAC."

Tim's pronouncement infuriated me. *Are you fucking kidding me right now? Are you seriously comparing me to Jimmy Lee, vice chair? The senior most dealmaker in the bank? Maybe even the industry? Who easily makes $20 million a year and can basically pick up the phone and talk to any CEO on the planet?*

Me, Jane Buyers Russo, mother, Sunday school teacher, corporate banker. Six levels down from the CEO. Three levels down from the head of the Investment Bank. *I* should have had a plan to prevent the largest, most disruptive financial crisis in history by cleverly outwitting the intentional fraud of my client, Lehman Brothers? This, three years after the systematic destruction of my business unit, a unit originally designed to at least have the *potential* to identify and protect against such events. Not to mention all the regulators, rating agencies, and our own senior management who were *also* without a plan and unable to identify the problem and protect us from it. But yeah, sure. I should have had a plan.

My face was a mask. I didn't dare reveal what I felt or thought and kept my mouth shut.

It was January 2009 and time for my annual performance review. I knew to expect trouble because it took both Tim and Susan to do it — Tim, who ran investment banking for financial institutions, and Susan, who ran corporate banking for the same client base.

I'd spent the year putting out fires. Ostensibly, my job was to generate revenues, but I'd been doing nothing but managing risk and making sure we did as little new business as possible and got out of whatever existing business we could.

EIGHT SEPTEMBERS

I had walked down the hall to Susan's office on the thirty-fifth floor of 383 Madison, the Bear Stearns building we'd inherited as part of the bailout of that firm, where she and Tim were waiting for me. I could tell they were nervous by the stiff and awkward way they were sitting in their chairs, my closed personnel files in front of them.

Joining them at the small round conference table, I offered a tight smile that did not reach my eyes. I braced myself for what might be coming. In the best of times, performance reviews were a mix of "you're great/you're not doing enough to justify your existence" — and this was definitely not the best of times.

Tim, who'd proven himself my advocate despite some headwinds, took the lead. He told me how much due diligence they had done to prepare for this evaluation, how many people they had spoken with, and how much background had gone into it.

"Everyone has tremendous goodwill toward you," he began with a half-smile.

I waited.

"People think you have integrity and really like you." I knew he believed this and felt that way himself. "But here's the deal." Tim believed in ripping off the Band-Aid all at once. I knew to brace myself.

Steady, Jane. Use your poker face now.

"You should have had a plan. You know, like Jimmy Lee did for General Motors."

And so went my forty-five-minute review, one minute of praise and forty-four minutes of setting me up to take the fall — *and* justify the 70 percent reduction in my compensation.

I worked my ass off for a bank that was ready to throw me under the bus to protect senior management from its own poor decisions.

Like Doug after 9/11, I knew after Lehman that I could no longer work in the industry. I knew that I needed a different kind of a life. I knew I needed to be a different kind of person. I knew that I did not have another crisis in me, just as surely as I knew another crisis would come, as dependable as a wave on the ocean.

CHAPTER 36

Walking Away

In the months following my January 2009 performance review, Susan and Tim would admonish me, saying, "Your heart's not in it," and they were right. After throwing myself completely into managing the crisis and then being criticized and punished in my review and in my pocketbook, I could not muster any enthusiasm or joy for the job, the firm, or the industry.

Instead, I saw an opportunity to get free, to find myself a new life and a new self that was undefined by work, released from the patriarchy, and outside of the hierarchy.

It would take some time to extract myself with my grace and dignity intact, though.

In February 2009, I had my uterus removed, joking that I'd rather have surgery than go to the office. I'd finally had a moment to see the doctor and found out I had fibroids, for which she recommended a supracervical hysterectomy. Jimmy kindly took me to and from the hospital, where he suffered the indignity of being asked by the doctor if he was "the boyfriend." He stayed in the upstairs apartment while I recovered downstairs, being cared for by William and our housekeeper.

After I fully recovered, I started looking for a place to live. The kids' therapist told us that more finality around our living arrangements would be good for the boys. I didn't think that Jimmy could get himself organized to find a place and move out, so I did.

My poor real estate broker tolerated my tears, often sitting with me in the park while I coped with my new reality. I found a great three-bedroom apartment overlooking the Hudson River, and my broker negotiated a manageable rent for me — one upside of the financial crisis.

I made sure that both homes would be familiar for the boys, leaving the brownstone mostly intact and only taking personal items and a few pieces of furniture, including my piano, to the new apartment. I brought the boys with me to go shopping for new beds and living room furniture. They would spend one week at each place, so I made sure the housekeeper followed the same schedule to ensure they would have that normalcy as well. Their emotional well-being ranked as the top priority for me.

Marriage counseling hadn't worked, so we moved on to mediation. That quickly became adversarial as we each engaged our own attorneys when Jimmy refused my choice of mediator. He insisted on being the one to file for divorce, needing to claim his role as the injured party. It didn't matter to me. I was willing to wear the scarlet letter if that was what he needed.

In addition to splitting our assets and getting alimony, Jimmy wanted a share of my future earnings, comparing me to a professional athlete and demanding his rights. I had the sinking feeling that, just like Leilani, when it came down to it, it was all about the money for him. It would take several painful years for us to come to an agreement.

Divorce is like a death, except there is no social protocol to provide comfort to the bereaved. I didn't only grieve the marriage, I grieved my *idea* of what our marriage was. I had to confront the lies I told myself, to see Jimmy for who he actually was — not who I wanted him to be — and to accept that I had failed at keeping my marriage together.

How much more would I be willing to let go of in order to find a new life?

***

I could have stayed at the bank and fought. I could have argued I'd been treated unfairly. I could have leveraged being one of only a few female managing directors into a better role, higher compensation, more seniority. After all, I was only fifty with plenty of working years ahead of me.

But how did I want to spend my life, my days, my minutes? Did I really want to be angry and combative, fighting the behemoth of J.P.

Morgan, to whom I would inevitably lose due to its size and resources? Honestly, the company and its people had already given me so much, including the possibility of walking away with financial security. Fighting for more to protect my broken ego seemed like ingratitude and an unproductive use of my time.

During the worst of it, I had taken to carrying around a list of my favorite scripture passages in my pocketbook. I would pull it out and read it whenever I felt scared or alone, which was often. The passages fell into two categories — fear not/protect me from my enemies, and peace/love/abundant blessings — and were a mix of Old and New Testament, the Psalms, Gospels, Epistles, and Prophets. My favorite was from 2 Timothy 1:7: "For God has not given us a spirit of fear but of power, love, and self-control." I took comfort and solace in the words, which connected me not only to my past but to something deep within me that was even greater than this woman I had become — the multi-tasking, uber-performing, hypervigilant *doer*.

Some days during the summer of 2009, I would leave the office and walk east until I reached the river, where I would pull out a cigarette and guiltily smoke, relieving my anxiety and taking a pause from thinking and feeling. I didn't know what was wanted of me. I didn't know whom to trust, and I wondered what would happen if I simply walked away. Everything seemed meaningless, and without the impetus of a crisis, something to react to, I did not know how to proceed.

Even Tim, who had been a stalwart for me, became erratic and elusive, fighting his own demons. Dominick became increasingly unsatisfying as a refuge, our relationship out of balance now that I had separated and he remained married. My sisters were still grieving and recovering from the loss of our parents and the weight of the work left in their wake. Jimmy — my partner for my entire adult life — had become a combative adversary, bent on tearing me down.

My only joy was my sons. But J.J. would be off to college on the West Coast in the fall of 2009, and Will suffered alone with the new routine of shuffling between parents and coping with high school. I worried about the echo of my own parents' abandonment, first when I was fifteen and they moved to Hawaii, and later with their divorce. I vowed that I would be emotionally available to my children, affirming their reality, supporting their experience of this moment, their need to fledge into adulthood.

I'd wanted to quit with a big "FU" the moment I finished that performance review. But after twenty-eight years, I was determined to leave with a severance package. It took all my self-control to exit the bank gracefully, cash in hand, reputation intact — or rather, as intact as it could be with certain people maligning me at every opportunity to cover their own tracks. But I finally understood what Dominick meant when he said, "It's not about you."

How could it not be about me? My fears, my concerns, my reputation, my career, my life.

What did he mean? I'd wondered then.

I understood it now.

The attack on me by my superiors wasn't about me. They were protecting *themselves*, maintaining their positions. I would have the last laugh: stepping out of the game, consciously choosing a new life, willing to walk into the unknown, trusting that something better awaited me.

But first I had to get through my retirement party on April 30, 2010. Tim had wanted it to be a big affair and promised to get all the senior folks to come. Hilary — who, according to Tim, had been calling the head of the Investment Bank once a quarter to see if I had been fired yet — put the kibosh on that. The room on the 49th floor at 270 Park Avenue ended up being too big for the forty or so people in attendance, but the intimate crowd included nearly everyone critical to any success and happiness I'd had in my career, so it satisfied me.

What I considered my real party we held at a local bar, attended by my old team and my closest clients and colleagues in the business. No speeches, I told them, just drinks and laughs like the good old days. I went out and bought the brightest, most flouncy floral dress I could find to announce my staid banking days were over.

***

I planned nothing, except to do nothing.

To sleep when sleepy, eat when hungry. To do what I felt like and not do what I didn't. Over time, I added in a few things: learning to make stained glass, studying astrology, dancing, exercising, meditating.

On my first day of retirement, I wore my pajamas when Will left for school. When he returned home that afternoon, there I was, still on the couch, still in my pajamas.

He eyeballed me and said, "So this is how it's gonna be now?"

And I said, "Yes! Get used to it!"

We both laughed and laughed.

I hadn't felt that good in a long while.

***

The sun shone in the blue sky dotted with puffy white clouds over the pier that jutted into the Hudson River. The dull roar of traffic on the West Side Highway droned on beneath the gusts of wind swirling bits of trash and causing whitecaps on the water. Dominick sat silently as he smoked, stoic behind his sunglasses, rigid on the metal bench. I stood behind him, my hand lightly on his shoulder, the George Washington Bridge in the distance.

He was sensitive enough to feel that things had been shifting over the past year. He tried to distract me, but the tide had turned. I was no longer married, and he still was. In my mind, that imbalance changed us from two people having an affair to my being his mistress, which did not sit well with me. He sometimes talked vaguely about a future life together, but I didn't see him doing any of the emotional work needed to make such a change. I'd had years of therapy, spiritual support, and my sisters — and it was *still* a struggle to cope with the end of my marriage. As far as I could tell, he had no support system.

EIGHT SEPTEMBERS

He knew he was losing me, and his two natures were fighting: the one that would say anything to get what he wanted, and the one that wanted only the best for me.

"I've raised the bar," I announced. "As you yourself said, I deserve more."

"Maybe too soon," he countered, as if he might attempt to meet the new bar. But we left it at that.

Later that afternoon, he sat in his car while I stood on the sidewalk. The wind blew off the river, messing up my hair. I bent down to speak to him through the passenger window.

"So?" I asked, pulling my sunglasses down slightly to look at him.

He looked away, took a long drag of his cigarette, and flicked it into the street before answering. He cleared his throat and glanced at me. "So," he echoed, followed by a cursory smile that did not reach his eyes.

Nodding slightly, I raised my eyebrows and sucked in my lips; there was nothing left to say. Pushing my sunglasses back in place, I stood as he pulled away from the curb, watching until he turned down West End Avenue.

That would be the end of that.

I wondered how much more pain my fractured heart could stand.

***

My piano shone in the corner, not a speck of dust on its high-gloss black finish, the bright sun and sparkling Hudson River shimmering through the wall of windows. The piano had accompanied me from my old life to my new, bearing witness without judgment.

I'll take lessons again, I suddenly thought.

Raising the lid to expose the keys, I ran the backside of my thumb from the lowest note to the highest. My pointer fingers trilled "Peter, Peter Pumpkin Eater" on the black keys, then both hands launched into the chords of "Heart and Soul."

This would be my home now. Time to start over.

EPILOGUE
Empowerment

"The only person you are destined to be is the person you decide to be."
—*Ralph Waldo Emerson*

September 2010

Hands planted on the counter, I leaned forward and stared directly into my eyes in the restroom mirror.

"I am in command of my energies," I declared, repeating my intention for the day for the umpteenth time. It wasn't even ten a.m.

Two entire days had been spent with the bank's attorneys, preparing me for the deposition today, going page by page through thousands of emails printed out in a thick black binder entitled "JANE BUYERS RUSSO, MANAGING DIRECTOR, J.P. MORGAN."

It contained every email I'd written or been cc'd on regarding Lehman: our credit lines and collateral calls, our deliberations and decisions, emails with my team, senior management, the Lehman folks, the regulators. They'd also taken my notepads and made copies of anything Lehman-related, trying to discern meaning from my cryptic shorthand and separating out the personal bits — therapist, divorce attorney, parents' estate tax returns, lawsuits in Hawaii.

The lawsuit between J.P. Morgan and Lehman was about whether or not we'd had the right to seize Lehman's collateral to pay off our outstanding loans. I was testifying as an employee, and the bank was paying for my legal representation.

Toward the end of the second day of prep, the senior female partner pulled me discreetly aside in the narrow hallway and showed me a thin binder, also with my name on it. "We need to review this too," she said as neutrally as possible, looking up into my eyes, the male lawyers mercifully disappearing on cue.

I guessed what it included but gave no outward sign my pulse had quickened. I'd been expecting it and steeled myself against it. Another set of emails, personal ones I'd sent to and received from Dominick and my husband. The inclusion of my husband's emails surprised me, since I hadn't considered they were probing for insider trading. Emails with Dominick — influential in the industry and deeply involved in the crisis as well — did not surprise me. They were probing for inappropriate disclosure of confidential information. They would find neither. Turns out, it's possible to retain professional integrity even while your personal standards are at an all-time low.

Forewarned, I would not allow myself to be surprised or shamed in the deposition by a dramatic reveal of these personal communications.

"Ready?" they asked when I returned from the restroom. My heart beat faster and I wiped my moist palms on my jacket. I closed my eyes and took a breath.

I am in command, I silently reminded myself.

I nodded and strode into the conference room, lawyers flanking me.

My seat at the head of the long, wide conference table faced a video camera trained directly on me. I wore a slate-blue Anne Klein pantsuit, professional and flattering, not too revealing. It felt odd and unfamiliar now that I'd retired and given up the uniform I'd worn every day for twenty-six years, freed from the tyranny of stockings and heels.

The large, windowed conference room high above Sixth Avenue was packed: attorneys for Lehman on one side, attorneys for J.P. Morgan on the other. Representatives from the bankruptcy court were there too. Everyone had a copy of my fat email binder in front of them. Hundreds of thousands of dollars of billable hours right there in that room, everyone getting paid — except me, the former banker, the star witness.

"Oh, we can't pay you for your time, Jane. If we did that, it would appear as if we were paying you for your testimony."

Of course. Let's just add insult to injury.

The court had mandated seven and a half hours of taped testimony from me, which would translate into an eleven-hour day. I'd shown up late, stuck in crosstown traffic — the deposition coincided with United Nations General Assembly week in New York, and cars, limos, black SUVs, and taxis crammed West 52nd, vying for an advantage one inch at a time.

I shrugged my shoulders and, unusually calm, told the cabby, "No worries. Don't stress about it. This is one meeting they can't start without me!" I'd had plenty of jitters up to this point, but today I was determined to be composed, in command.

Underneath the calm exterior, however, I was angry.

Angry with Lehman and Barclays and Bank of New York for lying to me. Angry with Hilary for disregarding my counsel and giving away our collateral, then trying to get me fired to cover up her error. I was angry with the regulators and rating agencies who were happy to throw the banks under the bus and not take any responsibility for their own lack of oversight and understanding. I was angry at the investment bankers who derided our commercial banking franchise, then detonated it with their love of leverage and take-no-prisoners competitive stance. I was angry at the world for blaming "greedy bankers" and not understanding their own complicity in a system that allowed them to buy houses and cars and run up their credit cards without consequence. I was angry with myself for being taken advantage of, personally and professionally.

In the two years since the financial crisis in 2008, I'd left my marriage, the bank, and the affair. I'd been working on myself. And I was learning to use my anger as jet fuel to propel me forward.

Today, I was determined.

I would be in command of myself. I'd be telling *my* story, the way *I* wanted to, the truth *I* believed.

The lawyers had coached me:

Answer with a simple yes or no. Don't elaborate.

Sit up straight.

Make sure you understand the question.

Pause before answering.

Read whatever it is they are referring to.

Don't get flustered. They are trying to trip you up. Don't get emotional. Stick to the facts.

Ask for a break when you need one.

Sitting straight in my chair — shoulders squared, hands in my lap, ankles crossed — I fixed my gaze on the far wall. My jaw was firmly set, my expression a mix between cooperative and contemptuous. Even though I didn't feel it, I'd been told I came across as intimidating, which at the moment didn't bother me one bit.

The lawyers were smart, and they'd done their homework. But this business was my bread and butter, and there wasn't anyone in the room who knew more than I did about how tri-party repo worked, how we valued and managed collateral, and how we funded our broker-dealer clients.

It was go time.

I answered questions, followed the lawyers' guidance. No emotions, no outbursts, no extraneous details. Confident, competent, consistent. The facts were the facts, regardless of how Lehman tried to twist them. The hours dragged on. They would not break me.

"Yes, the collateral call for $5 billion was necessary."

"No, Lehman was not being truthful in its financial disclosures."

Sure enough, at the eleventh hour, all else failing, they opened the slim binder, made a weak attempt to insinuate I'd crossed a line I hadn't crossed. I wouldn't bite. I sat coolly unresponsive, my green eyes hard, feigning disinterest as I watched them consider a personal attack — weighing that against my demeanor, my command of the facts, my relentless conviction that Lehman was in the wrong and J.P. Morgan had acted appropriately. I saw them fold, concede the deposition was over, close the binder. Noticed the flash of satisfaction in my attorneys' eyes, the repressed smiles of a game well played.

It would take another five years, but the court finally ruled in J.P. Morgan's favor. We had the right to the collateral we demanded. We had acted in good faith.

Vindication.

No one would call to thank me for my testimony.

The world had moved on.

And so have I.

Afterword

> "A journey of a thousand miles begins with a single step."
> —Lao Tzu

For me, that single step took place over thirty years ago when I attended my first Gam-Anon meeting. The thousand miles in my journey included years working the 12-step program, personal therapy, religious training, spiritual exploration, and, of course, life experience.

In the decade covered by this book, my stumbling blocks piled up internally and externally, creating a wall of isolation, doubt, and shame. Learning to step back, observe without judgment, and cultivate compassion was the introspective and restorative work that followed in the years since the events described in this book. Being willing to look honestly at those stumbling blocks and take responsibility for my own healing has made all the difference.

What I needed was to find my way back to the person I was when I arrived in this world. She who loved being alive, embodied, unconcerned with others' opinions and mandates. Not yet constrained by expectations and rules, guilt and shame not yet on autopilot.

This is the part of me that got lost. The part I starved and neglected. The part that would, miraculously, resurrect and rescue me when my life was in ashes.

The promise that part held? That if I listened deeply, if I honored the still small voice within, if I acknowledged and was willing to see things as they actually are, then I would be healed.

I would be free.

I would finally be whole.

EIGHT SEPTEMBERS

***

When I left Wall Street, aside from testifying on behalf of my former employer and a short consulting gig assisting with the creation of a tri-party repo clearing product, I turned my back entirely on that facet of my life. It took many years before I was able to look back at my experiences there, particularly the tumultuous years between the terrorist attacks of 9/11 and the margin call on Lehman Brothers, with any kind of objectivity or emotional distance.

But as I found ways to express and come to know myself — with my therapist and in personal development workshops, and through creative outlets like music and writing — the anxiety ebbed, and a new feeling took its place: gratitude. My appreciation for what I'd learned along the way, and the person I'd become in the aftermath of those challenging years, grew. When the pressure to keep my problems hidden behind a tightly controlled façade of perfection went away, my relationships with my sisters, my sons, and my friends deepened, enriched by my willingness to be open and honest with them about what I felt, thought, and needed.

I've remained friends with some of my former colleagues, and others I have not seen since I retired, but I am appreciative of the influence each and every one of them has had on me. They helped me mature, both professionally and personally, and I wish them well.

My sisters and I are closer now than we've ever been, and the house we built together in Maine has been the source of a great deal of joy. We are surrounded there by our family history — including photos, furniture, and mementos that belonged to our parents — and take great satisfaction in making memories for the next generation. It is gratifying to carry forward the love we were given and allow the frictions to soften with time.

Jimmy and I were last together at William's college graduation in 2016. We don't have much communication or contact these days, but we share a deep and abiding love for our sons, our greatest accomplishment.

Our sons have created successful, happy lives for themselves and were with me — as were my sisters — to celebrate my second marriage to a wonderful man in 2021. Together we've created a peaceful,

AFTERWORD

meaningful, emotionally honest and fulfilling life. Not a day goes by that I don't appreciate every step of the journey that led me to this life.

Acknowledgements

Writing may be a solitary act, but crafting a book is not. Many threads have been woven together to create this memoir. Beginning with that first impetus from my friend *Chris Moore*, to an initial one-day memoir intensive at Gotham Writing with *Melissa Petro*, to personal development workshops with *Mary Elizabeth Lynch* and *Mark Thurston*, to writing constellation workshops with *Suzi Tucker*, to one-on-one manuscript mentoring with *Tanya Shaffer* and *Nan Mooney*, and classes with *Gotham Writing* and *Laura Davis*, this has been a journey through my interior landscape as much as it has been an exercise in learning how to write.

My mentors spend their lives generously sharing their multitude of gifts and talents for the benefit of many people, not just me. But for me specifically, I would like to thank them for the following:

Mary Elizabeth, whose wisdom and compassion taught me how to *show* up for myself using nonjudgmental awareness and to generate the courage needed to excavate my own wisdom hiding beneath my wounds.

Mark, whose deep knowledge of personal transformation psychology, spiritual philosophy, and the nature of the will taught me how to *stand* up for myself to enable constructive growth and change.

Suzi, whose curiosity, insights, and unique understanding of systemic dynamics taught me how to *take my place* when all I could muster was to shuffle forward.

Tanya, whose enthusiasm, expertise, and Off-Leash classes enabled me to get out of the murky middle and finally complete a full first draft.

Laura, whose willingness to share her writing techniques and tricks of the trade allowed me to create a compelling and cohesive narrative that is (hopefully!) hard to put down.

Gotham Writing (including Melissa Petro and Nan Mooney), whose classes, instructors, and students taught me how to give and receive feedback;

EIGHT SEPTEMBERS

how to build character, plot, and narrative structure; and how to write a memoir.

When I moved to Florida, I found my peers in the Works in Progress group of the Amelia Island Writers, a branch of the Florida Writers Association. Each week we meet in our local bookstore, The Book Loft, to read our work to one another and offer feedback across genres, as well as share our learnings about the editing, publishing, and marketing aspects of writing a book. The group is committed, thoughtful, skilled in critique, honest, open, and fun. I am indebted to them for their belief in me and encouragement to continue. They have inspired me with their own writing and publishing successes.

Many, many workshop participants, friends, and family members gave me feedback early in my writing process, for which I am grateful. A huge thank you goes to early readers of my full manuscript, who offered detailed and critical feedback: *Katie Bleakie-Schuller, Becky Buyers, Ralph DeFalco, Cindy Goldman, Jane Hawthorne, Nils Johnson, Ned McCormack, Julia McDermott, Krisy McKown, Chris Plagge, Katy Plagge, Wendy Rains, Anthony Scianna, Linda Sexton, Bailey Symington, Jeannette Tighe, and Elsie Viehman.* My book is better as a result of your comments and questions.

Like many opportunities, *Tim McConnehey* from Izzard Ink Publishing magically appeared in my life at just the right time. His calm, grounded manner paired with his expertise and understanding of the publishing industry made him a great partner to shepherd me through the process of turning a manuscript into a book.

Tim connected me with my first editor, *Jenna Love Schrader*, who had a vision for what this book could be and to whom it might appeal. She helped shape the important before and after sections as well as the continuity of the entire narrative.

The team at DartFrog Books turned out to be the perfect publishing partner. From my first conversation with *Gordon McClellan*, who immediately understood the value of my story, to the team behind the scenes creating the cover, layout, and design, they have been professional, focused, and dedicated to delivering the best possible version of *Eight Septembers*. The amazing *Corey Stewart* provided the final edits that

ACKNOWLEDGEMENTS

elevated my book to a whole new level. I am grateful for her expertise, clarity, and enthusiasm.

Just as there were many people involved in helping to craft this book, there were many people involved in crafting my career. Only a handful are mentioned in the memoir, but I am thankful for so many others who taught me lessons large and small — especially my unnamed colleagues in the Broker Dealer Division, the Government Clearance Group, the Investment Bank, and at the Depository Trust Company. That thank you extends to the more challenging characters in my story, who pushed me to see things in myself that I otherwise may not have seen. I am grateful for all of it.

To my sisters, *Ellie and Becky*, whose love, support, and acceptance has been tangible day in and day out. Your encouragement, not just for this book but for me personally, has been one of the pillars that has held me up.

To my sons, *J.J.* and *Will*, two wonderful young men whose kind and generous hearts, intelligence, senses of humor, and caring natures make me so happy and proud. *I'll love you forever, I'll like you for always.*

To my husband, *Anthony*, whose friendship, constancy, and willingness to be honest even when it was difficult means so much to me. You bring joy, laughter, and loving companionship to my life every day.

About the Author

Jane Buyers was previously a Managing Director and senior banker with J.P. Morgan Chase. In 2025, she was named an Honorary Trustee of Simmons University. She is a former board member of the Collegiate Church, the Center for Hearing and Communication, the Robert Toigo Foundation, and C. Brewer & Co, Ltd.

After her banking career, Jane took up writing as a creative and therapeutic outlet. Her experiences taught her that people lead more satisfying lives when they are aligned with what matters most to them and have the freedom to navigate their choices in a healthy and balanced way. She endeavors to embody those concepts in her daily interactions. Jane brings warmth, integrity, humor, and compassion to her writing and interpersonal relationships.

Jane lives happily in Florida with her husband, Tony. Together, they have five children and five grandchildren.

Referenced Sources

Front Matter
Monda, Barbara J. *Rejoice, Beloved Woman!: The Psalms Revisioned.* Notre Dame, Ind: Sorin Books, 2004.

Introduction
Mollenkamp, Carrick, Susanne Craig, Jeffrey McCracken, and Jon Hilsenrath. "The Two Faces of Lehman's Fall." *The Wall Street Journal.* October 6, 2008.

Chapter 2
Munsch, Robert. *Love You Forever.* Ontario, Canada: Firefly Books, 1995.

Chapter 5
Ingber, Jeff. *Resurrecting the Street: Overcoming the Greatest Operational Crisis in History.* New York, NY: Jeffrey Ingber, 2012.

Chapter 8
A Search for God. Books I and II. Virginia Beach, VA: A.R.E. Press, 1992.

Sugrue, Thomas, and Mitch Horowitz. *There is a River: The Story of Edgar Cayce.* Virginia Beach, VA: A.R.E. Press, 1997.

Thurston, Mark. *Experiments in the Search for God: The Edgar Cayce Path of Application,* Virginia Beach, VA. A.R.E. Press, 1976.

Chapter 16
Case, James H. *Hawaii Lawyer: Lessons in Law and Life from a Six Decade Career.* North Charleston, SC: CreateSpace Independent Publishing Platform, 2017.

Reflection and Discussion for Readers and Book Clubs

Part One: Shock

September 11, 2001, revealed heroism in ordinary people who might have gone through their lives never called upon to demonstrate the extent of their courage."
—Geraldine Brooks

When I talk about being in New York City on 9/11, people ask: *Weren't you afraid? Why did you stay at work?* It never occurred to me to run away. My children were safe, and I had a job to do, so I stayed. I trusted that all would be well. I'm not sure if that was faith or simply a failure of imagination. The thing about shock is that it interrupts the status quo, so by definition it is disorienting. We can't know in advance how we might respond.

Before the terrorist attacks, I was feeling trapped and dissatisfied in my career, unable to envision a path to a more satisfying situation. The chaos that ensued underscored how critical my job was and how good I was at doing it. Attending to the work in front of me was a way to honor the first responders and those who had lost their lives.

Crisis often shifts our focus to what matters most.

- *What kinds of shocks or crises have you had in your life?*
- *How did you respond?*
- *Were you able to learn and grow from these experiences?*

Part Two: Recovery

"Every worthy act is difficult. Ascent is always difficult. Descent is easy and often slippery."
—Mahatma Gandhi

Certain situations I encountered required me to step up because I had made a commitment or assumed a role and was expected to follow through. I did not always rise to the occasion, though. Sometimes I excelled beyond my expectations in one domain of life while failing miserably in another. Sometimes I simply took on someone else's responsibilities and ignored my own.

There are many ways to understand what it means to recover. To recover from an illness. To recover from addiction. To recover remains from Ground Zero. To recover from trauma. To recover our former selves or interests. In most contexts, recovery means *healing* or *restoration*, physically, mentally, spiritually, and relationally. Recovery can happen naturally, but it is generally a choice. Choosing recovery is declaring, *I want to get better.* Sometimes it's easier said than done.

- *Is it time for you to step up and do something outside of your comfort zone?*
- *Are you being called to step back from something and recover?*
- *How have you recovered from difficult experiences in your life?*

Part Three: Adaptation

"Adapt or perish, now as ever, is nature's inexorable imperative."
—H.G. Wells

Whether I liked it or not, how I spent my time reflected my priorities. If I *rejected* that premise, I would continue to be frustrated by my inability to do the things I wanted to do. If I *accepted* that premise, I could create the capacity to figure out what was driving me to spend my time on the things I thought I did not want.

REFLECTION AND DISCUSSION

Because underneath that thing I might not want (the job, the spouse, the house, the addiction) were things I *did* want (financial security, emotional closeness, a safe space, relief from anxiety). If I could practice naming the driving force behind the things I didn't want, I could turn my attention away from my complaint and onto my true desire. No one stays in a situation unless a need is being met. In order to make changes, the trick was to understand what I needed.

- *When have you been called upon to adapt?*
- *What prompted you to follow that nudge instead of remaining frozen or stubbornly in place?*
- *How did knowing your motivations help you in making changes?*
- *What happened to you and those around you as a result of you adapting?*

Part Four: New Reality

> *"Every experience and condition is a useful experience, and these are either made as stumbling-blocks or stepping-stones."*
> —Edgar Cayce Reading 1424-2 (38)

Looking at life as a series of lessons gave meaning to everything I did. Each experience was an opportunity for either growth or avoidance. The choice was mine.

When I took on my new department head role at the bank, I was in uncharted territory. It was unnerving and disorienting. I had to figure out how to manage my responsibilities, my relationships, and my self-image. I put change into motion without knowing the consequences and without a roadmap. My guardrails were my belief that life is purposeful and my faith in a higher power.

- *What gives your life meaning?*
- *Consider how your difficulties have been opportunities to learn.*
- *Are there times when you've chosen to avoid life's lessons?*
- *What price did you pay for that?*

Part Five: Bombardment

> *"It always seems impossible until it is done."*
> —Nelson Mandela

We do not need to know the full plan. Being willing to take the next best step is the only way forward. My sisters and I came to rely on the mantra "Trust the process" because we learned over time that solutions would reveal themselves if we did what was before us and allowed things to unfold in due course.

In this stage of my story, external events started pushing into my life in an aggressive way. I found myself in continuous, reactive fight-or-flight mode. I saw myself in battle and armed myself accordingly. It was hard to be proactive or strategic, and I found my vision clouded by my assumptions and biases about what "should" be.

- *When has life bombarded you?*
- *What do you think was trying to get your attention?*
- *How were you able to step back and choose a different response?*

Part Six: Inundation

> *"You have power over your mind—not outside events. Realize this, and you will find strength."*
> —Marcus Aurelius

I considered that the chaos outside of me was a mirror of the chaos inside of me. My internal bully reflected back to me. One moment I am the victim, the next I am the tyrant. Two sides of the same coin. If I wanted to step out of that dynamic, I needed to address my inner turmoil so that my external world might settle down.

By the time my father died and my department was dismantled, events were spiraling out of control. I was angry and grieving and resentful. Still in reactive mode, multitasking and barreling through, I sought solace where I could — all while berating myself for not doing things "better" or "right." I had not yet gained power over my mind.

- *Can you identify any parallels between your inner monologue and your external experiences?*
- *When has changing your thoughts changed your perspective?*
- *How do you demonstrate power over your mind?*

Part Seven: Frenzy

"That which we hide from ourselves and others has power over us and robs us of our true power."
—*Spiritual Energy Principle #5*
Personal Transformation and Courage Institute (PTCI)

When I worked so hard to hide my guilt and shame, all of my energy was consumed protecting my secrets. I used wishful thinking, denial, and avoidance to blind me to ugly or hurtful truths. In my quest to hide, I ceded my ability to change. It was as if I stood with my arms restrained behind me, struggling to keep the darkness contained and concealed. It was not possible for me to reach out or even maintain my balance when my arms were so occupied. Dropping these habits had the potential to liberate me and give me a chance to move forward instead of staying stuck in an unhealthy dynamic.

When I look back on 2008, I often think of a giant apple tree being shaken so hard that the limbs hurl its fruit scattershot across the land. Many people were caught in the frenzy of that year. For me, it ended up being a wake-up call: What has been can no longer be.

- *Are there illusions or truths you create to avoid seeing what is directly in front of you?*
- *What are your fears about that particular unknown becoming known?*
- *How might you be different if you allowed that "thing" to see the light of day?*

EIGHT SEPTEMBERS

Part Eight: Calamity

"Calamity is the perfect glass wherein we truly see and know ourselves."
—*William Davenant*

I was overwhelmed and inundated on all sides. I had to find a way to cope. Sometimes I relied on old habits like isolating, smoking, and disassociating. Other times I relied on my faith. Faith in human nature, in goodness, in myself, in the Creator. But you can only balance the spinning tops for so long. There's a reason why reaching bottom was a necessary step for changing my life.

By the time 2008 ended, I had endured many consecutive losses: my father, my department, my retired colleagues, my mother, my marriage, my client base, my credibility, my hope. I was out of energy and no longer able to continue doing the same thing over and over. It was time to step back and take stock.

- *When in your life have you reached bottom?*
- *What was your response?*
- *Which responses helped and which hurt?*

Epilogue: Empowerment

"The only person you are destined to be is the person you decide to be."
—*Ralph Waldo Emerson*

I had a choice to make. I could remain entangled in the morass of my career, divorce, and affair, or I could let all of that drama go to find out what awaited in the unknown. Letting go was scary and yet it was also a relief. Letting go was the first step. I did not magically recover. Yes, time and space allowed me to rest and recuperate from exhaustion and stress. That gave me the opportunity to reflect and breathe, as well as eat and sleep on my own schedule. But the real inner work was facilitated by professionals in therapeutic settings and personal development workshops.

REFLECTION AND DISCUSSION

I had to expand my tolerance for discomfort and build my capacity for self-observation. From there, I had to get grounded in my own goodness — my unique gifts and talents — to create a strong foundation from which to face my inner demons. Learning to show up for myself and stand up for myself were important steps in reclaiming power over my life.

- *How do you use your power?*
- *In what ways do you give your power away?*
- *How have you reclaimed it, or plan to reclaim it?*
- *Who have you decided to be?*

www.ingramcontent.com/pod-product-compliance
Lightning Source LLC
LaVergne TN
LVHW040039080526
838202LV00045B/3403

PRAISE FOR
SHADOW OF ICE ISLAND

"Cole and Mistel are so sweet together. I really enjoyed the addition of the perspectives of Kurtz and Zanna and the tension and banter between them. The dynamic of this group made for some great reading, the continued slow burn romance for Cole and Mistel settled really well, and the action, danger, adventure, revelation of secrets, and political intrigue kept me flying through the pages. I can't wait to see what comes next for this group!"

—MICHAELA, GOODREADS

"BRAVO! Williamson has crafted an exquisite masterpiece! I was immediately immersed into the drama. Twists and turns kept me turning the pages. These characters will linger long after turning the final page."

— CARYL, GOODREADS

"I was thrilled to continue the storyline of Cole, Mistel, and Kurtz in the world of Er'Rets! Jill Williamson is a master at character building. This world is full of so many interesting characters with true to life hurts and hang-ups. Tagging along to see them grow, develop, and embrace redemption mid-adventure is pure magic!"

—JENNIFER, GOODREADS

"Okay, this was pretty amazing! I was really excited to jump back into Cole and Mistel's story, and it totally delivered! Romance readers will love it. The chemistry between Cole and Mistel was so good and kept me invested the whole time. By the end, I was already excited for the next book, especially because I really want to know more about Kurtz. He is such an interesting character!"

—JO|RUTH, GOODREADS